# Central Europe: Core Or Periphery?

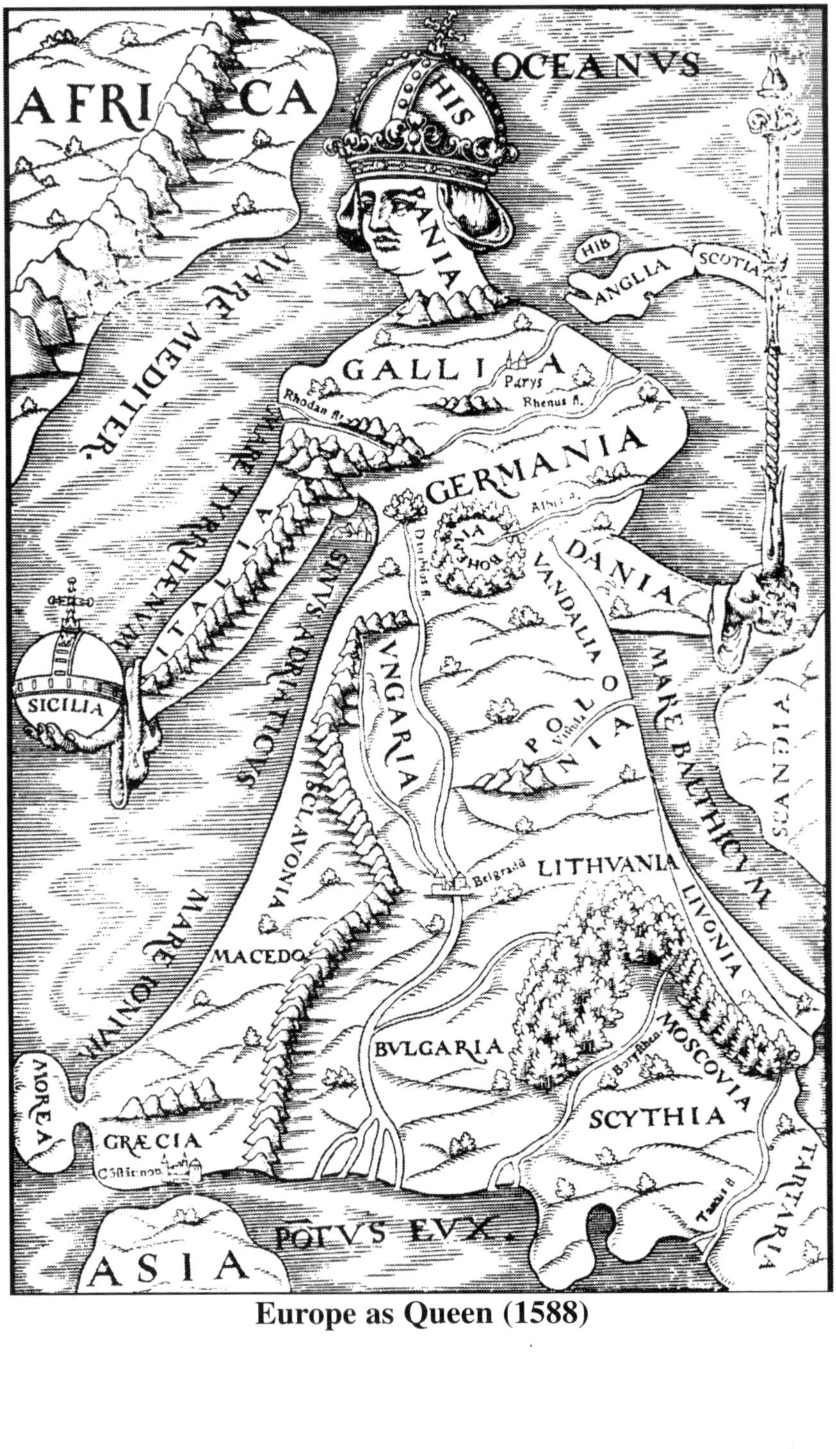


**Europe as Queen (1588)**

# Central Europe: Core Or Periphery?

Christopher Lord (editor)

COPENHAGEN BUSINESS SCHOOL PRESS
*Handelshøjskolens Forlag*

Printed in the Czech Republic
Set in Times and Helvetica by the Institute of International Relations, Prague
Printed by MIDAN TATRY s. r. o., Vrútky
Cover designed by Kontrapunkt, Copenhagen

ISBN 87-16-13447-8

Published in association with the Institute for International Relations, Prague, and the Eleni Nakou Foundation, London.

The Eleni Nakou Foundation is a charitable company, limited by guarantee, established under the Companies Act 1985 and registered in England and Wales. The aims of the Foundation are to establish a forum for wider appreciation of the dimensions and depths of European culture. The Foundation does not express opinions of its own.
The Eleni Nakou Foundation, 38 Montagu Mansions, GB-London W1H 1LD

*For Claire*



Distribution

*Scandinavia:*
Munksgaard/DBK, Siljangade 2-8, P.O.Box 1731
DK-2300 Copenhagen S, Denmark
Tel +45 3269 7788, fax +45 3269 7789

*North America:*
Copenhagen Business School Press
Books International Inc. P.O.Box 605
Herndon, VA20172-0605, USA
Tel +1 703 661 1500, fax +1 703 661 1501

*Rest of the World:*
Marston Book Services, P.O.Box 269
Abingdon, Oxfordshire, OX14 4YN, UK
Tel +44 (0) 1235 465500, fax +44 (0) 1235 465555
E-mail Direct Customers: direct.order@marston.co.uk
E-mail Booksellers: trade.order@marston.co.uk



Frontispiece: *Europe as Queen*, from Sebastien Münster, Cosmographia Universalis (1588)
photo: Basel University Library

# Table of Contents

## 4. CENTRAL EUROPE AND EUROPEAN INTEGRATION



## 5. RISK FACTORS



## 6. ISSUES OF IDENTITY

# Introductory

Petr Luňák, Claire Sneed, Otto Pick

# Foreword

Ten years ago Central Europe appeared (or rather reappeared) on the scene, not only in geopolitical terms, but also in the cultural discourse over what Europe actually is. For half a century Europe had had no centre, so to speak. It had been cut in two halves, with the dividing line running right through what was once seen at least as a geographical centre, and to many as something much more. There was Western Europe and Eastern Europe: but there was no Central Europe left in between them at all.

For the generations born after 1945, Europe had become synonymous with Western Europe. It seemed that it was here and only here that the 'true' Europe, both in its political and cultural dimensions, had been planted, and had further evolved during the Cold War years. The fact that the gruesome system that kept Eastern Europe in bondage for forty years was itself a brainchild of European thought was often forgotten. With only scanty and superficial contacts between the peoples, stereotypical concepts of social patterns and lifestyles on the other side of the divide grew up in both halves, with social and cultural life developing along two separate trajectories as a result.

When the Soviet Empire imploded there was an urge in the repressed areas to 'return' to Europe. Quite apart from the heartfelt joy of being 'free at last', this desire had many dimensions, economic, political, social and cultural. However, outside political rhetoric, this was not matched by a complementary desire in the West. Europe seemed to have got used to living without Central Europe - it had drifted so far westwards that its geographical centre had become a periphery.

Nearly ten years after the Great Revolution, Europe has still not been able to come to terms with the new map. Of course the shuttle of the loom of history which was dropped in 1939 (if not in 1914) cannot just be picked up again, and the idea of a European core that existed a hundred years ago may just be a myth. Central Europe may not exist. But there is a widespread feeling that we must be able to meet the call of history and heal the wounds that the twentieth century has left on our continent.

It was thoughts like these that prompted the Eleni Nakou Foundation to initiate our fourth symposium, this time with the slightly provocative theme of *Central Europe - Core or Periphery?* The Czech Republic more than any other place is representative of what was and is Central Europe, and Prague is the jewel in the crown of our European cultural heritage. I am therefore grateful to the Institute for International Relations and particularly to Professor Otto Pick who as director of the Institute in 1996 immediately responded both positively and enthusiastically to our proposal and undertook to organize the symposium. And I extend my thanks not least to the excellent Claire Sneed, who worked so hard to get all the many details of preparing an international meeting like this into place. The volume is much improved by the splendid photographs by Gorm K. Gaare (in black and white) and Prokop Paul (in colour, including the cover). Thanks are also due to Christopher Lord who gathered the manuscripts and ideas presented at the symposium and has done a fine job in putting them together and polishing the English where necessary.

The Eleni Nakou Foundation was established in 1990 with the aim of promoting cultural contact and understanding between the European peoples. Every second year we initiate a symposium related to European culture. The first was held in Crete in 1992, when a group of historians, sociologists, political scientists and journalists was invited to discuss the theme *Images of Europe*. In 1994 a second symposium was convened at the Louisiana Museum of Modern Art near Copenhagen to debate the question *What is European in European Modern Art?*; and in 1996 we held a third symposium, this time in Toledo and with the theme *Europe and Islam, Dynamics and Convergent Trends*. I should stress that the aim of these symposia is not to follow a narrowly academic and arcanely specialist agenda. Of course, specialists are invited. But our intention is to provoke searching discussions over a wide-ranging area. Nor are the books that we produce after these symposia presented as records of the proceedings. They are edited as self-contained publications in their own right. I am delighted that this volume, based on the discussions at Štiřín Castle, reflects these intentions so exactly.

*Dr Erik Holm*
*Director of the Eleni Nakou Foundation*

# Introduction

With the end of the Cold War, traditional labels were resurrected in various parts of Europe - in the mistaken assumption that a conceptual return to the status quo ante could easily be achieved by such means. 'Central Europe' was perhaps the most prominent expression of this political and cultural nostalgia, and Prague was touted as the urban epitome of this imaginative exercise.

Politically and historically the 'Central Europeans' of today look back to the allegedly golden era of the Habsburg Empire. In relative terms these were of course the good old days: the region was stable, and the Austro-Hungarian realm represented a common market and free trade area of some 70 million people. Its limited military capability suited its role as buffer between the growing power of Germany and the restless ambitions of imperial Russia. All this came to an end when the Habsburgs decided to throw in their lot with the Hohenzollerns. The regional balance of power in Central Europe was gone, and the rickety empire of Francis Joseph began to disintegrate in the face of pressures it had failed to foresee. The 1918 settlement which, according to E. H. Carr, introduced Europe's 'twenty years truce' simply replaced the multinational Habsburg empire with a mosaic of supposedly national states constructed on the basis of Woodrow Wilson's notions of self-determination. In their ignorance of conditions in the region, Western and particularly American politicians seem really to have believed that political and ethnic frontiers could be made to coincide in Central and Eastern Europe. In fact the treaties of St. Germain (1919) and Trianon (1920) provided the incentive for the ethnic cleansing which followed several decades later. Instability became the norm for the lands between Germany and Russia, and they were picked off one by one, first by Hitler and subsequently by Stalin. After 1948 Central Europe ceased to exist as a political concept and it disappeared gradually from the consciousness of the West.

All this changed in 1989. The urge to establish a regional political identity in Central Europe received some of its initial impulse from Prague, where there was at first a trend towards the abandoment of both bloc institutions and towards replacing them with some kind of pan-European security structure of which Central Europe could be the core. Visegrád was to some extent the outcome of this way of thinking. It is ironic that for a time Prague then emerged as the most vocal critic of the Visegrád approach. The disintegration of Czechoslovakia and the emergence of two smaller successor states transformed the regional balance and may have caused some apprehension that Poland could aspire to a dominant role within a regional grouping. Furthermore, the Czech government under Václav Klaus rejected regionalism in favour of rapid integration into Western structures, in the mistaken belief that the one excluded the other. The politicians in Prague also fell for their own propaganda, and they genuinely seemed to believe that their country was so far ahead in transforming its economy and developing its democratic institutions that any close association with its allegedly less successful neighbours would only serve to retard its inevitable and speedy progress towards the Elysian fields of NATO and the European Union.

For a time, the notion of Visegrád as a Central European concept appeared to have gone forever. Paradoxically, it received a new lease of life just as three Central European countries - Poland, Hungary and the Czech Republic - began to move towards full NATO membership. The government in Prague which came to power after the election in the summer of 1998 is much more positively inclined towards the idea of regional cooperation. Soon afterwards, the Slovak electorate removed the authoritarian Mečiar regime and this made the Slovak Republic acceptable as a candidate for NATO and EU membership and as a partner within the region.

The hiatus in regional cooperation had not been total. Some institutions survived, notably the more broadly based (though largely ornamental) Central European Initiative (CEI) and the much more pragmatic and therefore reasonably successful Central European Free Trade Area (CEFTA). Both these institutions, however, transcend the geographical boundaries of Central Europe. While it would be totally unrealistic and counterproductive if the three new members of NATO were to form some kind of Central European bloc within the Alliance, they are able to make a special contribution in view of their shared experience and regional know-how.

The cultural picture is less clear. Central Europe has in the past acted as a cultural crossroads for the continent as a whole. A walk through the older parts of Prague will quickly confirm this, at least as far as architecture is concerned. Especially the nineteenth century and the decades preceding the rise of Hitler in Germany saw the emergence of a special Central European cultural identity centred mainly on Prague and Vienna. Names like Kafka, Werfel, Max Brod, Alfons Mucha, Gustav Mahler, Alexander Zemlinsky, Oskar Kokoschka and others spring to mind in this connection. There certainly was a feeling of a shared Central European culture stemming from the multinational and multiethnic inheritance of the Habsburg Empire. This was especially true in Prague, where there was a fruitful symbiosis of Czech, German and Jewish cultures. However, it is worth saying again and again that the Jewish community provided the catalyst which made this achievement possible. The destruction of Central European Jewry at the hands of Hitlerite Germany changed all that beyond recall. The post-1945 settlement also brought about the expulsion of Germans from Poland and Czechoslovakia. Attempts to revive the post-war cultural identity of Central Europe are therefore little more than an exercise in nostalgia. Perhaps the time has come to encourage the adoption of a completely fresh approach to cultural cooperation, based on shared historical experience, but free from any attempt to mythologize the past. The Kafka industry which has emerged in Prague in recent years serves as a tourist attraction - it provides no basis for cultural development.

Nevertheless, a conference which attempts to examine the contemporary meaning of 'Central Europe' and of its role in the wider process of European integration is both topical and useful. It is hoped that the papers and discussion at the Štiřín meeting will have made a worthwhile contribution. Central Europe was always a vital and essential part of the whole continent, although it was almost forgotten for half a century. Its time has come again, but in a new context.

*Prof. dr. Otto Pick*
*First Deputy Minister of Foreign Affairs of the Czech Republic*

# Editor's Note

The subject of this book - Central Europe - is something that some people would deny exists. Indeed, we could perhaps have simplified the title of the collection to 'Central Europe?'; but that would have been too provoking. Our collection of learned analyses of various aspects of the situation of a group of rather idiosyncratic countries ends up with a discussion by Iver Neumann and Maria Todorova as to whether the term has any meaning at all outside the historical context of some scholarly debates of the past; and it is not entirely clear what our decision should be. Are these countries just a part of Western Europe which got stuck on the wrong side of the Cold War divide, through simple bad luck? Chris Cviic, for instance, would seem to be arguing that even the former Yugoslav republics - yes, even rotten old Serbia - qualify through their history and culture for membership in Western Europe, and that it is therefore only a question of time before they are 're-connected'. Other arguments presented here would seem to argue, contrariwise, that there is a special Central European cultural identity (Ewald Osers looks at the literature of the region, and Eliška Fučíková at its art production, to see if a true Central European identity can be discovered there), notwithstanding the differences of language and culture between the peoples and cultures of the region, which seem just as striking as any alleged similarities.

Perhaps a less contentious claim is that the countries of the region have something in common in their current economic situation. The analyses of two distinguished economists, Marie Lavigne and András Inotai, look at this question, and we must conclude from a look at these factors that there is at least in economic terms a regional identity of a kind - or, if we believe Prof. Inotai, several different possible identities, depending on which institutional and economic criteria you choose to look at. (Another economic view comes from Prof. Loukas Tsoukalis, who has been kind enough to offer us a short paper based on his reactions to what he heard at the conference from which this book arose.)

From a political and general historical perspective, the question is a lot more complicated, and we are fortunate to have two of the best possible guides through this labyrinth, in the shape of Professors George Schöpflin and Miroslav Hroch (a Hungarian and a Czech respectively), who explain the lie of the land for us: the cultural, linguistic and ethnic mix on the one hand; the effects of centuries of power politics on the other.

One traditional way to identify the region has been to talk about the lands in between Russia and Germany: and so it is natural that we should consider the situation today from a Russian and a German perspective as well as from the point of view of the countries themselves. From Moscow, Alexei Arbatov gives us a view of the region in relation to Russia, while Joachim Krause explains the German attitude - and Germany of course has always provided the single most influential foreign influence on the region.

Most serious observers would link the future of Central Europe with that of the European political institutions, and especially the European Union. Specialized treatments of this link are offered by Professors Helen Wallace and Ferdinand Kinsky, while in the same section, the current Swedish Ambassador to the Czech Republic (and noted author) Ingmar Karlsson offers some thoughts on the relation between the supposed European cultural identity and the identities of the various nationalities that go together to make up Europe. Slavenka Drakulić, the world-famous novelist and commentator on post-communist Europe, brings the book to a close with some personal thoughts about what it means to be a Non-West European, which is how she seems to understand herself now to be categorized by the Western Europe she longed for so earnestly back in the bad old days of the Eastern Bloc.

For it was the Eastern Bloc and not the Central Bloc, after all, that made these countries what they are today, at least as far as living memories are concerned; and as a Westerner, I cannot help remembering that all the countries under discussion in this collection were quite definitely in Eastern Europe not so long ago, as far as the ordinary usage of English at least was concerned. If I had been asked let's say in 1989 to make a list of Eastern European countries, it would simply never have occurred to me to leave out Poland, Czechoslovakia and Hungary... but times have changed, and so geography has apparently had to change as well to keep up. 'The Former Eastern Europe' would not really have done for a title either, though, although I have long felt this to be the most accurate term of art, so 'Central Europe' is evidently what we are stuck with for the time being at least. If some of our commentators are right, it is just a question of time - a few years, perhaps - before some of the countries discussed here will have made it into Western Europe, and so I suppose it is entirely possible that when they have reached that happy state, they will treat the idea of being Central with the same disdain they now reserve for the idea of being Eastern. (*Central European? But my dear fellow, you must understand, we have always had a completely Western civilization in our country!*) Conversely, I have often heard it said at conferences that such countries as Ukraine, Bulgaria and Romania are in reality Central and not Eastern; so perhaps, taking this strange geographical shift into consideration, we should be prepared for some future reader to pick this very volume from the shelf, blow off the accumulated dust, and raise an eyebrow of surprise that way back then in the twentieth century they really used to think of the Czech Republic, Hungary and Poland as Central European countries.

*Christopher Lord*
*Institute of International Relations, Prague, 1999*

RUSSIA
LATVIA
LITHUANIA
To Russia
Smolensk
Vilnius
Kaliningrad
Gdańsk
Minsk
WEST GERMANY
Berlin
Oder R.
BELARUS
Poznań
EAST GERMANY
Neisse R.
Warsaw
Leipzig
POLAND
Dresden
Wroclaw
U.S.S.R.
Praha
CZECH REP.
Kiev
Cracow
Danube R.
L'viv
UKRAINE
Munich
Brno
SLOVAKIA
Vienna
Bratislava
Kočice
AUSTRIA
Budapest
Debrecen
MOLDOVA
HUNGARY
Iași
SLOVENIA
Cluj
Odessa
Venice
Ljubljana
Zagreb
Szeged
Kishinev
Trieste
Rijeka
CROATIA
Timişoara
ROMANIA
BOSNA-HERCEGOVINA
Sarajevo
Belgrade
Zadar
Bucharest
Split
SERBIA
Constanta
YUGOSLAVIA
Danube R.
Ruse
ITALY
MONTENEGRO
Niş
Dubrovnik
Sofia
Varna
Rome
Cetinje
KOSOVO
BULGARIA
ALBANIA
Skopje
Naples
Tiranë
MACEDONIA
Edirne
Istanbul
Thessaloniki
Ioannina
GREECE
TURKEY
SICILY
MILES
0 50 100 150 200
0 100 200 300
KILOMETERS
Patras
Athens
Izmir
DODECANESE IS.
CRETE
1938 Borders
Western Boundary of the Warsaw Pact States, 1955–1991
GREECE NATO States, 1949–1991
Borders of New States, 1989–1991
LATVIA Names of New States, 1989–1991

# 1. Historical Background

Ewald Osers, Otto Pick, Ferdinand Kinsky

# 'Central Europe': The Rise and Fall of an Historical Region

*Miroslav Hroch*

In this paper I deal with the question as to whether or not the term 'Central Europe' can be used as a productive tool for the analysis of European history. This is not only a question of conventional terminology, but also one of actual and objective historical content. It is not then enough to ask whether and to what extent we are able and willing to imagine a territory, in our case Central Europe, which corresponds to this term. It is necessary to probe further to determine whether or not it is actually possible in European history to distinguish between macroregions, each of which would possess a population sharing a common historical fate, and would thus be capable of being differentiated from the populations of other macroregions. A simple glance at the map of Europe and a bit of grammar school knowledge should be enough to provide us with a positive answer to our question. But when we begin to work with concrete areas and concrete historical circumstances we are faced with a problem. Here I will attempt to lay out my opinion on the current existence, or rather non-existence, of Central Europe, once the situation has been considered in terms of its historical dimension.

Every attempt at an historical regionalization of Europe encounters the difficulty of actually defining Europe, or more specifically, of demarcating and limiting Europe as opposed to the other continents. If we put aside the sceptical view on the existence or possibility of defining Europe, we are left with two options. Either we can take the current geopolitical demarcation of Europe as stretching from the Atlantic to the Urals, project it into the past, and by this means find ourselves a term that continues to refer to the same territory, or we can proceed from a viewpoint that regards Europe as a territory composed of individual parts that gradually became tied to particular centres (the Byzantine and the Frankish), which were inherited from the ancient Roman Empire: and in this latter case the term we come up with will be a dynamic and changing one, and will refer to an ever larger area as our analysis progresses in time. Given the fact that in this paper I am making use of material from the Modern Age, that is, from the sixteenth century on, when Europe was more or less already in its current shape, I do not consider the second option a useful one, and will therefore adopt the first method instead. For the purposes of this paper Europe is to be understood as a continent bordered by the Atlantic, the Mediterranean and the Black Sea, and in the East, either by the Volga, or by the Urals.

In this context, a concept of the regionalization of Europe is one which dissects Europe into large territorial units which exceed the dimensions of a single state and, with respect to historical regions, at times also cuts across the territory of the states that exist today. Thus we are not speaking about regions in the sense construed by the European Union, say, but instead about some kind of macroregion.

The phenomenon of historical macroregions has a specific quality, in that such macroregions can be said to exist in two ways: as regions which actually exist in reality, and as constructs which have emerged in the realm of political and cultural discourse. Thus what we understand when we hear the name of a particular region can in some instances differ from reality: it can be possessed of qualities which neither correspond to reality nor appear demonstrable. Whether or not this is an issue of deliberate ideology or one of spontaneous displacement is not our concern here. What is important is that we interpret and accept the designation of a macroregion as an independent construct quite capable of holding its own in the realm of political discourse.

European macroregions are usually designated by two sets of terms, the first being derived from geographical indices, and the second being based on cardinal points - although the overlapping of the two is by no means ruled out. On the one hand we have regional designations such as the Baltic region, Scandinavia, the Balkans, the Alps, the Mediterranean, and so forth. On the other hand we have designations such as Northern, Southern, Western or Eastern Europe. In current literature we most often encounter an interpretation of these terms in a figurative sense, as constructs which have emerged out of a particular discourse. One popular intellectual game is to construe beforehand the qualities of a particular region and then to look for convenient geographical limits to suit it. The most notable example of this is found in the myth of the West and the East: to begin with, 'ideal types' were created for that which is West (in a positive sense) and for that which is East (as a collection of negative characteristics), and then in the moment of political necessity the appropriate regions were drawn in.

In this essay we will focus on the kind of terminology based on cardinal points. In this context, of course, it is necessary to remind ourselves of the elementary problem involved in every effort to delimit territory along such lines: it is dependent on the point of observation from which the question is viewed. In other words, the point of view can easily be relativized: the view from Paris places Toulouse in the South, but as seen from Seville it belongs in the North; as seen from Warsaw, Vienna is in the South, but from Venice it is in the North; and from Paris, Strasbourg is in the East, but from Prague it is in the West.

Such relativism could be overcome if we were to select an objective observation point and thus determine a centre. If we divide Europe according to cardinal points, we are then able to derive its imaginary centre. This 'centre' could be taken as a specific point on the map, calculated in geographic terms, or it could be a certain area or space. If we prefer a spatial interpretation of the 'centre', we must decide whether the area in question is simply a residual territory which does not belong in any clear way to a particular direction in terms of cardinal points (*Zwischeneuropa*: 'In-Between-Europe'), or whether the area is one marked by certain specific traits. The first suggestion offers merely a negative definition and can hardly be a useful analytical tool for our present purposes. The second suggestion presents us with the task of determining if the area, or 'our area', has within itself something that binds it, that is, something more than merely the temporary political interests of those who conceived the term 'Central Europe'.

The term 'Central Europe' appears to have been first used to designate a geopolitical entity at the time of the Congress of Vienna, and in connection with Metternich's conception of a European 'concert of powers', a political balance of powers. Between the Western powers, Britain and France, and the Eastern superpower, Russia, the guarantor of the balance of power was meant to be Central Europe, where the decisive role fell upon the newly emerging Austrian Empire. This balance was understood not only in terms of international politics but also in a cultural sense. Here we are dealing with a macroregion that actually existed but is at the same time a construct assigned with a mission in the general interest of all of Europe.

Leaving the question of terminology for a moment, we must ask if it is really possible to clearly mark out in the past a large region in the centre of Europe whose inhabitants shared a common fate: one distinguishable, that is, from the fate of the inhabitants of other regions lying to the east, west, north and south. In other words, did the historical experiences of the inhabitants of this region provide them with something more in common among themselves than with inhabitants in the West, North or East? Conversely, can we reconstruct any specifically Western European (or Southern European or Northern European) historical fates in which Central

Europe was not involved? Once again, we are not here to project current ideological constructs into the past, but to try and interpret historical relationships in themselves.

We could easily begin with the period of the late Roman Empire and ask what long-term consequences the border lines as laid out by the Roman *limes* held for this region. We could then also investigate historical fates in the period of the migration of nations; and after that, the character of mediaeval colonization and urbanization, the territorial dimensions of dynastic marriage politics, and so on. But all this would require the expert input of mediaevalists, and furthermore, we are now referring to periods too far off in the past to be relevant to this argument.

Let us begin, then, at the outset of the Modern Age, at which time we can notice the beginning of two processes of great importance in terms of demarcating Central Europe, in contrast both to the West and the East. These two processes were the overseas discoveries and the Reformation. The overseas discoveries and the ensuing expansions abroad were of decisive import in terms of the integration of states and societies in the West. The area to the east of France, though, participated only partially in this overseas expansion and was likewise only indirectly affected by its consequences - such as the Price Revolution, for example. In this, the relationship of Central Europe to the Western European powers and their commercial expansion also differed from that of Eastern Europe, which itself became a secondary target for Western merchant capital, and was thus brought into a position on the periphery of the emerging world system.

The Reformation, both its course and its outcome, also held specific consequences for Central Europe. That is not to say that the success of the Reformation was not felt in other parts of Europe, in the West and in the North (though not in the South or in the East); but in these areas the success was of a different nature. In the countries of the West and North of Europe the Reformation either achieved a complete victory, and became the state religion (England, the northern Netherlands, Denmark, Sweden), or after an initial success was ultimately defeated (France, the southern Netherlands). Unlike this type of clear outcome, the Reformation in Central Europe led, in the area between the Baltic region, the Alps, the Rhine and the Vistula, to a lasting compromise such as cannot be found elsewhere in Europe.

This was not a compromise simply founded on consensus. Instead it was a realistic recognition on the part of almost all those involved that, with two thirty-year wars behind them, their goals would not be achieved by force. Though 'religious toleration' meant primarily a mutual understanding between princes and sovereigns, in some parts of Central Europe (the Czech Crown lands, Poland, the Hungarian lands, Transylvania), several generations experienced a period of general cultural tolerance even on the level of townsmen and peasants. Tolerance, however, did not rule out friction and unrest, and in connection with this we must take note that many intellectuals in the region had already formed a picture of the enemy based on religious stereotypes before they had developed a picture of the enemy based on national stereotypes.

A certain tension between religious confessions could in some respects be stimulating. Religious tension persisted into the period of secularization in the nineteenth century where, for example, it is evident in the conflict between the Catholic and Reformation traditions in the historical sciences. Differences in the evaluation of the Reformation, and also the Counter-Reformation, arose, and these remained into the twentieth century an unignorable component in the historical consciousness of a wide stratum of newly forming national units. While in Germany and Hungary a dividing line cut through these units, in the Polish example it came to form an essential component of national identity.

In connection with the Reformation, though not only in this connection, the Thirty Years War, and along with it the temporally and territorially close Polish-Swedish War, was an experience of a specific nature in Central Europe. This was the last conflict in European history in which religious argumentation dominated. At the same time, it was the first conflict - and one surpassing all previous experiences of war in terms of the means and the destructiveness brought to bear - which had a Europe-wide character. Nevertheless, the focal point of the conflict lay in Central Europe, which over the course of events was also ultimately the most damaged by it. It was for this reason also that the conflict became so strongly imprinted in the historical conscious in the Central European region. In all Central European national histories the Thirty Years War occupies a meaningful place in history, or even acts as a temporal landmark. But however unusual it may sound, the war also contributed to the integration of Central Europe and of the other European macroregions.

Leaving aside religious differences, Central Europe shared another relevant experience in common during the early Modern Age, for which we can find the best analogy in the south of Europe. This experience was that of the 'Turkish threat'. The emerging pamphlet literature colourfully described the nature of this threat, and the regularly collected 'Turkish tax' mediated this perception even in parts of Central Europe which never came into direct contact with the Ottomans. For the Habsburg lands and for the Polish nobility it was, of course, an immediate and tangible problem, which then also had a place in creating an historical consciousness. Although the Turkish threat clearly lost its relevance in the nineteenth century, up until that time it remained an important factor in European thought.

In the early Modern Age, absolutism is usually noted as a Europe-wide phenomenon. But the success of the central powers had a markedly different impact in different regions. For Central Europe it holds true that long-term success was achieved only in two important states: the Habsburg Monarchy (specifically the western part) and Prussia. The Estates system survived among the central states, for example Meklenburg, Wurtemburg and Saxony. But Poland as a royal power was sufficiently weakened during this period that a concrete expression of this weakness, the Estates 'republics', emerged. The curious parallel existence of monarchic absolutism and the Estates system was typical for the Habsburg monarchy, where absolutist centralism didn't achieve complete success until the second half of the eighteenth century.

A significant feature of state development in Central Europe is the remarkable discontinuity of its evolution. None of the states in Central Europe evolved in continuity out of the Middle Ages and into a modern nation state: as we see in the cases of France, England, Denmark, Spain and Portugal. Some mediaeval states were engulfed by a larger unit during the early Modern period (Bohemia, Lithuania, the Hungarian lands), and none of the modern nation states in the region is able to refer back to an independent existence during this period. Here, suitable mention should be made of one quite specific political formation, namely the 'Holy Roman Empire', a non-state state which disappeared at the very time when the period of evolution into modern civic states set off. Except for the Balkans, we cannot find such a degree of discontinuity in states and their constitutions in any of the European macroregions as we find in Central Europe. This objective discontinuity clearly contrasts with the demands and aims of the nineteenth century national movements - which were established on the basis of a directly opposite interpretation of history.

But before we embark on this chapter of the development of Central Europe, it is worth mentioning another feature specific to this region: the exceptionally complex overlapping and cohabitation of identities, which was, on the one hand, a result of the disintegration of the Holy Roman Empire, and on the other hand, a product of the opposition of the Estates institutions and the interests of absolutism. A characteristic 'regional patriotism' was notable in this respect, and this was especially typical for the eighteenth century, though it was not always so clearly definable. Sometimes it overlapped with, and at other times it complemented, the dynastic patriotism of the small and middle-sized German states. Due to the strong survival of this regional patriotism, state identity could not (even in the conditions of an absolutist system) assert itself with such authority and consistent action as is seen in Western, Northern and Eastern Europe. To this overlapping of political identities and their ambiguous hierarchies it is important to add the ever-increasing strength of ethnic, or cultural, identities in Central Europe, which opened the doors for new national identities.

Ethnic diversity and national heterogeneity is generally considered the most obviously specific trait of the Central European area. This characterization is valid, but there are two stipulations which must be added. Firstly, the ethnic diversity of the Balkan macroregion is similar to that of the Central European region, if not even more pronounced. Secondly, the ethnic diversity in Central Europe is marked by one qualitative characteristic: this intertwining and overlapping was of ethnic groups whose size and economic stage of development were not necessarily comparable, as they were in the Balkans. Instead the groups were intertwined within the context of one dominating (in terms of numbers and of economic development) ethnic group and culture - the Germans. Although it is unfair to project modern national identities into the period preceding the rise of national movements, it is indisputable that even in the early Modern Age, all Central European ethnic groups and their cultures were to a greater or lesser degree affected by their relationship to the German cultural group.

With the rise of national movements this ethnic diversity acquired a character, in the midst of an imbalance of power, which was again specific to Central Europe. All the Central European national movements, in their early stages, had somehow to formulate a reaction to the significance and influence of the German national movement. We cannot find any similar predominance of one nation and one culture in Western or Northern Europe, although a certain parallel can be sought in the example of Russian predominance in Eastern Europe. Throughout the course of the national movements there emerged a stereotype of protecting national identity against German predominance, as in the Czech, Slovenian and Polish cases. In some instances a partial emancipation was achieved - in the Hungarian case for example - while in others the dependence on German culture was 'covered up' by a new threat, this time from the Hungarians (in the Slovak, Croatian and Romanian examples).

In this connection it is necessary to make note of yet another specific trait. Efforts toward national emancipation in other parts of Europe, whether Catalan, Welsh, Flemish, Finnish or Ukrainian, have emerged out of a distinct and culturally definable concept of the nation and national interests, and this preceded the emergence of the concept of a nation based on a political definition. But in Central Europe, national movements seeking emancipation usually subscribed to the same cultural and linguistic conception of the nation as that of the dominating German national movement. Perhaps for this very reason Central Europe became the 'classic' battleground for national demands and conflicts, where the models were formed for similar conflict in other parts of Europe.

Only after the unification of Germany under Prussian hegemony did the cultural and economic predominance of the German element become one with political dominance. Out of this emerged a conception of the cultural mission of the Germans in Central Europe which, for the Second Reich, became a part of the ideology of territorial claims and expansion in this part of Europe. This was a shift that had, of course, its obverse side: on the basis of such experience the majority of non-German national movements in Central Europe developed a stereotype of a perennial German threat, which was even projected back into their own histories.

Apart from this, ethnic multiformity in Central Europe has yet another peculiarity: the strong participation of the Jewish population in the formation of individual national cultures in the region from the end of the eighteenth century. We can, of course, find evidence of the Jewish Diaspora throughout Europe (perhaps only weaker in Scandinavia), but nowhere did intellectuals and artists of Jewish origin participate so markedly and in such numbers in the intellectual and artistic life of individual nations as they did in Central Europe. The roots of this can be found in the fact that the eastern part of Central Europe neighboured the zone in which the concentration of Jewish inhabitants during the early Modern Age was exceptionally high; and during the first half of the nineteenth century this was above all a consequence of an increasing portion of the Jewish minority identifying itself with the ruling German culture and consequently even with the German nation. During the second half of the nineteenth century, however, alternatives to this identification with the German nation emerged. More specifically this meant an identification with the cultures of the non-German nations that were establishing themselves: at first with the Hungarian and Polish cultures, and then with the Czech. At the very end of the century the Zionist alternative appeared. It is essential to add that identification with a particular culture was not necessarily accompanied by complete assimilation, by the resignation of Jewish identity and a change to the national one. Thus the result was an even more complicated overlapping of identities in Central Europe.

Probing further, is it possible somehow to determine the place of Central Europe in the process of modernization? The common polarization of European development as characterized by the dynamic progress of the advanced West and the stagnation of the backward East tells us very little. The attempt to apply this pattern to Central Europe, dividing it into a more advanced western part and a backward eastern part, founders on the fundamental reality that Central European industrialization took off equally quickly in the west, in the Ruhr basin, and in the east, in Saxony, in Bohemia and even in Silesia. Dortmund and Aachen were as much at the forefront of industrialization as were Berlin and Vienna. In some regards it is even possible to say that the polarization within Central Europe in the early Modern age is rather more characterized by a contrast between the delayed agrarian and backward north, and a more advanced south. But even this polarization loses substance during the course of the nineteenth century.

If we apply the concept of a 'world system', as I. Wallerstein worked it out, we could say that Central Europe belonged until the middle of the nineteenth century to that area known as the 'semi-periphery'; that is, to the territory between the dominant 'heart', occupied by north-west Europe, and the 'periphery', to which eastern and south-eastern Europe belonged. This 'semi-periphery', unlike the 'heart', in no way determined the tempo or direction of development in the system on the whole, but unlike the 'periphery', was not dependent on the 'heart' for its economic growth. For the early Modern period, Wallerstein situated the 'semi-periphery' in the area lying between Scandinavia and the Mediterranean. This perspective even makes it possible for us to regard Central Europe as the main part of the 'semi-periphery': as a sort of centre of gravity.

But following the process of industrialization in the second half of the century the situation changed: the industrial heart of the world system clearly shifted to Central Europe, but did not encompass it entirely. If we consider in this connection that at that very time the unification of Germany had just come about, and if we regard the German territory in its entirety, then it seems that at the end of the nineteenth century we can place Germany in the 'heart', with the rest of Central Europe remaining on the semi-periphery. Thus an important fissure emerged in the historical macroregion of Central Europe, and unlike the situation in the sixteenth and seventeenth centuries it did not divide the macroregion into an advanced south and less advanced north, but instead into a more advanced west and less advanced east. We will see that this was not the only fissure.

In addition to industrialization, mention must also be made of another component in the modernization process, namely education. If we consider literacy as one of the basic markers of education, and thus even as a criterion for modernization, then we can confirm that the conception of Central Europe as occupying an intermediate position between an advanced West and backward East is an invalid one. The average ability to read and write, though with variations in individual countries, was in fact higher in Central Europe at the beginning of the nineteenth century than anywhere else in Europe. This is usually accounted for in the concept of education as a bounden duty, as it was adopted from absolutism, particularly in its later, enlightenment phase, and which was particularly notable in Central Europe. The aforementioned conflict between the three religions of the region must also be included as a mobilising factor in terms of education. The single-minded commitment of the state to a policy of education, which was typical for absolutism, was also adopted in Central Europe as one of the basic tasks of the modern constitutional state. The notion of the state as having the decisive role in and responsibility for the education of the population remains to date as characteristic for all the states which were at one time in the Central European region.

There exists yet another noteworthy distinction: the inhabitants of Central Europe had acquired literacy and the other basics of a general education before they were influenced by the ideas of liberalism and democracy. This could possibly be defined as a Central European paradox, in that in the late absolutist environment people acquired a general education before they acquired a political one. This fact ought to be analysed as a socio-psychological factor which affected the formation of the moral profile of the mass of the population in its relationship to politics. More important for us, however, is the impact it had on the nature of the programmes and aims of the Central European national movements. In all cases (excepting perhaps the Polish resistance to the division of the territory) cultural, educational and linguistic demands were formed earlier than political demands and programmes. (This is not entirely specific to Central Europe, as a similar order of events can also be found in the national movements in Eastern Europe.)

None of the European macroregions can be limited to precise boundaries that would be valid for all periods. Partial shifts occurred everywhere, and for this reason it is necessary to take into account some transitional zones. This is true also for Central Europe, particularly in its western and eastern extremities. The boundaries formed by the sea in the north and the Alps in the south leave only a little room for transitional zones. There were, however, such territories: Schleswig, toward the European north, and Croatia toward the south. At the western end of Central Europe the Swiss cantons (especially in the Rhine Valley) and the left bank of the Rhine formed a transitional zone, and at the eastern end, particularly in earlier times, Transylvania was also such a zone. More complicated was the situation of the Polish-Lithuanian state. Its eastern, Lithuanian and Ukrainian part could have been considered a transitional zone in an earlier period, but from the time of its division from Poland it must be considered as a part of Eastern Europe, with the exception of Lithuania proper, which had a close cultural relationship with Poland proper, due to the Catholicism they shared in common.

In connection with this it is necessary to make mention of the construct 'East Central Europe' that is consistently invoked in German historiography (*Ostmitteleuropa*), and which designates an area encompassing the non-German parts of Central Europe and the non-Orthodox (that is, the Catholic and Protestant) parts of Eastern Europe. This construct has substance insofar as it enables us, particularly in cultural history, to consider as a unit those lands whose political and economic relations were significantly disparate and whose orientation tended in some areas toward the western part of Central Europe, or in other words the German states (the Czech lands, Poland, the Hungarian lands), and in other areas tended toward an Eastern European orientation (nowadays, Poland and Latvia; in the nineteenth century Lithuania and East Galicia).

Where does Central Europe stand in the history of international relations? This question brings us to an extremely serious aspect of our problem, since it has very often become a subject and source of argument in current politicizing, or even ideologizing. By way of introduction, we may note that international relations up until the sixteenth century evolved as relationships within macroregions, and at times between neighbouring macroregions. Thus, for example, the Hundred Years War was a Western European conflict *par excellence*, with some marginal influence in Central Europe. The battle with the Order of Teutonic Knights affected Central and Eastern Europe, while the Livonian wars were a Northern and Eastern European affair. The sixteenth century French-Habsburg struggle over Italy and the battle against

Ottoman expansion were more comprehensive, but still by no means Europe-wide. Whoever would like to doubt the existence of Europe as an internally linked and interactive unit could easily find supportive argumentation in the sphere of international relations. The first conflict that more or less involved the sovereigns and diplomacy of all of Europe was the Thirty Years War.

Throughout the period of the early Modern Age it is valid to state that Central Europe was never the starting point for power-political expansions into other regions of Europe, with the exception of the struggle for influence in northern Italy. Quite the opposite was true: the region itself became a repeated target for expansion from the outside. Next to the already mentioned rise of the Ottomans, there were also the repeated French attacks of the seventeenth and eighteenth centuries, and the successful Swedish expansion of the seventeenth century. In searching for a specific characteristic of international political development in Central Europe, we could look to the internal polarity of the region, which from the sixteenth century was represented by the unending struggle for Habsburg hegemony in the area. Rivals of Habsburg power in Central Europe were always to a considerable degree supported from the outside, but in the eighteenth century a rival of the Habsburg monarchy emerged within the region itself, one which was capable of standing its own, and that was Prussia. For the following period, and especially after the disintegration of the Polish-Lithuanian state, it is possible to view the contest between Prussia and Austria as the dominating polarity in Central European politics.

The balance of power system worked out at the Congress of Vienna for the first time in history enabled the Central European powers to participate decisively in the political evolution of other European regions and in the relationship between European powers in a Europe-wide context. This system operated successfully for several decades, but in the middle of the century it reached a crisis point that peaked with the emergence of a unified Germany. From that time on, Central Europe ceased to be a target of external power politics, and instead became a centre of political expansion. Moreover, it tried to gain a share in imperialist world expansion, and thus even in this way to be part of the 'heart' of an expanding world system. It is symbolic that this shift coincided with the emergence of the rather similar expansionist ambitions of another power, and one which up until that time had also been more of an object than a subject with respect to external relationships: Tsarist Russia. It was not until this more modern period that that erroneous generalization which has often been projected far into the past finally proves true: Central Europe found itself lying between two centres of great power expansion - the western great powers and Russia.

This change, a consequence of the emergence of a new great power, Germany, also became one of the first decisive turnabouts which led to the disintegration of the entire macroregion. Unified Germany overturned the balance of power in Central Europe: and even the crucial Prussian and Austrian polarity - not only in the sphere of international relations, but also in the sphere of economics. From that time on, Central Europe became a German sphere of interest. Nothing can change this important fact, not even if we remember that with the emergence of the Second Reich, Central Europe was inherited by Austria-Hungary, which by contrast is of little relevance for us here.

This shift in power in Central Europe evoked reaction from the other European great powers and laid the foundations for the rise of an enormous and tragic conflict, which was rightly termed the First World War. (I do not intend to question here whether or not this conflict as such had to be.) What is important for us is that at the beginning of the war the concept of *Mitteleuropa* was born, and through the course of the war Central Europe was actually a definable region. Firstly, the polarity between Germany and the other states of Central Europe ceased to be a regional matter and instead reflected a Europe-wide polarity. Secondly, the establishment of an anti-Soviet *cordon sanitaire* reached into Central Europe and turned it about to face East.

The third and definitive step toward the decline of Central Europe was taken by the establishment of a system the foundations of which were laid at Jalta, and which was altogether petrified in the Cold War. The Iron Curtain divided Europe into the West and the East, and Central Europe became a mere memory, that perhaps for some still found a reference point in relic form with the existence of a neutral Austria. Not even after the disintegration of the Soviet bloc did this political reality change. The Iron Curtain was replaced by the Schengen agreements. Optimists of course emphasise the temporary character of these agreements, but the question as to whether a larger European Union will make space for the renewal of Central Europe, or whether Central Europe will be preserved in the already mentioned *Ostmitteleuropa*, still remains open. But to pursue this contemporary question would take me beyond the limits of my theme.

In sum it is possible to say that the construct of Central Europe as one of the European macroregions is a functional and altogether legitimate tool of historical analysis. But for a discussion on the current regionalization of the continent it is of very limited use. A program for its 'renewal', either as an ideological postulate or as an economic or political reality, should take into consideration that the idea or project of a return to the pre-1871 or pre-1914 conditions is merely an illusion: an illusion that, as with all such a-historical illusions about 'returning' to the past, is more of an ideological dead-weight than a source of inspiration. This does not mean that certain, and sometimes even important, relics of the period when Central Europe was a macroregion do not survive in the mentality and in the economic reality alike. A fate shared by the inhabitants of a region through centuries cannot be erased from the minds of the population, and the ties which emerged in this context have left in their wake more than one tangible souvenir, from the alpha of architectural progress to the omega of railway development.

# Central Europe in Art History

*Eliška Fučíková*

The term 'Central Europe', which Professor Hroch has discussed here at some length from historical and political viewpoints, does not in fact enter the official terminology of the cultural area. It is used only as an auxiliary term for the territory, if we want to examine the culture in this area in the present sense of the word. As a professional, I had used the term Central Europe for part of the title of a large exhibition project which I headed and which aimed at mapping one important period in Czech history. Prague deserved its place in the heart of 17th-century Europe, whose maps were stylized as figures of a queen, as during the reign of Rudolf II it became the imperial residence for the second time in its history.

I am an art historian by profession, and I have some experience with the problem of whether Central Europe is the core or periphery, as a few years ago I chaired an identically named section at an international congress on art history in Berlin. I can thus refer to certain general conclusions at which those talks and discussions arrived. Admittedly, these were concerned with art history exclusively, but up to a point they seem also to be relevant to other areas of culture, namely to literature, music, theatre, etc.

In art history, Europe tends to be divided by the Alps, rather than by the actual state frontiers. On the one side, we have the area of classical ancient culture, but inherited mostly by Italy rather than Greece. The other part is the territory beyond the Alps, in which the seeds of this classical culture gave rise to new cultural centres in England, France, the Netherlands, Germany, and elsewhere. These centres were not always identical with the administrative or political centres of these countries. They were often, but not always, related to royal courts; and sometimes it was monastic orders and their associated monasteries that provided the cultural spark: for example, the famous mediaeval monastic scriptoria, whose products - illuminated manuscripts - spread visual art culture, besides disseminating wisdom, and not only in the areas of their production, but also in the other countries where the manuscripts were sent. Important cultural centres also sometimes originated around art-loving aristocrats. There was, for example, the group of artists, headed by Rubens, around the archducal pair of Albrecht and Isabella in Antwerp and Brussels in the first quarter of the 17th century. There were important artistic centres in the cities too, of which we could name, for example, Utrecht in the 16th and 17th centuries; but these circles were also formed around outstanding art personalities, such as Dürer and Cranach within the German lands.

If by Central Europe we mean the part of the continent linked by its common history within the Holy Roman Empire of the German nation, then it is necessary to say that since the Middle Ages there have been important artistic centres which influenced art production in Europe in general, and which could be compared with those in Italy. What I have in mind are, for example, the Rhine valley and the Danube areas in the Middle Ages, Nuremburg and Budin in the 14th century, and 16th-century Saxony. However, unlike in Italy, the art that was produced there was not always the work of local artists. From time immemorial, Central Europe was crossed by important trade routes, which not only served the purposes of commerce, but which also spread knowledge and culture. At the crossing points of these roads, foreigners settled, and became active in all sorts of occupations. The examples which I cite are from the Czech lands, as these are naturally closest at hand for me, but the general conclusions are also applicable to other regions. When Charles IV became the Holy Roman Emperor and chose Prague for his residence, this city not only became an important political centre, but it also excelled in culture. Thanks to his journeys all over Europe, Charles was a connoisseur of the best that was to be seen on the continent at the time. To realize his bold artistic plans, which were closely linked to his political aims, he invited artists from various countries to come to Bohemia. Matthias of Arras came to Prague from France, Tommaso da Modena was from Italy, Peter Parler came from Gmünd in Swabia, Master Theodoricus was possibly of Greek origin... and we could continue listing other nationalities then working at the imperial court. Each of these architects, sculptors, stonemasons, painters, illuminators, goldsmiths, and other craftsmen brought to Prague what he had come to know in the place of his training. The environment into which he had moved and the subsequent commissions visibly influenced his works and gave rise to new qualities. At the court of Charles IV, an important artistic centre was formed, which radiated all over the Empire. At that time, Prague was the heart of the Holy Roman Empire, not only as Charles' residence, but also because it turned into a source of inspiration for at least the whole of the area which at present we name Central Europe. When, for example, Charles' daughter Anna married the English prince Richard, she brought to England not only a numerous train, which also included painters, but also

a

b

c

d

e

f

g

h

i

a Illuminated manuscript: *Uber Viaticus* by Jan ze Středy
b Cathedral of St Vit, Prague
c *St Václav* (1372) - in Cathedral of St Vit
d *Medal of Rudolph I*, Antonio Abondio
e Valdštejn Gardens, Prague
f Karlštejn Castle, interior
g Crown of St Václav (1347)
h Karlštejn Castle, interior
i Church of St Mary, Prague, decoration by J. B. Santini (1710?)

All photos in this section by Atelier Paul, Prague

some rare illuminated manuscripts. Even though the members of her entourage were soon sent back to Bohemia because of misbehaviour, the influence of the art which Anna brought to her new country was even reflected in the wall paintings in Westminster Abbey. Although during the reign of Charles IV the whole area of Central Europe as it is conceived of today displayed the Gothic style and the culture of the High Middle Ages, its standards differed dramatically in various countries, and even in various locations within a single country. Whereas Prague was undoubtedly a real centre, in which new art of a European standard was created, in various other parts of Charles' empire buildings and works of art came into existence which could not compare with these. In those places this new art was not reflected, nor was it perhaps known, as new impulses came there with considerable delay and in a reduced, distorted or folkish form, in a form symptomatic of areas denoted as peripheries, notwithstanding the fact that Caroline court art found its way, as has already been mentioned, as far as England. At that time, artists went around Europe spreading knowledge of new forms and aesthetic views as far as the farthest outposts of the continent. The standard of their information, however, varied, depending on the environment where they had come from. The nationality of the artist was irrelevant; only his qualities and abilities counted.

The co-existence of artists from various artistic centres in one place considerably influenced the established styles. In the case of Caroline art we are speaking of the highest quality both of inspiration and of the ensuing results. In other cases, inspiration of, say, a rather provincial character could contribute to a specific expression of undoubted high qualities in the new environment. From the early 16th century on, Italian architects, stonemasons, stuccoers, and masons came to Bohemia. Coming from the Italian-Swiss border regions, they had not become acquainted with the art of the Italian High Renaissance in Rome, Florence or other important centres, but their information was mediated by various architectural handbooks and drawn models. They mostly stayed in Prague or other towns during the building season only, from spring to autumn, but some of them settled there and made it their home. The new environment inspired them, changing their production into a specifically 'Czech' art expression of high artistic value. Renaissance stately homes, town halls and burghers' houses are still the dominant points and most admired buildings of Bohemian and Moravian cities and towns. In their quality, they are certainly comparable with the outstanding Renaissance buildings in Munich or Augsburg, which also draw on Italian inspiration, but they took a different view of the style.

Until the 17th century, Central European art shows influences of various cultural centres, which resulted in local variants of a standard depending on the person who commissioned the work, their taste and, up to a point, on financial possibilities. After the Thirty Years' War, when various Central European regions ostensibly closed in on themselves, with religious orientation playing an important role, there was a smaller number of artists who came from abroad and set the tone of local production. A classic example is Czech Baroque art. Among the architects there were many with Italian names, who had been born in Italy, but who had found a new home in Bohemia. Still others were their descendants. Their works still resound with Italian inspiration, but they are so specific, so outstanding both in quality and in creativity, that we can easily speak of an important artistic centre having been formed in Bohemia at that time. The painters of the Czech Baroque only rarely travelled - as had been the custom in the past centuries - to acquire their knowledge abroad. Imperial and aristocratic galleries provided enough inspiration in the paintings of the Italian, Flemish, Dutch, Austrian, and German masters exhibited in them. Painters developed their talents under their influence, but not in direct training. Artistic exchange in the 17th and 18th centuries was much more focused on the Central European territory, being carried out within the German lands, Austria, Bohemia, Moravia, and Silesia. Even these regions started to form an original culture which definitely cannot be marked as provincial or peripheral, and which shows features characteristic of the area in question.

An essential turning point in the characteristics of cultural production came about in the 19th century. With the growing national awareness, the demand for national art came increasingly to the foreground. Efforts to get rid of foreign and especially of German influences show up principally in the contents of the works of art. The search for new forms was neglected, however, resulting in the fact that artistic production shared in the search for national identity, but to the detriment of artistic quality. Efforts to eliminate any foreign influence led to provincialism and the lowering of artistic standards. It was only when Central European artists looked around the world again and travelled to countries which then held a leading place in European culture - to France, above all - that they began to emerge from a provincialism influenced by this local patriotism. The aim of their journeys was not so much education, learning their trade, or improving their personal style, but rather getting to know the freedom of artistic creation, the immense scope of the means of expression, and the right of artists to create works independently of social commissions, out of their inner needs.

Paradoxically, it was only then that the various national schools began to differ. They held on to their characteristic features well into our century. The 20th century again shook the Central European region in a slightly different way - compared to that of the Middle Ages and early modern times. Classic centres of European culture, mainly Paris, were conquered by artists coming from the 'provinces', from the areas which until then had mostly just accepted influences from outside. I don't have in mind only such figures as Picasso from Spain, but also the Russian Kandinsky, Mucha and Kupka from Bohemia, and so on. A new art was created, without national or nationalistic borders, and thanks to the easy flow of information in print, by picture and by sound, it was spread to all places where people were interested. Only after World War II, when Central Europe was divided by the Iron Curtain into East and West, did the growing isolation that resulted begin to influence art production again: not only through a lack of information about what was happening elsewhere in the world, but also through the greatest talents escaping into emigration, and political pressure being asserted on the artists to accept the Communist ideology and its corresponding form of expression in art.

When the Iron Curtain fell in 1989, a somewhat strange situation arose. Opening the borders brought not only the possibility of free movement of people and information, but also the possibility of confrontation and comparison between what had been created in the West and in the East. Besides an enthusiastic reception for this possibility from many people, voices reminiscent of those of 19th-century patriots have arisen too. Nevertheless it seems that in spite of that, the influence of those factors which had in the past brought definite positive results in Central Europe, and led it out of cultural provincialism, is beginning to be felt once more. This was perhaps one of the reasons why the exhibition *Rudolf II and Prague: the Imperial Court and Residential City as a Spiritual and Cultural Centre of Central Europe* [Prague, May-September 1997 - ed.] was so successful: not only with the general public, but also with contemporary artists. It pointed to a period in which in one place, in Prague, enormous spiritual and artistic potential had gathered from various countries in Europe. Thanks to an enlightened monarch, various artists and scholars and scientists found another home, freedom of creativity, and even the appreciation of the public. This is why Karel van Mander, a famous Dutch painter and biographer of Italian, Netherlands and German painters, both from the past and from his own time, could recommend in his book (published in 1604) that young would-be artists should travel to Prague, if they wanted to know a genuine Mecca of art. How different this is from the fairly recent past, when every artist coming from beyond the Alps headed automatically for Italy if he wanted to broaden his training and education. This happy situation, however, soon vanished, when the local conditions changed drastically. When Rudolf died, he was succeeded by his intolerant brother Matthias, who did not like art and who was the cause of many Protestant scholars and artists leaving the country. The Czech Lands changed into a province that expelled talented people and drove them to escape abroad. Wenceslaus Hollar and Comenius should be cited as the most well-known examples.

The debate at the 1990 Congress in Berlin ended with a statement that thanks to its geographical position, Central Europe had played an important part in political, economic and spiritual history. At the time when it opened up to the world, when its political arrangements were built on a multinational basis, it was able to compete in the area of culture with the most important traditional centres. When it lacked this possibility, or when it prescribed itself nationalism as a programme, it could not do as much as at other times. Just to quote another example from the Czech lands, after World War I, the exceptional interest and quality of Czech culture was conditioned by its successful interweaving of the influences of three ethnic groups then living in the area: the Czechs, the Germans and the Jews. Two of these ethnic groups, the Jews and the Germans, and thus their inspirational contribution, vanished almost completely from this environment after World War II. Czech culture still nostalgically recalls the years between the two wars and lives on their inspiration. Some of its artists do so so vehemently that they try to follow the styles of that period, avoiding any inspiration coming from outside or from more recent history, and merely imitating. Prague, however, seems to be very attractive to foreigners and during the few years after the revolution it had enchanted a fresh community of them. Besides the Americans, English and French people, also Russians, Slovaks and artists from the former Yugoslavia have settled there.

It is impossible to answer the question whether Central Europe is the core or periphery of Europe: there is no unequivocal reply. It depends. In its territory, there are certainly some places which have never contributed anything significant to international culture. Its situation within European culture was formed in the same way as it was formed geographically: that is, from a number of larger and smaller states; and this cultural character persists even today. In its territory there is perhaps not a single place which would occupy a similarly permanent position in the cultural world as for example do London, Antwerp, Paris, Florence, and Rome. However, in the past, Central Europe has never been, and hopefully it never will be in the future, entirely peripheral. This situation will last especially if the area preserves its openness to foreign influences and to those artists who come to settle and create there; if it gets its inspiration from what they are bringing, and if it will in turn influence them by its *milieu* in such a way that they, together with local artists, can create new values and thus a new artistic and cultural environment in which to live.

# Is There a Central-European Identity in Literature?

*Ewald Osers*

In the literary sphere the concept of a Central European identity is not as easily defined as it is in economics or political science. Try as one may to discover objective scholarly criteria, one finds oneself, ultimately, reduced to subjective, often unverifiable, judgements, feelings, or even hunches.

Perhaps I should declare my position straight away: personally I believe that, certainly in late nineteenth-century and twentieth-century writing, there is something that sets the writers of this geographical area apart from those outside it. At the recent conference at Štiřín Otto Pick asked the question: 'Is Franz Kafka a German-Jewish writer who happened to be born in Prague, or is he a typical Central European writer?' This extreme formulation set me thinking - more precisely, the word 'typical' set me thinking. What would make a Central European writer a 'typical' one? Had Professor Pick said 'clearly a Central European writer' I would have said 'yes' without giving it another thought.

It seems to me that the only even faintly scholarly approach would be to look at a handful of authors from inside and outside this hazily defined Central Europe, both novelists and poets, writing (like Kafka) in German, and to try to discover what characteristics, if any, those 'inside' have in common and what characteristics, if any, distinguish them from those 'outside'. As a next methodological step we might look at some authors writing in Czech and see whether they share any characteristics with their German-writing colleagues inside the area. Care would, of course, have to be taken not to confuse an author's choice of *realia* with whatever Central European characteristics he might have.

If we begin by looking at Jaroslav Hašek's *Good Soldier Švejk* (*Hašek; 1993*), Joseph Roth's *The Radetzky March* (*Roth; 1974*), and Arnold Zweig's *The Case Of Sergeant Grischa* (*Zweig; 1947*) - three novels all set in an army milieu - we find that the atmosphere, the spirit, of the first two is noticeably different from that of the third. The heroes (or anti-heroes) of Hašek (1883-1923) and Roth (1894-1939) are neither supporters nor real opponents of the army of His Sacred Imperial and Royal Majesty, or of the system that army supports: they find it, and the political system behind it, faintly ridiculous. Not evil, but outdated and a bit of a joke. There is a kind of *je-m'en-foutism* about it, a certain resignation, fatalism, laxness and *Schlamperei.* An unheroic and perhaps subconscious focusing on the absurdities. Take the open-air Mass celebrated - in *The Good Soldier Švejk* - in front of a portable folding altar, by the *Feldkurat* Katz. No mention is made of the fact that Katz is a typically Jewish name - but a Czech reader would know. I am not, of course, suggesting that Jews do not convert to Christianity elsewhere than in Central Europe or that they do not sometimes take holy orders: after all we have a Bishop Montefiore in England. But in its place in the book this incident serves to emphasise, and is clearly intended to emphasise, the comicality of the whole setting.

Joseph Roth's *Radetzky March* marvellously reflects the atmosphere of an empire that has outlived itself, that lives, in its civilian and military society, on its past glory - the young Lieutenant Trotta unable to live up to the legend of his grandfather, 'the hero of Solferino' (even though that legend, perhaps typically, is proved to be a sham) - an empire that, politically, was crumbling at its edges and that was presided over by a tired old man, an emperor who was beginning to show signs of senility. A key passage in the novel is the duel to which the Jewish army surgeon is compelled to challenge an aristocratic fellow officer who had insulted him: he realizes the stupidity of the code of honour by which he considers himself bound, yet he complies with it. Both duellists are killed and a senior officer's only comment is 'Nothing one could have done about it.' Again a kind of shoulder-shrugging, unprotesting acceptance of the folly of a system. A more hilarious picture of the imperial Austrian army and its officer class is *The Storming of Sarajevo* (*Meyrink; 1913*) by Vienna-born Gustav Meyrink (1868-1932). Written in what might be called officers' mess Viennese, this short story describes how an army unit which had lost its way mistakes Sarajevo for the enemy's capital city and, with considerable loss of life on both sides, storms and captures the town which had long been part of the Austrian empire and was garrisoned by Austrian troops.

The spirit that informs *The Case Of Sergeant Grischa* by the non-mid-European Arnold Zweig (1887-1968) is very different. To him - as to his fellow-German Erich Maria Remarque, author of *All Quiet On The Western Front* - the army is not a joke, but a cold, unfeeling institution which does not even function well.

One of the most important Central European authors between the two world wars, an author who was shortlisted for the Nobel Prize, was Karel Čapek (1890-1938). A close personal friend of President Thomas G. Masaryk, he shared his political ideas and ideals, and later published his conversations with him under the title (in the English translation) *President Masaryk Tells His Story* (*Čapek; 1941*). Not a person, therefore, who could be accused of sharing Joseph Roth's mood of pessimism and impending doom. But even he, it seems to me, betrays a mid-European identity at least in some of his writings. His novel *War With The Newts (Čapek; 1998*), a social and political satire in science-fiction form, never ceases to be cosily amusing and entertaining, and it ends, reassuringly, with the Newts not taking over the world. His other great science-fiction satire, the play *R.U.R. (Rossum's Universal Robots)* (*Čapek; 1923*) ends not with the robots gaining mastery over mankind, but with two robots, a male and a female one, discovering love, laughter and tears - the progenitors of a new human race. It lacks the frightening vision of the future which characterizes Aldous Huxley's *Brave New World* (*Huxley; 1994*) or George Orwell's *Nineteen Eighty-four* (*Orwell; 1993*) - two authors outside our mid-European zone. And if we look at Čapek's short stories we find in them a good-humoured *Gemütlichkeit* that seems to me entirely mid-European.

One is tempted, from considering the satirical and absurdist authors of *Mitteleuropa*, to go one step further and look at the unwritten jokes of the region. I believe that there is a type of Central European joke that would not be found in Germany, or in Italy, or in France - though just possibly in Israel, as a kind of mid-European humour brought to the Middle East by immigrants from Central Europe. But I am not thinking here, or not primarily, of Jewish jokes. There is that vast range of Viennese Count Bobby jokes. Slightly goofy aristocrats are surely not confined to the old Austrian monarchy - one need only think of the characters in P. G. Wodehouse's books - but there is an endearing gentleness about Count Bobby and his friend Rudi that I think is lacking outside our region. There is the equally wide field of Frau von Pollak jokes, rooted anywhere between Prague and Vienna, and possibly at home even in Budapest. Again, social climbers and parvenus are not exclusive to Central Europe, but I think that outside this area jokes about social climbers would be rather more aggressive and condemnatory; they would lack the forgiving note that surrounds Frau von Pollak's pretensions. (It is worth noting that the English television series *Keeping Up Appearances*, increasingly popular now also in America, is, by comparison, explicit farce.) When Czechs added to the ubiquitous slogan posters '*Se sovětským svazem na věčné časy*' [With the Soviet Union in all Eternity] the words '*A ani o minutu dýl*' [And not a minute longer], then this seems to me the same kind of mid-European humour as the Poles' interpretation of the initials RWPG, which stood for the Polish of Council for Mutual Economic Aid, as *Ruskim wszystko, Polakom gówno* [For the Russians everything, for the Poles bugger-all]. Surely this is the same kind of humour as in the Austrian joke, in the mid-thirties, when the (then illegal) Nazis began to stage attempts on the lives of Austrian leaders: 'The penalty for shooting at a public official is ten years' imprisonment. The penalty for shooting at a member of the government is twenty years' imprisonment. To shoot at the President of the Republic is altogether forbidden' [*Auf den Herrn Bundespräsidenten zu schiessen ist überhaupt verboten*]. What these jokes - Czech, Polish, Austrian - have in common is a determination to see the funny side even of a desperate situation. This attitude is perhaps most succinctly expressed in the famous persiflage of a First World War Austrian high command communiqué: 'The situation at our front is hopeless, but not serious.' I have a strong feeling that outside our mid-European area these things would not be joked about. Or if joked about, then there would be more militancy in these political jokes, almost certainly more crudeness, and not the same degree of amused tolerance of the situation.

Leaving humour aside and returning to serious writing, we come back to Otto Pick's question about Kafka. There is no obvious similarity or parallel between the haunted and haunting work of Franz Kafka and the angry, contemptuous sneering of Thomas Bernhard. Yet in a way both authors, using very different means, expose the horror and the absurdity of the world around them - Kafka the helplessness of the individual trapped in a machinery he does not understand, Bernhard the superficiality, the meanness, the falseness and the complacency of Austrian society. One would look in vain for anything similar outside the mid-European area - Thomas Mann, Günter Grass, Heinrich Böll or Jean-Paul Sartre are quite different.

There is, I would suggest, some similarity between *The Last Days of Mankind* (*Kraus; 1974*) by Karl Kraus (1874-1936) and *The Tragedy of Man* (*Madách; 1998*) by the Hungarian Imre Madách (1823-1864), in spite of the time gap between them - an awareness of doom, but with a markedly satirical undertone. Only in the work of a Central-European writer - in this case Karl Kraus, born in Bohemia but working in Vienna - would the final scene of his apocalyptic vision of the end of humanity be accompanied by a group of hyenas dancing a Viennese waltz on the dead bodies of the killed, or (the final line of the play) the reported (but possibly apocryphal) remark of the Emperor Franz Joseph, 'I did not want this,' be placed in the mouth of God.

From a writer in Germany or in Russia one would expect a deeper blackness, an unrelieved gloom.

Whether we look at Stefan Zweig (1881-1942) or Robert Musil (1880-1942) or Joseph Roth, it is hard to avoid the impression that, for all their differences, they have one thing in common - an atmosphere of overripeness, a world past its peak, a society on the decline. This is not necessarily a negative value judgement. The sympathetically described emotional and social entanglements in Schnitzler's stories and plays could probably not exist in a society that was still militantly, aggressively, on the way up, any more than could the delicately portrayed relationships in Stefan Zweig's later books - I am thinking here of *Erstes Erlebnis*, *Amok*, and *Verwirrung der Gefühle* (*Zweig; 1928a, 1923*: some of the stories from the first two of these volumes are translated in *Zweig, 1928b*). The Austrian Robert Musil's *Man without Qualities* (*Musil; 1935*) seems to me very different from the German Hans Fallada's (1893-1947) equally famous *Little Man* (*Fallada; 1933*) - the mid-European being the psychologically much more complicated of the two.

There are, I think, two aspects worth noting - first, this atmosphere of decline, of an irresistible downward slide, did not come to an end with the collapse of the Habsburg monarchy, but continued into the twenties; second, there is, in all the authors I have named, an air of acceptance of the inevitable, perhaps even a reasonably happy, resigned acceptance.

The more we focus on what may be a Central European identity in the field of literature, the more we find ourselves inclined to define its geographical extent as coextensive with the old Austro-Hungarian monarchy, particularly perhaps with its heartland - Austria proper and its historical crown lands of Bohemia, Moravia and Silesia.

I had hoped to extend my proposition to the area of poetry. I had hoped to show that Rainer Maria Rilke, born in Prague into a German-speaking family, was essentially different from Stefan George, who was born in the Rhineland. I had thought that in the Christian imagery of Rilke's *Stundenbuch* (*Rilke; 1941, 1995*) or *Marienleben* (*Rilke; 1951*), on the one hand, and the neo-classical pagan world of Stefan George's *Jahr der Seele* (*George; 1982*) or *Teppich des Lebens* (*George; 1984*) on the other, a difference between 'mid-European' and 'non-mid-European' would be found. But I have to confess that any such characterization would be contrived. Indeed on re-reading some Rilke and some Stefan George I was struck by the number of poems which could (or almost could) have been written by either of them. Clearly not every author born within our area bears its traces. It could, of course, be argued - in defence of our thesis - that Rilke only spent his younger years within the area, after which he travelled around and then lived in Paris and in Switzerland, quite apart from the fact that there was probably a deliberate effort on his part to be not a Central European but a European poet. And perhaps our thesis continues to be valid so long as most of the authors born and working within our area, or at least a sufficient number of them, display some of the aspects of a mid-European identity.

I have no hesitation in claiming Hugo von Hofmannsthal for my proposition, and perhaps also Ernst Trakl, even though, a native of Salzburg, he was born within a stone's throw of the periphery of the area. The extensive correspondence (*Hammelmann and Osers; 1961*) between Hofmannsthal and Richard Strauss (who had a brashness often thought of as 'typically German') highlights the Viennese poet's overculturedness, oversophistication and basically pessimistic view of the world. He could almost be a character from Joseph Roth or Arthur Schnitzler.

If we accept the existence of a mid-European identity in the literature of the territory of the former Habsburg monarchy, the question arises whether this identity has survived the political and social upheavals of the thirties and the Second World War, including of course the virtual annihilation of the Jewish population of the region. One imagines that, even with the original nutrient soil no longer existing, this 'mid-European identity' would, at least for a time, continue to be present through the operation of inter-generational tradition. Indeed, I believe that Bohumil Hrabal, Vladimír Páral and Miroslav Holub can be seen as direct heirs to the Švejk tradition in literature, even though Holub has, I would claim, one foot outside our mid-European area: his black humour is focused not so much on the foibles and follies of Central-European man as on the absurdities of humanity generally. (In much of his writing there is an affinity with the American Joseph Heller.) If we compare these writers with German satirical or humorous writers, with Erich Kästner, Christian Morgenstern or Joachim Ringelnatz, we find that they are, in a way not easy to define but, I think, clearly perceptible, rather different.

In conclusion one is bound to ask whether a politically restructured and nationally fragmented Central Europe will continue to sustain a mid-European identity in literature. Might there not be a deliberate change of climate from inward-looking, gently self-pitying fatalism to a European-Community-oriented optimism? A deliberate effort to shake off whatever spiritual heritage is left of the old monarchy and to become 'Westerners'? In the tug-of-war between mid-European tradition and West European strivings - one is tempted to say: between inherited and acquired characteristics - which will prove stronger in the future?

# 2.
# Interrupted Progress

Jiří Musil, Christopher Cviic

# Discontinuity in Central and South-Eastern Europe

*George Schöpflin*

Discontinuity is conventionally understood as a fragmentation of power, as a result of which neither the individual nor the community has adequate control of its fate, and the nature of coherence is threatened. (*Eliade; 1954*) In Central and South-Eastern Europe it is all but a cliché that the region has suffered from the repeated experience of discontinuity and the resulting threat of incoherence. In terms of self-images and perceptions of history, the past is seen as a constant series of foreign invasions, subjections, conquest and cæsuras. (*Milosz; 1983*) The outcome is a strong sense of powerlessness, of being buffeted by alien forces, of being the plaything of history.

In this context, we should look first at real and perceived history and compare these histories to the experience of those collectivities which are seen in Central and South-Eastern Europe as having an integral past, i.e. the West. There is an apparent contradiction here. The history of the West is far from having been untroubled by cataclysms. Even a casual look at the histories of countries like France or Britain will show massive cæsuras. Thus in the 20$^{th}$ century alone, France has undergone two world wars, two foreign occupations (one partial), the terrible losses in the First World War, the need to reintegrate Alsace-Lorraine after 1918 and again after 1944, loss of empire, the influx of three million refugees ethnically cleansed from North Africa and then the arrival of a further 3-4 million immigrants, a semi-civil war in the early 1960s, three constitutions, and a far-reaching socio-economic transformation which saw the end of the traditional peasantry. Yet this history is not seen as discontinuous in the Central and South-East European sense. So why, then, is history conventionally defined as fragmented in that region and not in the West?

A number of long term, interlocking historical events have combined to create this sense of powerlessness. In the first place, the area has evidently been subjected to a series of invasions and occupations from outside, though that in itself is not a sufficient explanation, given that various Western countries have had a similar past (e.g. Ireland, Italy, Netherlands). What is significant in this connection is that invasion was followed by repeated attempts to transform the local institutions and customs according to the needs, aspirations and wishes of the alien invader. The most important of these for our purposes was the expansion of empire from the 16th century onwards. The destruction of the local systems of power and their incorporation into imperial projects have left an ambiguous legacy. None of the empires was powerful enough to eliminate local institutions and traditions entirely. These persisted sometimes in combination with imperial power, at others as a source of contest. The outcome has been an incompleteness, as neither imperial nor local aspirations were ever fully satisfied. The idea of incompleteness and intermediacy is strongly felt throughout the region; it is a recurring theme in the literature and historiography of every tradition there.

Thus, by way of example, the Ottoman Empire had remarkable military capacity for its time (14th and 15th centuries), but it lacked the ability to transform the lands that it conquered into integral parts of itself. The ambiguity can be seen most acutely in the intermediacy of the tributary states of the Danubian Principalities and Transylvania. (*Makkai et al; 1986, Boia; 1997*) These lands remained under native princes and thus were able to retain their own institutions, but these institutions were continuously subjected to interventions from the Porte, as a result of which their functioning was disrupted and their ability to establish themselves as coherent entities was constantly undermined. This meant that the relationship between rulers and ruled was a distant one, with very little sense of community, in which the reciprocity of power was either non-existent or very restricted. That in turn brought with it an alienation from all political institutions, which tended to be regarded by the majority as remote, exploitative and arbitrary. The local elites were content with the enserfment of the bulk of the population and the peasantry had little reason to identify with the institutions of their rulers. In that sense there was a discontinuity within the population.

Something analogous applied to the Hapsburg-ruled lands. Vienna controlled them, but could not reshape them when state modernization reached the imperial agenda in the 18th century; likewise in Prussia and Russia. Local institutions not only survived but were able to fight off the challenges launched by the imperial centre. What they could not do, on the other hand, was to launch modernizations of their own. Indeed, in the most conspicuous case - that of Poland in 1791 - the empires moved rapidly to squelch the potential threat that a modernized Polish state might represent to them, and partitioned what was left of Poland.

The role of the state, it should be clear, is a key aspect of this analysis.

While the differences between the mediæval kingdoms of West and East existed, these were not insurmountable. (*Szucs; 1983*) It was the coming of the modern state, from the 16-17th centuries onwards, that began to effect the transformation that has given rise to the experience of discontinuity. In the West, the newly developed technologies of organization, rationalization and classification that underlie the growth of state power and capacity gave rise to the modern state that is marked by its ability to maximise its taxing and coercive power. (*McNeill; 1983*, *Mann; 1993*) Inevitably, this process impacted repeatedly on the Central and South-East European region, where neither social capital, urbanization, agriculture nor trade had evolved to the level where a similar intensification of state capacity was feasible.

The contrast between this region and, say, Italy is instructive. At the end of the 15th century, France had acquired a remarkable lead in artillery technology and was able to devastate Italy, which was largely defenceless against the new fire-power of the French. (*Keegan; 1993*) Yet because Italian intellectual, economic and organizational capacity was eclipsed only temporarily, within two generations the gap was closed and a new fortification system was designed that largely nullified the earlier advantage. In Central and South-Eastern Europe, the gap could not be closed, essentially because the local capacity for generating power and intellectual capital was lower than that of the intruding empires. Much the same applied to taxing capacity as did to coercive capacity. (*Tilly; 1975*)

The outcome of the difference in state capacity turned out to be vital in the development of the two regions of Europe. The rise of the modern state created the preconditions in which the state, in order to operate efficiently, demanded a growing input of consent on the part of the ruled - modernity implies mounting complexity and greater complexity means that neither coercion (or the threat of coercion), nor reliance on only a part of the ruled, would function as successfully as reliance on the consent of the bulk of the governed. Here in the rise of state capacity one can see the origins of democracy, so that the weakness of state capacity had far-reaching implications for the retardation of the spread of democratic forms of government in Central and South-Eastern Europe.

The consequences of the gap went beyond the foregoing, however. There is a persuasive argument to the effect that the forms of the public sphere, the public thought-styles and thought-worlds which a society encounters when it enters modernity leave a lasting impress on the collectivities concerned. Hence it becomes important to scrutinise closely the context in which these societies were brought to the encounter. Clearly, it is significant that Central and South-Eastern Europe entered modernity antagonistically, in the form of a collision. Broadly in the West, the process of modernization was 'organic' in the sense that conflicts over 'modern' forms were either domestic, as between different socio-political actors within one polity, or between one or more international actors with their own models of modernity (e.g. as through war between France and Britain or between America and Britain).

In Central and South-Eastern Europe, domestic models of modernity, as argued above, were weak and not based very directly on local socio-economic patterns, but were imported from outside, often as a response to the intrusion of a power that was perceived as alien, and as a defence against that intrusion. This process of importation inevitably distorted the nature of modernity as it had evolved in the West, because the domestic context was different and the aspects of modernity that were taken over were inevitably partial. Technology has a cultural context and the reception of technology without its enveloping culture changes its impact. Hence the repeated attempts to make 'a forced march through history' and to catch up with Europe never achieved their objective.

The outcome of this pattern for the region was manifold. It created a state of affairs where local patterns tended to be devalued, whereas imported aspirations had high prestige. Local institutions were on the whole not trusted, and power was often seen as arbitrary and uncontrollable. In all human activity, however, power operates simultaneously at two levels - the institutional and the symbolic - and when power cannot be secured at one of these, compensation will be sought in the other. (*Hankiss; 1997*, *Kertzer; 1988*, *Mach; 1993*) This is what regularly evolved in the region. The institutions of the alien empires were distrusted, domestic institutions were fragile, and to secure the coherence of local communities the symbolic sphere was invested with a significance far greater than has been the case in the West, particularly in the Anglo-Saxon West. But this created a difficulty of its own. When political power is primarily generated and exercised in the symbolic sphere, it cannot easily be made transparent and accountable, because symbolic action (rituals, liturgies, myths) inevitably gives rise to ambiguity. Symbolic power then quite understandably functions in an arbitrary way, which triggers off mistrust and uncertainty.

The second dimension of modernization-as-resistance concerns the reception of the ideology of nationalism. This is a particularly long and complex process which demands very extensive analysis for which there is no space here, but in essence the local elites sought to mobilise and strengthen their power by relying on the ideology of nationhood. (*Schöpflin; 1998b*) Here again, the difference in the history of institutions proved to be crucial. In the West - particularly in the so-called core states of France, England, and the Netherlands - the reliance on nationhood for the mobilization of society took place within a political culture of 'organic' institutions, so that civic and ethnic forms of attachment were in some kind of a balance. On the other hand, where (as in Central and South-Eastern Europe) civic and state institutions were weak, ethnicity - which depends strongly on symbolic action - tended to predominate in sustaining coherence. This further reinforced the already high significance of symbolic politics, with a corresponding difficulty in finding a way to make power predictable and transparent. This pattern of power has persisted to the present day, though the intervening period of the last 200 years added its own distortions.

It was against this background of belated and uneven modernization, with sizeable sections of society still to be modernized, with a rather low socio-economic base (predominantly peasant agriculture, limited industry, low state capacity, restricted forms of knowledge) and with a penchant for relying as much on the symbolic as on the institutional sphere that the region weathered (or not) its first phase of independence from 1918 to 1939. The Second World War represented a major cæsura, not least in breaking the will to rule of the pre-war political elites and thereby indirectly assisting the communist take-over.

Communism itself should be seen as another discontinuity. It completed the project of modernization, but the modernization that it brought was very one-sided, distorted as it was in favour of an eccentric model of narrow industrialization (with its exclusive emphasis on heavy industry) and the monopoly of political power. It is particularly important to note here that the reliance on monopoly power to effect modernization was founded on a non-consensual understanding of power. Consent was dispensed with as superfluous because the communist ideology was declared perfect. Once again, the imposition of an externally generated model of modernity failed the region and, even more vitally, was seen to have failed it by those who lived there. (*Gellner; 1991*)

The post-communist experiment in democracy is still young and it would be quite premature to offer anything more than an interim assessment of it. However, two factors stand out. One is that the ideals, institutions and legitimating aspirations of democracy were once more imported, though this time the fact that they were imported from the West and not the East added to their attractiveness; and, though democracy was a transplant, it has shown a fair measure of resilience in its first few years. Many changes of government have taken place and these have all resulted from democratically conducted elections.

Nevertheless, the post-communist systems exhibited features common to many of their historical and socio-cultural antecedents. The institutional sphere - crucially, commitment to self-limitation and the acceptance of procedures as authentic - was operating only intermittently, and often only in relation to major aspects of the power system and much less regularly in everyday life. Encounters between the individual and the state have remained opaque and unpredictable. Correspondingly, the symbolic sphere has played a disproportionate role.

In the political evolution of the region, the West has a very particular role to perform. It is Central and South-Eastern Europe's 'idealized other'. It is the West as myth, as an alternative, superior world against which whatever is happening at home can be measured and generally found wanting. In this pattern of reasoning, the discontinuities of the West are screened out cognitively and the West is reinterpreted as the area of stability and continuity; and hence - it is the next step in the logic - the West owes a duty of care to the East, because the East is its most ardent imitator.

This myth-West has not that much to do with the sociological and political reality of Western Europe. It is constructed out of best-case examples and the negative factors are ignored, as they must be if the mythic function of the West is to work. This myth-West is broadly speaking internalized and made a part of the implicit cognitive world of the region - a part of 'doxa' in Bourdieu's language (*Bourdieu; 1993*) - and cannot easily be challenged other than at the mythic level. Naturally, it has a negative counterpart among those who decry Europe, currently the radical right. (It is, incidentally, wholly misleading to label representatives of these social currents as 'Eurosceptics', because that term implies a degree of engagement with the European integration process, whereas the radical right denies Europe or at least the Europe that exists now.)

The problem of this myth-West is that it frequently runs up against the real West: the institutions and states that actually comprise Western Europe, with their own interests, ideals, agendas and, for that matter, their own mythic universe. The real West does not always behave in the way in which an idealized other should behave, and this triggers off disconcertingly harsh responses from Central and South-East Europeans. These are the responses of betrayal. These feelings of betrayal should not be seen as some kind of a 'typical, infantile' response, but as an intelligible reaction to an inexplicable phenomenon that disturbs one's coherent picture of the world and counts as a discontinuity. All this is exacerbated by the weakness of trust in institutions in the region. The West's 'businesslike' approach, based as it is on a belief in institutions and procedures, is not understood on the same terms as it is offered, but is interpreted against a background of discontinuity. Inevitably, misunderstandings and misperceptions ensue, which then relaunch the cycle.

Thus the overall problem of discontinuity in Central and South-Eastern Europe is not the outcome of some inherent irrationality but is the product of specific historical and sociological circumstances. It follows that it will only disappear when the conditions that gave rise to it will be made irrelevant by changing the underlying causal patterns. The difficulty here is that the legacy of the past makes this endeavour harder than it has been in the West; and it may even be that it is impossible to eliminate them all and to create a broadly Western-type coherence.

If one looks at the existing discontinuities in the region, one sees that there are some major ones, with serious implications for democracy and the immediate problem of eastward enlargement, and also a number of minor difficulties that should diminish in their significance with time. In the first place one should look at what might be called the ontological discontinuity. Given the weakness of trust in institutions inherited from the past, the existing democratic order is largely accepted at the symbolic level, but less so in concrete terms. Fundamental aspirations and value-orientations - the secularization of values - remain unintegrated, with the result that the political contest only seems to resemble the kind of democracy that is the norm in the West. There are deep underlying cleavages that are difficult to reconcile within a framework of compromise, give-and-take or the acceptance of diversity. This is quite logical, seeing that political actors are disposed to view the 'other' as constituting a threat to the moral order of which they tend to see themselves as the sole representatives.

Political parties reflect these deep-level ontological divisions, making the political contest far more polarized than in the West. From this perspective, it is clear why political parties are not inclined to trust their opponents with power, treat their time in office as the legitimate exercise of near-monopoly power, and regard the loss of office as cataclysmic. *(Offe; 1998)*

Then there is a major discontinuity between the public sphere and the private sphere. Different moral and practical criteria are applied, essentially to the effect that the rules of consistency and trust do not apply in the former, though they do in the latter, because - and this is inherited from communism - the public sphere is not authentic. Here again, the weakness of institutionalization is evident. This discontinuity extends to the law and preparedness to internalise legal norms; these are weak, understandably if one takes the view that abiding by legality may result in some major disadvantage.

A third discontinuity is in social stratification. While in the post-war years the West very largely eliminated the worst aspects of social divisions, not least through the effective functioning of the welfare state, communist modernization exaggerated such cleavages by investing class with moral virtue (a pattern not entirely absent from the West either, though much weaker since 1989). The consequences of this are still in evidence - as much a result of the absence of agreed criteria for integration as anything else. In these circumstances it is not surprising that ethnicity is accorded such a salient role in creating the kind of coherence that modernity demands. The problem with basing the creation of coherence on ethnicity is that it works poorly in establishing the ground rules for a neutral public sphere, because this is not what ethnicity does (ethnicity is central in sustaining the implicit rules of solidarity, but is poorly adapted to act as the organising principle of a public sphere). (*Schöpflin; 1998a*) Crucially, a public sphere based on ethnicity cannot cope with citizenship when members of several ethnic groups are involved. There are countless examples to support this proposition.

Less important but still relevant discontinuities include the sizeable gap between town and country, in which the legacy of the peasant past remains real. When Gellner once remarked that 'every Czech has a peasant granny', that was his implicit meaning. The proposition is literally or metaphorically true for practically everyone in the region. The wider implication is that patterns of upward mobility are more fragmented than they are in better integrated societies and poverty, particularly rural poverty can be so serious a handicap that equal life chances - a precondition for a successful democracy - are still a long way in the future. Also noteworthy in this connection are the growing regional disparities that can be observed throughout the region. Whereas some regions show a considerable prosperity, others appear to be capable only of reproducing poverty. This can reinforce the appearance that one party's gain is another's loss, i.e. a zero-sum game. (*Jowitt; 1992*). Thus western Hungary is very well-to-do, while eastern Hungary is much poorer. The same can be said for Transylvania and the Regat, for Silesia and eastern Poland, and so on.

There is one final question to be raised in the context of discontinuity - the likely impact of EU integration through eastward enlargement. There is a certain danger that access to the EU might come to be perceived as yet another externally imposed reordering, so that membership will be followed by various forms of resistance, thereby weakening or undermining the enlargement project. From some sections of society, and not just those who are without a voice, this is very much to be expected. Opposition to the kind of Europe that is on offer exists on the political right (the Republicans in the Czech Republic, the Hungarian Justice and Life Party, Radio Maryja etc.).

There are wider aspects to this opposition, however. There are those who dislike the model of European integration because they see it as a form of neo-colonial domination, as being aimed at the homogenization of society and the consequent dilution of community. Attitudes of this kind may be found on the left, among those who view 'Europe' as neo-capitalist and exploitative and who cannot or will not recognise that the integration process involves continuous bargaining and that the criteria of Europe are subject to ongoing modification. These currents will be tacitly supported by those who have a deep-seated fear of the future; they exist in every society, but in the post-communist world their fears are enhanced through lack of cognitive capacity and low intellectual capital.

Further discontinuities can be expected from the key difficulty of low state capacity. It is an open question whether even in the five early access states the entire *acquis* can be enacted and administered in time before membership. Another serious discontinuity is in the widely differing metalanguages of the public sphere. In Central and South-Eastern Europe, these metalanguages tend to be weighted with references to past injustice, coloured by pathos and couched in explicitly symbolic terms. The 'businesslike' language of the West may, therefore, be interpreted in these symbolic terms and not understood in its own context. Crucially, if communication is seen as strongly symbolic, the idea that exchanges can be based on the underlying principle of a positive-sum game becomes meaningless. All too often, accession to the EU can come to be perceived as yet another inevitable overlordship.

Is there a way out of this vicious circle of weak institutions resulting in lack of trust resulting in excessive reliance on symbolic action which then reproduces the cycle? Improvement of state and social capacity should help to enroot a sense of predictability and transparency. At the same time, if the institutionalization of politics operates over time, this should gradually diminish reliance on symbolic action. But this must also take place at the symbolic level. The long term stability of the region and the bridging of its discontinuities require solemnized public action aimed at stabilising the public sphere. It is very much open to question whether this kind of strategy can be achieved from the resources of the Central and South-East Europeans alone. They will need the containing force of the West and its institutions, assuming that the societies of the region have the will and the commitment to accept this kind of external securing. On the one hand, leaders from the region have been asking for precisely this - hence the demand for the eastward enlargement of the EU and NATO - but as against this, the habits and mindsets inherited from the past, the burden of implicit meanings and the particular forms of social knowledge of the region will all make the process troublesome, though not in the end impossible.

# Re-Connecting the Southern Flank

*Christopher Cviic*

*This interpretative essay reflects on the theme of continuity and discontinuity in Central Europe, with particular reference to its 'southern flank' - the region made up of today's Slovenia, Croatia and Bosnia. That region came to be de-coupled from Central Europe earlier in the twentieth century. At the century's end, following the break-up of Yugoslavia, it is moving back into Central Europe, within the broader framework of the European Union.*

---

Any discussion of continuity and discontinuity in contemporary Central Europe faces the obvious problem of the choice of a starting point. Should it be 1918, the year of the break-up of the four dynastic empires which, between them, had ruled Central and Eastern Europe (including South-Eastern Europe) up to that time? Or should it be 1945, the year of Europe's enforced division in the aftermath of the Second World War? Or should it perhaps be 1989, the historical watershed marking the end of the post-1945 division of Europe into two hostile blocks?

For Central Europe's 'southern flank', the most significant watershed is undoubtedly the break-up in 1918 of Austria-Hungary, of which Bosnia, Croatia and Slovenia had been part - the first admittedly only since this province of the Ottoman Empire came under Austro-Hungarian administration in 1878; but the other two for several centuries. Here (as elsewhere in Central Europe), it is important not to lose sight - as many in the West often do - of the fact that Central Europe's peoples, though for long subjects of alien empires, are old nations with a strong sense of identity and a long history. Many of them had once lived in states of their own until for one reason or another they came under foreign rule. For most of them, foreign rule ended only in the twentieth century - for some as late as its second half.

The main reason for the Central Europeans' preoccupation with their national history and, in particular, their national identity, which the West Europeans and Americans find so anachronistic and hard to comprehend, has nothing to do with tactics, but everything to do with their historical experience. This differs significantly both from that of the United States and from that of Western Europe. The European immigrants who built up the United States were anxious to repudiate their (mostly unhappy) past in the old continent and forge a new, American identity. Today's Americans can, therefore, sympathise and even identify with those in Europe who want to forge a new, supranational polity not unlike that of the United States. That was what made so many Americans, including those who were not Communists, so interested in, even fascinated by, the post-1945 federal Yugoslavia. Admirers of supranationalism have little patience with the Central Europeans, who keep recalling their national past, often even the very distant past; failing to see that behind it lies not sentimentality but politics. In Western Europe there is also a good deal of distaste for Central European historicism; but the reasons for that distaste are different: history in Western Europe is taken for granted by its nations, most of which have for generations felt secure in their identity within their own established nation-states.

By contrast, insecurity has been the rule in Central Europe and that is why the Central Europeans care about their identity. All the nations of the region have at some time in the past seen not only their territory but also their national identity, language and historical culture threatened. The threat has not diminished with the passage of time. The old empires, which dissolved in the early years of the twentieth century, were by no means perfect, but the national states that followed them were almost invariably worse.

For example, the strongly legitimist Habsburg Empire recognised some of its peoples as 'historic nations' under the Habsburg Crown, with important consequences for their position. The historic rights of established states under the Crown were upheld. This was demonstrated, for example, in separate coronations, but also in the work of governmental institutions, up to the level of national legislatures. Whenever an attempt was made to do away with any of them, a serious political backlash occurred - coupled with a strong demand, usually in the end granted, for the restoration of those rights. This happened, for example, during the so-called era of 'Absolutism' under Alexander Bach (1851-60), when a centralised structure was imposed on the whole Empire. Or, before that, under the enlightened and modernising but autocratic rule of Joseph II (1780-90). Those rights included broad religious and national toleration. In fact, the introduction of the Patent of Toleration by Emperor Joseph II in 1781 enshrined an already existing practice.

On the other hand, where - as in the Russian, German and Ottoman Empires - there had been a total break with the subject peoples' era of independent statehood, it was usually the Church that took on the role of the guardian of national traditions and identity. It was the Roman Catholic Church which played that role in those parts of Poland that had come under Prussian and Russian rule following the Polish Kingdom's partition among Austria, Prussia and Russia. (This was in contrast to the Roman Catholic Church's attitude in the Habsburg Empire where the hierarchy and the bulk of the clergy remained close to the imperial 'establishment' right up to its break-up in 1918.)

The Ottoman Empire abolished all the political institutions of the states it had conquered in South-Eastern Europe, but it operated the so-called *millet* system of semi-autonomous religious-national communities. The Moslem *millet* embraced no unified territory nor any homogenous ethnic group or people of the same political and legal status. It held a position of superiority over the others because it was the only one that shared the religion and the laws of the ruling Ottoman class and was supported by it financially and in other respects. The non-Moslems were free to organise their religious, legal and educational institutions, but had to do so from their own resources. In that sense, the system held the non-Moslems back but, at the same time, it enabled them to preserve their religious and ethnic identity under the leadership of the Church. In the Ottoman Empire, this meant the Orthodox Church, which the ruler found both a comfortable partner, and a useful Christian counterweight to the Roman Catholic Church whose leader, the Pope, was a strong ally of West European Christian princes in their resistance to Ottoman invasions. It was thus that religion and identity became inextricably linked, with the Orthodox Church assuming an important role in the public life of the individual Balkan nations.

The real threat to national identities came in the last decades of these two empires: in the Habsburg Empire the Slavs felt threatened by pan-German and Hungarian nationalism, while in the Ottoman Empire the non-Turks saw as the main threat the attempt by the Young Turks to create a modern Ottoman identity. In the more confined space of some of the new nation-states established after both empires broke up, nations whose members remained on the wrong side of the border became exposed to a variety of dangers - from discrimination and assimilation to expulsion or even physical annihilation, This was demonstrated, most tragically and spectacularly, in the case of the Jews, who after 1918 exchanged a relatively safe existence in the generally tolerant and benign supranational Habsburg

Empire for a much more exposed and precarious life in the successor-states: a change of status and social position which, in the Second World War, led to the Nazi Holocaust. It is worth noting that, if the Nazis had triumphed in Europe, the survival of certain other Central European peoples would also have been threatened - particularly if they happened to inhabit regions earmarked for direct inclusion into the German Reich. This applied, for example, to the Czechs, the Poles and the Slovenes.

In South-Eastern Europe after 1918, for some of the nations previously under Ottoman rule, such as the Albanians and the Macedonians, predatory neighbours not all that much bigger or more numerous than themselves proved more deadly than the old Ottoman Empire ever was. Serious threats to the national identity and even the survival of such peoples had continued to grow in the post-imperial era and in former Yugoslavia had, in the second half of the twentieth century, twice exploded into mass slaughter - under German and Italian occupation from 1941 to 1945 and during the wars in Croatia in 1991 and Bosnia from 1992 to 1995. A third explosion has now occurred in the predominantly Albanian-inhabited province of Kosovo in Serbia.

Not surprisingly, threats to identity and physical survival - in Central and in South-Eastern Europe alike - have helped to strengthen the bonds linking members of each individual nation to one another at the expense of class and ideological or even religious bonds - to the despair of proponents of universalist ideologies such as Marxism, but also to the despair of those with ideas based on liberalism. That is why nation rather than class has been the main political category throughout the region's history: and to an extent this is still true today.

There are various theories seeking to explain why the Habsburg Empire, which was home for centuries to a variety of nations - including the Slovenes and the Croats (as well as some Serbs and Moslems) on whom this essay focuses - collapsed. Some argue that it would have collapsed anyway because of its increasingly acute internal problems - even if it had not been militarily defeated, along with the German, Russian and Ottoman Empires, in the First World War. The view can be heard that the crisis of the Habsburg Empire had first begun as far back as the end of the seventeenth century - with the end of the Ottoman danger and thus the loss of its *raison d'être* as a shield protecting the peoples in the front line (as well as the rest of Europe) from Ottoman invasion. An illustration of this role was the decision taken in 1527, when the Ottoman danger was at its height, by the Croat and Hungarian nobles who made up the political class at the time, to opt for the

Habsburgs: following their defeat by the Turks in the battle of Mohacs in 1526, and the death of their joint king, Ludovic. (It has to be said, however, that the Habsburg option was not the only one: some Hungarians as well as some Croats opted for accommodation with the Ottoman Empire; but that option - though tried out for a while in Transylvania - did not prevail.) The end of the Ottoman danger meant that nations which had found protection within the Habsburg Empire could begin to look at other possibilities, including independence.

The Hungarians did just this in 1848-49, but were defeated - with help from Tsar Nicholas I of Russia as well as from the Croats, who had felt threatened by rising Hungarian nationalism, and who saw the Emperor in Vienna as an ally. But weakened by military defeats - notably by Prussia in 1866 - the Monarchy had to give in to pressures for change from within. In 1867 the Habsburg Empire transformed itself into Austria-Hungary by an agreement (*Ausgleich*) between Vienna and Budapest. This agreement was followed by another in 1868 between Budapest and Zagreb which restored the old constitutional link between Croatia and Hungary: a link dating back to 1102 but which had been broken in 1848. The deal provided Croatia with a modest degree of autonomy within the Hungarian half of the Monarchy. In contrast, the Slovaks - also in the Hungarian half of the Monarchy, but lacking the status of a 'historic nation' - failed to secure any autonomy from Budapest, which continued to regard the areas inhabited by Slovaks as 'Upper Hungary', and as open to 'Hungarization'.

Like the Slovaks in the Hungarian half, the Slovenes in the Austrian half of the new state lacked the status of a 'historic nation', and in a similar manner failed to secure any autonomy from Vienna. More seriously for the future of the Dual Monarchy, no accommodation proved possible in the Austrian half between Vienna and the Czechs. On the eve of the First World War the Dual Monarchy was in a bad way politically - though not economically.

In economic terms, Austria-Hungary was in many ways a success story. Though its economic space was anything but homogenous, the individual regions having reached the stage of industrial revolution at very different times, there was a rough balance between the industrial core in Bohemia in the west and the largely agrarian eastern half; with finance for a heavy programme of investment in infrastructure coming chiefly from Vienna but also from other European financial centres. There was wide disparity in per capita income of different regions, but official policy had, nevertheless, succeeded quite remarkably in integrating the Monarchy's disparate regions into a functioning unit protected by high tariffs against foreign competition. The forces threatening to tear the Monarchy apart were not economic but political in character.

In the Austrian half, there were strong tensions due to the failure of attempts to reform the antiquated political structure which allowed only extremely limited access to political power for most of the population. Universal franchise and the secret ballot had been achieved by 1907, but the relationship between Czechs and Germans in Bohemia (and to a lesser extent also in Moravia) was deteriorating. In the Hungarian half of the Empire, too, cautious democratization was beginning to take place, but the Croats were frustrated by the failure both of Budapest and Vienna to agree to their demand for a formal union of all Croat lands (including Bosnia, Dalmatia and Istria) under the autonomous government in Zagreb. Some Croats were actively looking for an alternative solution in the shape of a new Southern Slav state, within the Monarchy, if possible, but if not then outside it - in a union with Slovenia, Serbia and Montenegro. This latter option was strongly supported by Croatia's influential Serb community which was part of the ruling coalition in Zagreb (*Hrvatsko-srpska Koalicija*).

It is, nevertheless a fact that among the Southern Slavs - the Slovenes in the Austrian half of the Empire and the Croats in the Hungarian one - the bulk of the political class, though disenchanted and disaffected, continued to think up to the very end in terms of a political solution within the Empire. A major political initiative, the so-called May Declaration, on 30 May 1917, by the so-called Yugoslav Club in the parliament of the Austrian half led by Dr Anton Korošec, a Slovene deputy, and backed by Czech deputies, demanded that all regions of Austria-Hungary inhabited by Slovenes, Croats and Serbs be united into one body under the Habsburg Crown.

This preference for solutions within the Dual Monarchy was even predominant within the political class in Bosnia, which had come under Austro-Hungarian rule in 1878, and which had been formally annexed in 1908. The Monarchy, though initially welcomed only by Bosnia's Croats and bitterly opposed by the province's Moslems and Serbs, had gradually earned even its opponents' respect for its large investment programme in the province's health, education and transport systems: something which had produced a dramatic improvement in living standards. There was some success, particularly among the province's Serb and Croat youth, for the idea of a union of the Monarchy's Southern Slavs with Serbia. This idea was actively promoted from Serbia, which had long aspired to the province of

Bosnia; had hoped to get it, with Russian help, in the wake of the Russian-Turkish war of 1877-78; but which had been frustrated in this aim. Active help for anti-Habsburg revolutionary terrorism in Bosnia from Belgrade started in 1903 when nationalist Serb officers brought the Karadjordjević dynasty to the throne in Belgrade, having previously assassinated the unpopular King Alexander from the rival Obrenović dynasty and his wife. The annexation of Bosnia in 1908 outraged Serb nationalists and led to an increase in active help to anti-Habsburg elements in the province but also in Croatia and Dalmatia. Serb victories in the Balkan wars of 1912 and 1913 increased Serbia's popularity and prestige among all Southern Slavs. It was from the ranks of Bosnia's revolutionary youth that the assassin came who killed Archduke Franz Ferdinand and his wife in Sarajevo in June 1914, sparking off the war between Austria-Hungary and Serbia which quickly grew into a world war.

The Central Powers' military defeats in the autumn of 1918 sealed the Dual Monarchy's fate. On 29 October 1918, a day after a similar declaration in Prague, the Croatian Parliament (*Sabor*) in Zagreb severed all political and constitutional links with Austria and Hungary and proclaimed a new state of Slovenes, Croats and Serbs on their entire ethnic territory. Dr Anton Korošec was made chairman of the National Council, with - as vice-chairmen, Dr Svetozar Pribičević, a Serb, and Dr Ante Pavelić, a Croat, whose notorious namesake became leader of the quisling regime in Croatia from 1941 to 1945. Rapid advances by Italian troops into Slovene- and Croat-inhabited territories on or close to the Adriatic coast, in line with promises made to it by Britain, France and Russia in 1915 to induce it to join the war on their side, caused panic in Zagreb and Ljubljana. Afraid of large-scale territorial losses to Italy, Slovene and Croat politicians, dispensing with all but minimal preliminary negotiations, plunged into unification (*ujedinjenje*) with Serbia and Montenegro under the Karadjordjević dynasty on 1 December 1918. (Bosnia's politicians had already voted for unification separately.) The ruler of the new Kingdom of Serbs, Croats and Slovenes was Prince Regent Alexander (he became King in 1921 on the death of his father, King Peter I and in 1930 gave the state the name Yugoslavia.)

Those were the circumstances under which - after sharing for many centuries the same multinational Central European state with German-speaking Austrians, Czechs, Hungarians, Italians, Poles, Romanians, Slovaks and the Ukrainians of Galicia - the Croats and the Slovenes found themselves for the first time in history in a new state together with the Serbs of Serbia and the Montenegrins. They shared a common language but little else (while the Slovenes, with a completely separate language of their own, did not have even that in common with the other two). The fact that they had never before lived together in one state was in some ways an advantage. It meant an absence of the enmities that often result from living together.

The victorious Entente Powers saw the new state as an element of the new, essentially anti-German order in Europe, named after the punitive Treaty of Versailles of June 1919. The new Yugoslav state had a dual use for the victors: as part of the *cordon sanitaire* against the new brand of Communism now coming from the Soviet Union; but also as a bulwark against the restoration of Austria-Hungary and the return of German influence to the region. And so Yugoslavia duly became, together with Czechoslovakia and Romania, a member of the French-sponsored Little Entente.

But Yugoslavia soon found itself abandoned to its own devices by its original sponsors. The United States opted out of European politics because of the onset of isolationism after 1919. Britain and France were engaged in other parts of Europe and in their colonial empires. The only European power to pursue an active policy in the area was Italy, a victor of 1918 but not happy with its territorial gains. And so Italy started to back, against the pro-status-quo Little Entente, the anti-Versailles, 'revisionist' governments in Austria, Bulgaria and Hungary. In the 1920s and the 1930s it was those states, together with Italy, that provided backing for the disaffected elements (mainly Croats and Macedonians) opposed to the existence of Yugoslavia.

There were plenty of those from the start: Yugoslavia soon turned out to be one of those states that are long on problems but short on solutions. The basic concept behind the new state was the then fashionable Romantic one: that of a common or similar language as a strong bond between peoples and a solid foundation for common life. Officially, Yugoslavia was the state of three equal Southern Slav 'tribes' (*plemena*) - the Croats, the Serbs and the Slovenes - making up the South Slav (*Yugoslav*) nation: but in reality the Serbs were dominant in every sphere of national life. As the largest 'tribe' (though without an absolute majority), the Serbs saw themselves as the liberators of their oppressed Slav brethren, and therefore as entitled to special privileges, not least because of the large casualties and material damage sustained by the Serbs in the Balkan Wars of 1912-13 and, later, in the First World War, during most of which Serbia was occupied by the Austro-Hungarian army.

For the non-Serbs, Yugoslavia proved to be a bitter disappointment. This was particularly so for the Croats, the new state's second largest nation. This was ironic because in the nineteenth century and the early years of the twentieth, Croat intellectuals and churchmen had been among the most enthusiastic advocates of the idea of the union of all Southern Slavs (including the Bulgarians). In 1918, with Italy busy occupying territories allotted to it by the Entente, union in a new Southern Slav state with Serbia, a member of the victorious coalition, had seemed the best protection. But post-1918 Yugoslavia failed to stop Italy from acquiring most of the territory it had been promised.

Another important reason for Croat discontent was the fact that within Yugoslavia Croatia lost the admittedly modest but still well-defined autonomous status it had enjoyed up to 1918 in the Habsburg Empire. Yugoslavia was from the start Greater Serbia under a different name, a centralised state modelled on France, with a Serbian dynasty on the throne, the Serbian Orthodox Church as the *de facto* official church, an army where the majority of officers and non-commissioned officers were Serbs and where the Serbian variant of the official Serbo-Croat language was the language of command, and a police force, diplomatic service and bureaucracy where the Serbs had a vast preponderance. The lack of full recognition for the Croat identity and national autonomy in the unitary Yugoslav state aggravated the Croats' sense of insecurity with regard to the Serbs. The Croats felt directly threatened by the possibility of Serbianization, disguised as campaigns for 'Yugoslavism': as for instance in King Alexander's abolition of, and ban on, all national symbols in the early 1930s. Ironically, the linguistic closeness of Southern Slavs, instead of forming a basis for a more harmonious common life than had been the case with the supposedly not-so-close non-Slavs - such as the Germans, the Hungarians and the Italians - turned out to be a divisive factor, since it brought with it the threat of assimilation. Many Croats felt that, in this as in many other ways (and notably in the economic field) they had jumped from the frying-pan of Austria-Hungary into the fire of Yugoslavia.

From the early 1920s on, the bulk of the Croats supported the opposition Croatian Peasant Party led by Stjepan Radić, who had been educated in Prague and who had married a Czech woman. Radić, a republican and a pacifist and a great admirer of Thomas Masaryk, one of the most respected figures in Czech political life and later the first president of independent Czechoslovakia, abandoned his republicanism in 1925 and joined the royal government in Belgrade. He died in August 1928 following an assassination attempt on him by a Montenegrin deputy in the Belgrade parliament in June. Two other Croat deputies were killed and two others seriously wounded in the same incident. The suspension of the Constitution by King Alexander in January 1929, the dissolution of political parties and the appointment of the commander of the royal guard, a Serbian general, as the Prime Minister, ushered in a period of harsh repression. This, in turn, led to a radicalization of political life and the emergence of terrorist movements in Croatia and also in Macedonia, which had been subject to systematic Serbianization since 1918. In 1934, in a joint Croat-Macedonian terrorist attack, a Macedonian terrorist killed King Alexander in Marseilles.

Four years later, in August 1939, on the eve of the Second World War, prospects for Serbo-Croat accommodation seemed to improve somewhat. Croatia became a separate unit, called *Banovina Hrvatska* - though with less autonomy than it had enjoyed in Austria-Hungary between 1868 and 1918. The autonomy deal (*Sporazum*) was supported not only by the majority of Croats but also by the majority of Serbian residents, who had grown to mistrust their fellow-Serbs running the government in Belgrade and had come to feel that their interests would be better protected by the authorities in Zagreb, the Croatian capital. However, the new autonomous Croat unit within Yugoslavia, which was announced as only the first stage of a thorough constitutional reform for the whole state, was rejected by most of the political parties in Serbia and also by the bulk of the Serbian intelligentsia. This rejection echoed the vehement opposition of the Serbian Orthodox Church in 1937 to the proposed concordat with the Vatican which would have given the Roman Catholic Church equality of status with the Serbian Orthodox Church. It became clear soon after the August 1939 Croat-Serb deal that any deal that broadly met Croat demands would be unacceptable to the majority of Serbs, with the exception of those in Croatia. But it was equally clear that any solution in the final version of the reform that fell short of full autonomy for Croatia would not satisfy the Croats. Radical nationalism, reflecting a growing rejection of any version at all of 'Yugoslavia', was on the increase.

Despite the evident problems involved in reaching a durable Croat-Serb accommodation, a *conditio sine qua non* for the long-term future of any version of Yugoslavia, Yugoslavia's existence was not seriously threatened. The Slovenes had managed to work out a *modus vivendi* with the government in Belgrade, partly thanks to Slovenia's semi-detached position in the north-west of the country but partly also thanks to the skill of political leaders like Korošec. Some other ethnic groups - like the Macedonians and the Albanians - with anti-Belgrade grievances even more acute than those of the Croats, were too weak to challenge the *status quo* - certainly without outside help.

Belying dire predictions of an imminent break-up after King Alexander's assassination in 1934, Yugoslavia's international position had actually stabilized. After Austria's *Anschluss* with the Third Reich in 1938, the outlook seemed to worsen; but by that time Yugoslavia was on quite good terms with the Axis Powers, Germany and Italy, the only ones likely and able to threaten its existence. Hitler, while as an Austrian no friend of the Serbs, had no plans for Yugoslavia's dismemberment. The Germans were happy with the government of Milan Stojadinović, a prominent Serbian banker who had taken office in 1935, a year after King Alexander's assassination. He had immediately set about distancing Yugoslavia from its partners in the Little Entente and, even more importantly as far as the Germans were concerned, had embarked on close economic co-operation with the Third Reich. Berlin had right from the start given a cold shoulder to Pavelić's Croat extremist *Ustaša* movement, which was too closely tied to Italy for Germany's liking. Mussolini's Italy, too, had in 1937 reached an accommodation with Stojadinović, an authoritarian figure who professed pro-Fascist sympathies and whose followers, modelling themselves on Mussolini's Black Shirts, wore green shirts and hailed Stojadinović as their *vodja* (leader).

There was no trouble from Yugoslavia's old backers, Britain and France. The Laval government in France, far from disapproving, actually encouraged Yugoslavia's rapprochement with Italy. And so, with the friendly Stojadinović in office in Belgrade, Italy decided to send Pavelić and his followers, who had been sheltering in Italy since King Alexander's assassination in 1934, into internment. Externally, Yugoslavia's rapprochement with the Axis had, at least temporarily, helped its stabilization as a state. Internally, it did not make much difference: even before the introduction of the royalist dictatorship in 1929, Yugoslavia had not been a functioning democracy, and it had become even less of one after 1929. In that sense, it was not that different from the other successor states of the Austro-Hungarian Empire, among which only Czechoslovakia could be called a Western-style parliamentary democracy.

The outbreak of the war in September 1939, only days after the conclusion of the Croat-Serb deal in Yugoslavia, changed the situation dramatically. Stojadinović had gone, and had been replaced by Dragiša Cvetković, a close ally of the Anglophile Prince Regent Pavle

Karadjordjević . It was Cvetković who had negotiated the *Sporazum* with Vladko Maček, the Croat Peasant Party leader and Radić's successor. Both Prince Pavle and Cvetković wanted to keep Yugoslavia out of the war. Their determination grew stronger after France's defeat in 1940, and the clear indication from Britain that no military help would be available for Yugoslavia in case of the war extending to South-Eastern Europe. But it did: in October 1940, with Mussolini's attack on Greece. In early 1941 Hitler, as part of his preparations for an invasion of the Soviet Union, wanted to secure his southern flank by expelling the British from Greece. He was planning to attack it from Bulgaria, whose compliance he had already secured - as he had also done with Romania. Pressure was put on Yugoslavia to join the Tripartite Pact and, more particularly, to allow Yugoslav territory to be used by the Wehrmacht *en route* to Greece. Prince Pavle continued to resist, but in the end agreed to Yugoslavia joining the Tripartite Pact.

On 25 March 1941 Cvetković signed the Pact in Vienna, in the presence of representatives of Germany, Italy and Japan as well as Bulgaria, Hungary, Romania and Slovakia. The signing ceremony was followed by an exchange of diplomatic notes specifying concessions obtained by Prince Pavle at his negotiations with Hitler. They were: a formal guarantee of Yugoslavia's territorial integrity; an undertaking that German troops would not use Yugoslav territory in their operations against Greece; that Yugoslavia would not be asked to provide military assistance to Germany; and that Yugoslavia would be given control of the Greek port of Salonika.

On 27 March a group of Serbian Air Force officers, who had been working closely with British intelligence, overthrew the Cvetković government and replaced it by one headed by General Dusan Simović. The new government immediately repudiated the Pact, arrested Prince Pavle and sent him via Greece into the keeping of the British, placing on the throne in his place the still under-age Prince Peter, the late King Alexander's eldest son. The coup proved wildly popular in Belgrade, not least because it was widely seen as a repudiation of the 1939 deal on Croatia's autonomy and of the men - Cvetković and Prince Pavle - who had been responsible for it. In the rest of the country, the coup's reception was subdued. The coup was a source of joy in a Britain which was then standing alone in Europe. Winston Churchill said that 'Yugoslavia had once again found its soul'. But rejoicing was premature. Attacked on 6 April by German and Italian forces supported by Hungarian and Bulgarian troops, Yugoslavia was defeated in a *Blitzkrieg* which ended with a formal surrender by the Yugoslav High Command on 17 April. King Peter and the government had left the country for the Middle East two days before.

The process of Yugoslavia's dismemberment was quick. Slovenia was divided between the German Reich and Italy. Hungary occupied the northern provinces of Medjimurje and Vojvodina. Bulgaria took most of Macedonia including Skopje, its capital. Italy attached western Macedonia and Kosovo to Albania which it had occupied in 1939. It also annexed Montenegro, and took from Croatia a large part of its Dalmatian coast. Quisling regimes were placed in power in Zagreb and Belgrade. The one in Serbia was headed by General Milan Nedić, a pro-German former Minister of Defence. Serbia's Jewish population was quickly rounded up by local Serb police and sent to German concentration camps. In Croatia, the Germans tried to persuade Vladko Maček, leader of the Croat Peasant Party, to head the government, but he refused. He was later sent to the notorious concentration camp in Jasenovac for 5 months, and spent the rest of the war in internment on his farm. Maček's 'no' to the Germans opened the way for Ante Pavelić, a Mussolini protégé, who became *Poglavnik* (ruler) of the so-called Independent State of Croatia. Pavelić immediately introduced Nuremberg-style laws and embarked on a policy of genocide against the Jews, the Serbs and the Gypsies. The break-up of Yugoslavia and the proclamation of Croat independence had been popular with the Croats, but disillusionment set in in May, when Pavelić signed away Dalmatia to Italy and accepted an Italian prince as Croatia's king. Pavelić's repressive and genocidal policies began to unite Croats and Serbs. The Communists, led since 1937 by Josip Broz Tito, an experienced Comintern official, by nationality half-Croat and half-Slovene, stood aside at first - the Molotov-Ribbentrop Pact was still in force in ex-Yugoslavia, as it was elsewhere in Europe. But the Party, small but well-organized, went into action after Hitler's attack on the Soviet Union in June 1941 and soon took over the leadership of the anti-Pavelić resistance as well as the anti-German and anti-Italian resistance in Slovenia.

An early, Communist-led uprising in Montenegro was crushed by the Italians. So was a Communist uprising in western Serbia in October 1941 led by Tito - who was forced to flee from Serbia, only returning to it at the end of 1944 when it had been liberated by the Soviet Army. Tito's Partisan movement's operations were mostly conducted in Croatia and Bosnia as well as in Slovenia. By 1943 there was a large territory administered by the Partisans in Croatia and Bosnia. The anti-Axis but non-Communist and largely royalist supporters of General Draža Mihailović, who was appointed Defence Minister by the Yugoslav government-in-exile in London preferred to lie low, biding their time. They hoped to be liberated by the Allies coming from the direction of Salonika - as they had been at the end of the First World War.

Tito's success in gaining support during the war among all the peoples of Yugoslavia should be put down mainly to the fact that he played down the Communist character of the struggle and played up the anti-Fascist national resistance to the occupying authorities and their increasingly discredited domestic allies. Thus Tito managed to forge a broad political front that became the basis of his post-war regime in Yugoslavia. Internationally, his Yugoslavia was recognised as the successor of pre-1941 Yugoslavia, whose dismemberment had never been accepted by the Western Allies. (The Soviet Union had accepted it briefly while its pact with Nazi Germany lasted, but reversed its de-recognition decision after Hitler's invasion in June 1941 and the formation of its alliance with Britain and, later, the United States.)

It is true that in 1945 there was not the same widespread, almost naive enthusiasm for Yugoslavia as there had been in 1918. Many people, in all parts of Yugoslavia, did not want to see it re-constituted, but they were not able to offer viable, internationally acceptable alternatives. And so Tito's Yugoslavia became the lowest common denominator. This was particularly true of the Serbs in Serbia (*Srbijanci*) who had been disappointed in the pre-1941 royalist Yugoslavia - not least because it had, as they saw it, caved in to the Croats in 1939. They were even less happy with Tito's state, which had banned the King from returning to Yugoslavia and had executed Draža Mihailović as a Fascist collaborator. But those Serb critics were in the end ready to accept the new Yugoslavia because it had at least once again brought together all the Serbs in one state. But not all the Serbs thought like this: Tito could count on the support of the Serbs of Croatia and Bosnia, the so-called *prečani* ((people from over there') who formed a large segment of his Partisan movement from its beginnings in 1941.

From 1943 on, Tito's willingness to engage Axis forces ensured him the crucially important military and diplomatic support of the British, who were the dominant force in the Mediterranean during the Second World War. As a Communist he had the support of the Soviet Union, whose army, in the autumn of 1944, helped liberate Belgrade and most of Serbia, leaving it to Tito's Partisans to complete the liberation of the rest of the country by May 1945. All three wartime Allied governments supported the restoration of Yugoslavia under a government made up of Communists and of members of the wartime government-in-exile. The monarchy was formally abolished in 1946, and Yugoslavia was made a federation consisting of six republics.

Croatia and Slovenia became federal republics along with Serbia, Bosnia, Montenegro and Macedonia. Both Croatia and Serbia were augmented by territories in the Adriatic region taken by Italy after the First World and recovered from it after the Second. Thus Tito had made good most of the territorial losses of the post-1918 royalist government. Equality was what, at least on paper, the post-1945 Tito Yugoslavia offered to its republics: in contrast to the pre-1941 arrangement, which had clearly been based on Serb supremacy.

But Tito's Yugoslavia soon began to face the same problems that had beset its predecessor, royalist Yugoslavia. The first Yugoslavia's life was cut short by Hitler's and Mussolini's invasion, and so it is impossible to say whether, if it had not been dismembered, it might not have become a viable state. However, despite strong Serb opposition to the deal with the Croats in 1939, it is conceivable that it might have developed into a latter-day version of the Dual Monarchy, with the Croats and the Serbs sharing power, and Slovenia enjoying a separate status and keeping the balance between the two. At that time, neither the Kosovo Albanians nor the Macedonians figured as political actors, though the Bosnian Moslems were a political force that would have had to be accommodated.

The second Yugoslavia, of course, had to cope with the terrible legacy of the Second World War, including personal traumas and a huge amount of destruction. But it also had several important advantages over pre-war Yugoslavia. One was that, in Tito, it had a charismatic leader who was also a skilful political manipulator of (and arbiter among) all the different Yugoslav nationalities and interest groups. Another was the country's economic prosperity, based to a large extent on massive Western external assistance in the 1950s and 1960s and, in the 1970s, on extensive external borrowing, helped by Tito's international prestige and with him acting as the country's credit card. Yet another glue holding post-1945 Yugoslavia together was the sense of external danger from the direction of the Soviet Union in the east, which, from 1948 on, when Yugoslavia was expelled from the Soviet bloc by Stalin, helped maintain a sort of unity in the country. Its exposed position between east and west in the Cold War made it virtually immune to the territorial claims by neighbours which had been a problem before 1941. Under Tito, any attempt to de-stabilise Yugoslavia could be seen as a danger to the European balance of power: something which neither NATO nor the Warsaw Pact wanted.

This extremely secure position, bolstered by strong international support, lessened the need for internal reforms while Tito was alive. They did happen, however, but always as a result of decisions taken at the top by Tito and his circle. A good example is the 1974 Constitution, which made Yugoslavia into a *de facto* confederation - to the fury of many Serbs, who saw this as a prelude to Yugoslavia's eventual disintegration, something that would leave Serbia as a rump minus not only Bosnia, Macedonia and Montenegro, lost back in 1945, but also minus Kosovo and Vojvodina. While Tito was alive he could rely on his own authority, backed by the Party and the Yugoslav People's Army (JNA) to maintain this complicated structure.

In fact, Yugoslavia's unravelling had begun long before the onset of its terminal crisis in the late 1980s. Ironically, it was precisely the generous Western economic and financial assistance, given to help keep Yugoslavia together as a barrier to Soviet expansion on NATO's southern flank, that helped the centrifugal forces in the country. Relying on large-scale Western aid from various sources, individual Yugoslav republics were able to pursue, within the framework of official 'Yugoslav' development policies, their own, unstated parallel policies. For instance, the decision to build the port of Koper on the small strip of Adriatic coast that the previously land-locked Slovenia had gained after 1945, with the much larger, already well-established Rijeka lying just below on the same coast, can be understood only in terms of those unstated but very real national strategies.

This 'national' development strategy, more appropriate to a sovereign country than to a member of a federation, is seen even more clearly in the project completed in 1976 of a railway linking Belgrade with Bar in Montenegro, on the southern Adriatic coast and close to Albania. The project, which also included the building of a modern port at Bar, was criticised as commercially dubious (which indeed it proved to be). But it made sense in the context of land-locked Serbia's search, ever since 1879, for direct access to the sea via a railway avoiding non-Serb (i.e., Moslem and Croat) areas and ending in Montenegro, regarded by all Serbs as a Serbian land.

These distinctive 'small-state' strategies lay behind the building of most of the duplicated capacity - steelworks, oil refineries and other factories and installations - in individual Yugoslav republics since 1945. Competition for investment projects involving public money exists of course in nationally homogenous countries, too, but in Yugoslavia it was bound up with separate national agendas that individual republics continued to pursue. In the 1970s the country went on a huge borrowing spree: a spree conducted by hundreds of banks, each backed by a local political bureaucracy, and each allowed to raise capital abroad. No thought was given to how the debts would be repaid. Here lay the roots of Yugoslavia's steadily rising inflation in the 1980s, which ended with a debt just below $18 billion.

Tito's death in 1980 marked the beginning of an economic and financial crisis that exposed the fragility of Yugoslavia's economy, and destroyed the population's confidence in the future. The sense of external danger finally disappeared in the late 1980s and the Party broke up at its last, abortive congress in Belgrade in January-February 1990. The JNA worried about Yugoslavia's evolution into a loose confederation and still more about it being split into smaller states, depriving the army of its *raison d'être*, its legitimacy and its hitherto comfortable and secure financial base. Of equal importance to the JNA's leadership was the continuation of the socialist order in the country (96 % of officers were Party members) which they saw as being threatened by the arrival in power in 1990 of non-Communist governments in Croatia and Slovenia.

Serbia's Party leadership shared the JNA's dedication to socialism, but it was primarily interested in maintaining power in Serbia and in as much of the rest of Yugoslavia as possible. The main item on its political agenda was rolling back Yugoslavia's federal system, as enshrined in the 1974 Constitution. Dissatisfaction with Tito's brand of federalism had been rife in Serbia since 1968 when Kosovo was first given a significant degree of autonomy, an autonomy which was further extended and consolidated in 1974. It was under Slobodan Milošević, who took office in 1986 and grabbed full power in Serbia in 1987, that the Serb anti-federal sentiment found effective political expression. In 1988-89 Milošević forged a new populist alliance with Serb nationalists dreaming of a Greater Serbia and brought Kosovo (by the use of brutal force against a resisting Albanian majority) and Vojvodina (mostly by pressure and intimidation) under Belgrade's rule. In 1989 a coup in Montenegro extended Belgrade control to that republic. In Bosnia, Milošević's local Serb allies assisted by the Orthodox Church had begun as early as 1987 to organise the local Serb population (31 % of the republic's population) against the tripartite (Croat-Moslem-Serb) government in Sarajevo, invoking fears of eventual 'Islamic fundamentalist' dominance based on the Bosnian Moslems' high birth-rate. A similar campaign began in Croatia among the local Serb population (12 %), accompanied, as in Bosnia, by secret arming by the JNA of local Serb paramilitary groups.

This Serb campaign of reassertion alarmed Yugoslavia's non-Serb majority. By 1989, Milošević's Serbia had gained three extra seats - those of Kosovo, Montenegro and Vojvodina - in addition to its own on the post-

Tito eight-member collective state presidency of Yugoslavia, which was the JNA's commander-in-chief. Acting in response to public feelings, the governments elected in the first multi-party elections in Slovenia and Croatia (in the spring of 1990) embarked on a course that was eventually to lead to independence, but which for a while at least kept the door ajar for a possible accommodation with Serbia. However, joint Croat-Slovene proposals for a looser, confederal structure, preserving a broad Yugoslav framework but at the same time protecting the non-Serb republics from a Serb take-over, were twice blocked at the federal level by the Serbian voting bloc (Serbia proper, Kosovo, Vojvodina and Montenegro) with Bosnia and Macedonia poised uneasily in the middle.

A serious additional blow to the waning confidence of non-Serb political and business leaders in the possibility of any sort of accommodation with Belgrade was dealt by the monetary 'coup' in December 1990. What happened was that the Milošević regime, using Serbia's own National Bank, helped itself to more than a billion and a half dollars' worth of money from the Yugoslav National Bank - the bulk of the fresh money supply earmarked for 1991. A few years before, fears of economic fragmentation and the resulting loss both of markets and of sources of raw materials might have been an argument for staying together - even at a political price. But this potentially powerful element of cohesion had already lost most of its force in the early 1980s, as a result of the dramatic deterioration of economic relations among Yugoslavia's republics. They ended up trading far more with foreign countries than with each other.

However, not everybody drew the same conclusions from this. Croatia and Slovenia saw it as another reason for saying goodbye to Yugoslavia. Not so Serbia or, even less, the JNA. Indeed, economic factors played an important role in the decision by Serbia and the JNA to try and stop those two republics from leaving the Federation. The JNA had an important stake in the status quo as a privileged organization, virtually a state-within-a-state, regularly spending half or more of the annual federal budget. Neither Serbia nor the JNA, therefore, welcomed the prospect of Croatia and Slovenia leaving the Federation. With only 8 % of Yugoslavia's total population, Slovenia in the 1980s accounted for a third of the country's gross national product as well as a quarter of its exports. In Croatia's case, the attraction was its large hard-currency income from tourism, its substantial natural gas and oil reserves, and its rich agricultural lands in eastern Slavonia, western Srijem and Baranja in the east close to Serbia.

The war in 1991 was the result of miscalculation on both sides: of overconfidence on the Milošević-JNA side and of a certain *naïvété* on the other, especially about the attitude likely to be adopted by Western governments. The army, often referred to as Yugoslavia's 'seventh republic', had been hoping for a solution like that adopted in Poland by General Jaruzelski in December 1981, but failed to secure enough political support. In the end both it and Milošević concluded that the Croats and the Slovenes would not dare to go ahead with their independence bid and that, even if they did, they could be quickly defeated. Milošević was ready to let Slovenia go. The army wasn't: but both hoped that Slovenia would be unable to make it on its own and that it would be forced to ask to rejoin Yugoslavia. On the Croat and Slovene sides (more especially in Croatia) there was a calculation that the predominantly Serb-officered but conscript (and therefore all-Yugoslav) JNA probably could not be used against them but that, even if it was, the international community - despite its oft-repeated negative attitude towards their independence plans - would come to their aid.

All those calculations of course proved wrong. The tragedy that happened subsequently is too fresh in everybody's minds and too well known to need to be rehearsed once again here. The conflict, which is not over yet (there is still unfinished business in Kosovo) has left behind a legacy of hatred and mistrust among the peoples of the region that is making even normal good-neighbourly relations difficult. It is clear from many different signals coming from the international community - the European Union, in particular - that hopes for a new Yugoslavia, entertained for a long time after Yugoslavia's bloody demise, have been given up. This is not least because any such idea is totally rejected in Slovenia and Croatia. In 1997, Croatia went as far as enshrining a provision banning the country from any new South Slav body or association in the country's Constitution. Yet, because of President Tudjman's involvement, with President Milošević of Serbia, in plans to divide Bosnia and, less controversially, as one of the signatories (with Bosnia and rump Yugoslavia) of the Dayton Agreement of 1995, Croatia is a 'Daytonland' with at least one foot in the dreaded Balkans.

Croatia and Slovenia are now firmly looking northwards and westwards - towards Central Europe and the European Union. (And so, now that it has become a *de facto* Western protectorate, is Bosnia and Hercegovina.) There is a marked and in many ways regrettable (though probably understandable) lack of interest in developments in other regions of former Yugoslavia (except of course Bosnia.) Croatia's and Slovenia's march westwards had begun very discreetly in the early 1980s when, though still republics of Yugoslavia, they joined *Alpe-Adria*, a low-key grouping which also included Italy's northern regions, several Austrian *Länder* and the three westernmost counties of Hungary. This has developed, under strong Italian influence, into a sub-regional organization of 16 member states called the Central European Initiative (CEI) with a total population of 241 million people and an area of 2,015,137 square kilometres. Its member states are: Albania, Austria, Belarus, Bosnia-Herzegovina, Bulgaria, Croatia, the Czech Republic, Hungary, Italy, Macedonia, Moldova, Poland, Romania, Slovakia, Slovenia and Ukraine.

Apart from the CEI, an organization which, though useful in several ways, is of no great international weight, Slovenia also belongs to the Council of Europe and the Central European Free Trade Area (CEFTA). More important, it is in the 'first wave' of candidates for European Union membership and a strong candidate for the membership of NATO to whose Partnership for Peace Programme it has belonged from its inception. Croatia is not yet in CEFTA and, though it managed to get into the Council of Europe with some difficulty, is not yet a candidate for EU or NATO membership. It is dogged by its patchy human-rights record and by its disastrous policy towards Bosnia, for both of which President Tudjman, its leader since 1990, is chiefly to blame. But its economy is well integrated with that of Western Europe and so the barriers are political and are likely to start being overcome only after the change of regime. Tudjman is 77, but his last presidential mandate expires only in 2002. However, his party has become immensely unpopular and may lose the elections due by January 2000 for the lower house of parliament. Either way, a change of regime and with it a likely improvement in Croatia's fortunes in the West is on the cards. For Croats who are in favour of change, the defeat of the Mečiar government in Slovakia in 1998 was an encouragement.

Despite the fact that almost 80 years have passed since the break-up of the Dual Monarchy, the sense of belonging to Central Europe is strong both in Croatia and Slovenia, as well as in Bosnia: though all of them of course look principally towards the European Union as the framework for today. Bosnia is in fact - if not in name - already an EU dependency. The process of European unification will eventually involve the whole of South-Eastern Europe, which means also all the successor states of Yugoslavia, including Serbia. This will help prevent the erection of new barriers and the appearance of new fault-lines in that part of our continent. The process will be slow but it is, in my view, irreversible.

# 3.
# Economic Factors

Marie Lavigne

# The Backyard of Western Europe?

*Marie Lavigne*

Let us begin with the forgotten economist who founded the economics of development, nowadays a very much neglected field of economic research. In 1943 he published a seminal article, dealing with Eastern and South-Eastern Europe, i.e. 'the whole area between Germany, Russia and Italy' (*Rosenstein-Rodan; 1943*). He was concerned with what would happen in the region after the end of the Second World War, which he evidently assumed was to be won by the Allies, as he expected that there would be war reparations from Germany. He believed that this region was not going to follow the Russian way: not politically, and not economically (by developing heavy industries and aiming at self-sufficiency). He proposed a pattern of industrialization based on labour-intensive industries, and sustained by international funding through an 'Eastern European Industrial Trust' (EEIT). The word 'transition' is to be found in the article - but in the meaning of the phase between end of war and the re-establishment of peaceful conditions. What the article conveys is that this part of the world needed to be developed so as to fit into the international division of labour. To achieve that aim, the West would have to contribute to the EEIT, but the East would have to do so as well. Both sides would participate in the Trust at parity: 'creditor' and 'debtor' countries would each acquire 50 per cent of the shares 'of a trust formed of all the industries created in the region' (p. 209). The Eastern contribution could be provided, inter alia, through financing the training of peasants to become industrial workers. Establishing of factories might also be a form of contribution. The commitment of the creditors would not exceed ten years.

Thus the people of Central and Eastern Europe would have to work hard: Rosenstein-Rodan assumes that a 48-hour week would be the rule. The West would also have to accept some sacrifices. The three following ideas put forward in the article look very modern more than 50 years later. The rich West might have to reduce its competitiveness and accept 'a part of their share in economic expansion in the form of more leisure', with its wage-earners working only for 40 or perhaps 35 hours per week. It will also have to buy the exports of the East 'in processed goods and light industrial articles' (p. 209). Finally, because the industrial restructuring will still leave many people unemployed, 'emigration will still have to supplement industrialization' (p.211).

Of course, one may say that such proposals are no longer relevant, or that they are not adjusted to the present situation either in the East or in the West. What the author tells us however contains some quite relevant points:

- the integration of Eastern Europe in the world economy will result from a co-operative effort by the international community of nations - with a participation by the private sector, but not through 'the automatism of *laissez-faire*';

- the Eastern European countries would have to co-operate among themselves as well;

- the West would have to open its borders to the goods and the people of the East;

- the transformation would have to be quick (twelve years, including the two years of 'transition' from war to peace conditions);

- it would bring external economies to the whole region.

Now let us get back (or forward) to the situation at the end of the 1990s. How can we assess the present specificity and the future of Central Europe? First we have to define the circle of countries included in this supposed geopolitical unit. Conventionally Central Europe includes three (or four) core countries: Poland, Czechoslovakia (since 1993 the Czech and Slovak Republics), and Hungary. We shall also include in this group Slovenia, a Republic of the former Yugoslavia.

These five Central European countries display definite similarities, as shown in Table 1. Their GNP per capita in USD, at purchasing power parities rates, ranges from 5,400 to over 10,000, with a weighted (according to population) average of USD 6,550. The largest country by population, Poland, is also the poorest. The average GNP par capita of the Central European countries amounts to 38 per cent (1995 data) of the average of the EU-15 Western European countries. It is about half of the 'poor-4' EU-15 countries. It is about 30 per cent of the geographically closest (Austria) country's GNP per capita (*Baldwin et al.; 1997*, p.130).

Poland stands out as both the biggest and the poorest country in the group, with a population more than half than the total of the Central European countries, and a total GDP a little less than a half. It has also been a leader in transition (though Hungary claims that it had already initiated some genuine market reforms during the Communist regime). It was the first country to resume growth (in 1992) and to catch up with its 1989 level of GDP (in 1995, see figure 1).

These countries are predominantly industrialized. The share of agriculture in their GDP, however, is 6 per cent, which is twice as large as the share of agriculture in the EU-15 countries (but matching the share of agriculture in the EU-4 'poor', and three times less than the share of agriculture in Greece's GDP).

In most of these countries the share of industry in overall output has dropped sharply by comparison with the centrally planned period, and the structure of output is now moving toward that of the developed countries. Most of them are still over-industrialized, which is a legacy of the Communist period. This means they still have to get rid of their inefficient industries, geared to the Soviet market, which were used after the beginning of the transition to redirect exports to the West of such goods as steel or chemicals. The output of services has expanded significantly in absolute figures and as a share of GDP, without yet reaching the Western level.

Another common feature is that the Central European countries belong to the group of countries in transition that is considered as the most successful from the point of view of systemic transformation, although not one of them has yet completed its structural reforms. Attached are figures showing that in all these countries growth has now resumed (fig. 1), that inflation rates have stabilized (albeit at a level much higher than in the EU countries) (fig. 2), that budget deficits are now everywhere under 5 per cent (though there has been an increase in all Central European countries in 1997, see fig. 3), and finally that unemployment has stabilized at rates similar to those of Western European countries (except for the 'anomaly' of the Czech Republic, where unemployment remains surprisingly low, see fig. 4).

The liberalization of trade, which has been part of the initial macroeconomic policies of 'stabilization-cum-liberalization', has led to an increased openness for these economies (see Table 1). The ratio of exports to GDP now matches the openness ratio of the smaller Western European countries. At the same time, there has been a reorientation of trade to the West and especially to Western Europe.

One may thus have the feeling that the Central European countries are smoothly moving 'back to Europe', gradually catching up at least with the

Figure 1 GDP index, 1989-97: Central European countries (Source: ECE/UN, 1998)

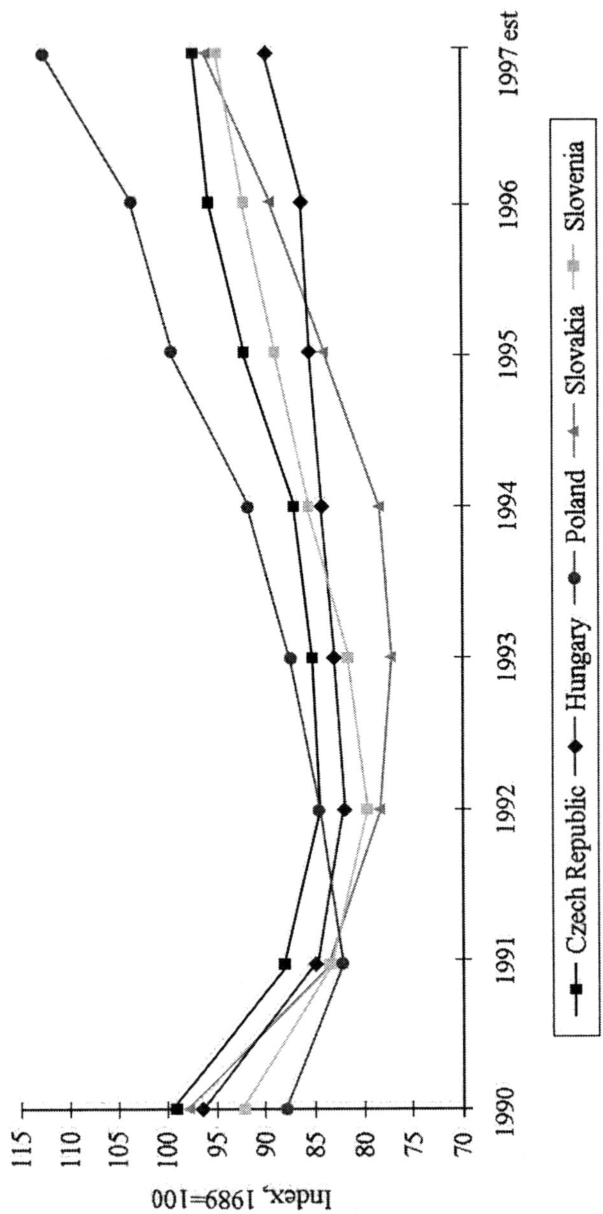

Figure 2: Consumer prices, 1990-7 : Central European countries (Source: EBRD 1997)

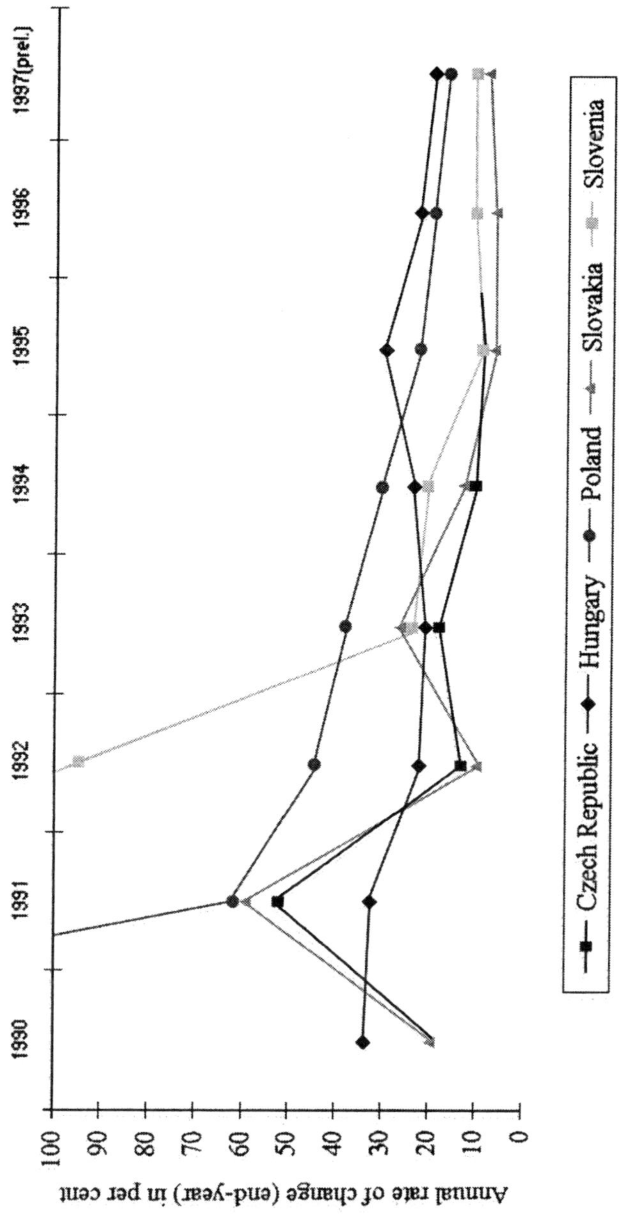

Figure 3: Budget deficit, 1990-7: Central European countries (Source: EBRD, 1997)

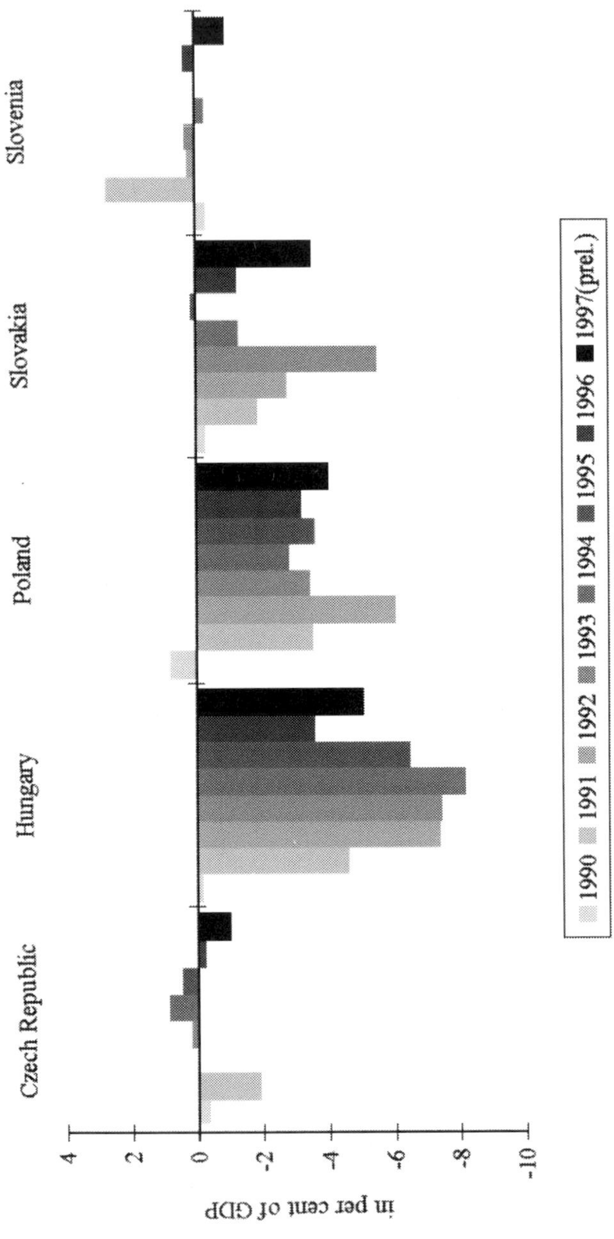

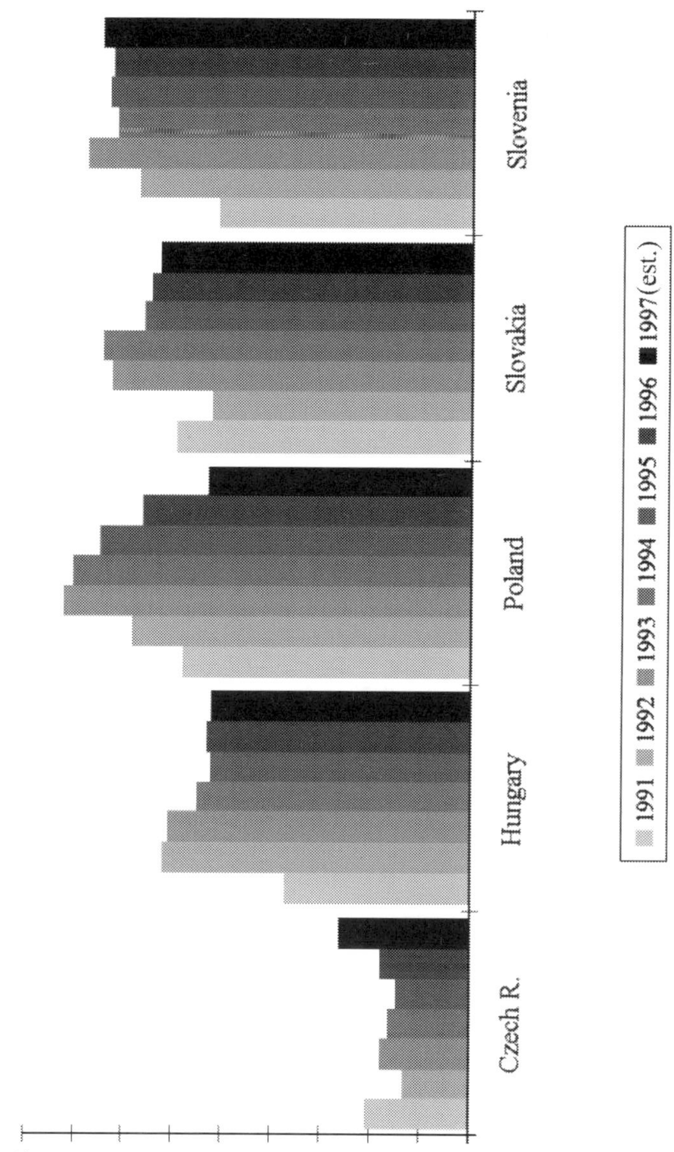


Figure 4:Unemployment rate, Central European countries, 1991-7 (Source: ECE/UN 1998)

Table 1: Basic data on the Central European countries (in comparison with EU)

| | Population, million,1995 | GNP per capita in US$, PPP-based, in 1995 | Composition of output in 1995, in p.c. agriculture** | industry** | services** | Ratio exports/ GDP, in p.c., in 1995 |
|---|---|---|---|---|---|---|
| Poland | 38.6 | 5400 | 6 | 39 | 54 | 25 |
| Czech Rep. | 10.3 | 9770 | 6 | 39 | 55 | 50 |
| Hungary | 10.3 | 6410 | 8 | 33 | 59 | 35 |
| Slovakia | 5.4 | 7320 | 6 | 33 | 61 | 63 |
| Slovenia | 2.0 | 10594 | 3 | 38 | 59 | 59 |
| **CEC, average*** | | **6547** | **6** | **37** | **57** | |
| Greece | 10.5 | 11710 | 16 | 31 | 53 | 29 |
| Portugal | 9.9 | 12670 | 6 | 36 | 58 | 33 |
| Spain | 39.2 | 14520 | 3 | 36 | 61 | 24 |
| Ireland | 3.6 | 15680 | 8 | 34 | 66 | 67 |
| **EU-4 poor, average*** | | **13740** | **6** | **35** | **59** | |
| Austria | 8.1 | **21250** | 2 | 34 | 63 | 39 |
| **EU-15** | | **16200** | **4** | **31** | **65** | |

* Weighted average (by population)
** Value-added.share in GDP.
Sources: World Bank, World Development Report, 1997; Hrncir (1997, p. 106); ECE/UN (1998).

least developed part of the European Union, and ready to become a part of the 'core' once they have joined the EU. The periphery is thus moving eastwards, encompassing the countries that were not included in 1997 for the first round of negotiations, opening in 1998, for accession to the EU: two of the Baltic countries, Latvia and Lithuania, and two so-called 'Balkan' countries, Bulgaria and Romania,* not speaking of the countries which have not been named at all so far. In this last, most peripheral group would figure the former Soviet Union countries west of Russia (Belarus, Ukraine and Moldova), as well as the countries of former Yugoslavia (save Slovenia) and Albania.

Are the Central European countries really ready to be part of the European core in a few years? To answer this question, we are going to explore several issues :

• what are the competitiveness factors of the Central European countries in CEC-EU trade?
• is it possible to look at them as a specific regional 'bloc'?
• *vis-à-vis* the global economy, what are their liabilities and assets?

## East-West Trade

The Central European countries account for hardly 4 per cent of the EU-15 imports, while directing 55-65 per cent of their exports towards their Western European partners. This asymmetry is critical to the future of the region. Are these exports enhancing the development prospects of the area, or are they the outcome of a regressive specialization in types of production that are declining in the West? We look first at the institutional status of the Central European countries in relation to the EU, as associates and soon as members (we are not elaborating on the process of accession, which is underway but might be delayed as the EU member states have become resigned to, but not enthusiastic with, the enlargement to the East). We then

* Actually Estonia was retained for the first round of negotiations - an obviously political move, as the Nordic EU members have pressed for the inclusion of a Baltic country. On the other hand, Slovakia has been 'sanctioned' for its un-democratic regime, though its economic performances would have qualified it for inclusion in the first round. The change of majority following the Slovak elections of September 1998 clearly reopen the issue. We put 'Balkan' between inverted commas because the countries in the area (including the former Yugoslavia countries) consider the term as despicable and meant to give a negative image.

discuss what is making the Central European countries competitive on the European market.

## The institutional framework

The three core Central European countries were the first to conclude Association Agreements (also called 'Europe Agreements') with the European Economic Community in 1991. Later, in 1993, these agreements were renegotiated with the Czech and the Slovak Republics separately, following the split of Czechoslovakia. Slovenia was the last in this group to sign a Europe Agreement in 1996. These agreements provided for the removal of all quantitative restrictions in trade of industrial goods and for the immediate removal of tariffs for goods other than 'sensitive' goods and goods regulated by other arrangements (the Multi-Fibre Arrangement, European Community for Coal and Steel). 'Sensitive' goods include a number of commodities defined according to the EU Common Tariff in such commodity groups as chemicals, textiles, base metals, clothing and footwear. The Europe Agreements did not cover agricultural goods, as these are regulated on the EU side by the Common Agricultural Policy, which cannot be affected by negotiations with third countries; processed agricultural goods are also included in the sensitive items of EU-CEC trade. All these items taken together accounted for about 40-45 per cent of the Central European countries exports to the EU in the mid-1990s.

Did the Europe Agreements improve market access to the EU? On the basis of a careful analysis of the Europe Agreement provisions and of the actual situation in the Central European countries, (*Drábek; 1997*) shows that 'the market openings provided by the Europe Agreements for the Central European countries are estimated to be relatively small, primarily during the first five years of the Agreement, with some improvements in the sixth year and, mainly, thereafter' (p. 33) - that is, essentially, after 1997. In addition, many of the provisions included in the Europe Agreements were already granted to the Central European countries in earlier agreements such as the trade and co-operation agreements concluded during the communist period, or in the General System of Preferences (GSP) granted unilaterally in 1990-1.

The first years of implementation of the Europe Agreements were marked by various conflicts over the surge in exports of sensitive goods. Among the most visible episodes, there was the anti-dumping case against steel pipes exports of several East European countries, that was won by the Western

European steel-makers in November 1992 (*Messerlin; 1993*, *Hindley; 1993*, *Wang and Winters; 1993*). In the following years, anti-dumping cases periodically erupted. Drábek (*Drábek; 1997*, p.35) identifies 24 anti-dumping cases against the Central European countries between 1990 and 1995. These cases were initiated by the EEC (EU) and notified in GATT (WTO). The Czech Republic and Slovakia faced 12 of these cases, jointly or separately, Poland nine and Hungary three. The commodities affected were mainly iron and steel and chemicals; some cases were directed against wood and minerals exports.

Agricultural goods exports suffered from oblique restrictions. An agricultural 'war' erupted in 1993 when the EC Commission imposed a one-month ban on livestock, meat, milk and dairy products imports from all East European countries, because a case of foot-and-mouth disease had appeared in Italy and had been traced to imports from former Yugoslavia. Hungary, Poland, and the Czech and Slovak Republics retaliated by banning imports (including transit) of the same goods from the EC, using the same pretext. Though the ban was lifted as scheduled, as well as the retaliatory measures, it left hurt feelings and was expected to trigger further protectionist measures. There were other bans on agricultural imports for health reasons (such as the ban on Polish milk imports in December 1997), that the Central European countries were quick to interpret as disguised protectionism. The latest conflict (at the time of writing) was about apple exports, and emerged between the Czech Republic and the EU. The Czech authorities had imposed a discriminatory tariff on apples imports from the EU countries above a quota of 24,000 tons a year, claiming that the apples exported from the EU (40,000 tons in 1997) were heavily subsidized, while the Czech apple exports to the EU were restricted (*Financial Times*, 5 May 1998).

Was the initial export specialization of the Central European countries a rational one, or did it display a 'distress strategy' in which one sells whatever is at hand? Indeed, the sectors which produce the 'sensitive goods' are declining. The chemical industry was developed on the basis of cheap Soviet oil, and has no future at normal prices for fuel. Processed agricultural goods have been crowded out of local demand by the role of the multinational retail chains, which are supplying their outlets with Western goods bought from their usual suppliers. They have not much future in export, except for such items as alcoholic beverages. Textiles and clothing look more promising, but basically with the region operating as a sub-contracting workshop for EU producers: about two thirds of the imports of clothing from the East by EC countries in 1992 were already due to 'outward processing trade' (OPT) whereby Eastern subcontractors manufactured finished goods with Western material, design and equipment (*Corado; 1994*).

Calculations show that the competitive advantages related to the export of sensitive goods have receded since the beginning of transition, except for some goods in some countries (for instance, iron and steel in Slovakia). When the Central European countries become members of the EU in the early 2000s (with the reservation for Slovakia already mentioned), will they still rely mainly on such exports?

## Competitiveness

Are there more competitive export sectors in the long term? Following a much-referred to study (*Hamilton and Winters; 1992*), it has been assumed that the Central and Eastern European countries had a comparative advantage in industries that are relatively intensive in human capital. Hughes and Hare (*Hughes and Hare; 1991*), using the DCC (domestic calculated costs) methodology, have shown that the most competitive sectors differ from one country to another, but that food processing (except in Bulgaria and to a lesser extent Poland and Hungary) is not competitive. In general, the most competitive areas would be the labour-intensive products included as sensitive in the Europe Agreements. Another author, using the revealed comparative advantage methodology (*Neven; 1994*), finds that the comparative advantage of Central and Eastern Europe lies in products that are both capital-intensive and *unqualified*-labour-intensive.

We have thus to explore the factors of competitiveness of the Central European countries. First, is the labour force in the Central European countries highly qualified or rather unqualified? The conventional view is that the industrial workers are indeed rather more qualified than in countries with similar income and development levels. This assumption rests on the image disseminated during the communist period: *viz.* In socialist countries people are literate and well-educated, especially in technical fields, since these are countries where the values associated with scientific and technical progress are highly respected. But there was also another image of the 'real' socialist worker: somebody who would shun work on the factory floor, especially as the Soviet-type enterprise would always hoard too many workers so as to be able to respond to surges in planned tasks. The socialist worker would not be fit for a competitive world despite the clichés of 'communist competition'; his initiatives would not be rewarded by higher earnings or improvement in his job position as the latter would mainly be determined by his position in relation to the Party. Thus, new skills and new attitudes would have had to be developed during the post-communist period: i.e. precisely at a time when funding for education had to fall drastically in the wake of fiscal austerity programs. Hence, it would probably be better to assume that compared to South-East Asian workers the labour force in the Central European countries is of no better quality.

But this labour force is cheap, and located closer to the Western European markets. Is this comparative advantage to last? This in turn depends on internal factors such as the trends in real wages (nominal wages deflated by an index of inflation, usually the consumer prices index or CPI) and in productivity. Indeed there has been a fall in real wages wherever the stabilization policies have been stringent, and in recent years a trend toward an increase associated with the success in stabilization policies and with the resumption of growth (fig. 5).

The cost of the labour force is also determined by the exchange rate policy. At the inception of transition, stabilization policies were often anchored to the nominal exchange rate, with a very strong devaluation of the domestic currency. Later the real exchange rate (nominal exchange rate deflated by the CPI) displayed a tendency to appreciation whenever the nominal rate was fixed or managed (in the case of a managed float) (fig. 6). There was also an increase in the nominal wage expressed in dollars (fig 7), which eroded the competitiveness of the Central European countries. However the wage differentials with Western Europe and even with the most developed newly industrialized countries are still high and may remain the best competitiveness factor for many years to come (*Havlík; 1996*, p. 19). The composite index of the unit labour costs (ULC), adjusted to the exchange rate changes, expresses the combined effects of exchange rate movements and trends in productivity and wages. Figure 8 shows that even for Poland the ULCs are still less than half the Austrian level, while Hungary and the Czech Republic are significantly lower.

So Central Europe seems to be developing into the backyard or the assembly line of global firms (European- or US-based multinationals), making use of the cheap local labour. Indeed, the increase in intra-industry trade of the Central European countries since 1995 seems to be closely linked with the activities of multinational companies, especially in the car industry (*ECE/UN; 1997b*, p. 46). The growth of OTP activities goes in the same direction.

The present structure of the Central European countries' exports to the

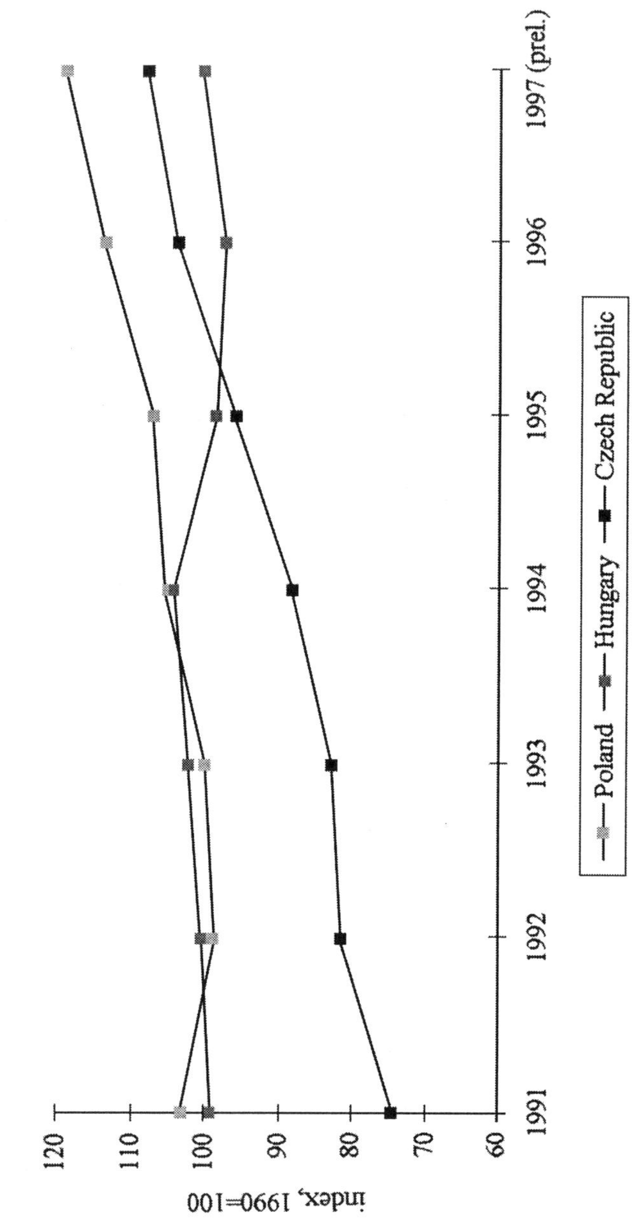


Figure 5: Real wage index, CPI-based, 1991-7 (Source: ECE/UN, 1998)

Figure 6: Real exchange rate index, CPI-based, in national currencies per USD, in selected CECs, 1991-7 (Source: Podkaminer, 1998).

A declining line means a real appreciation of the exchange rate

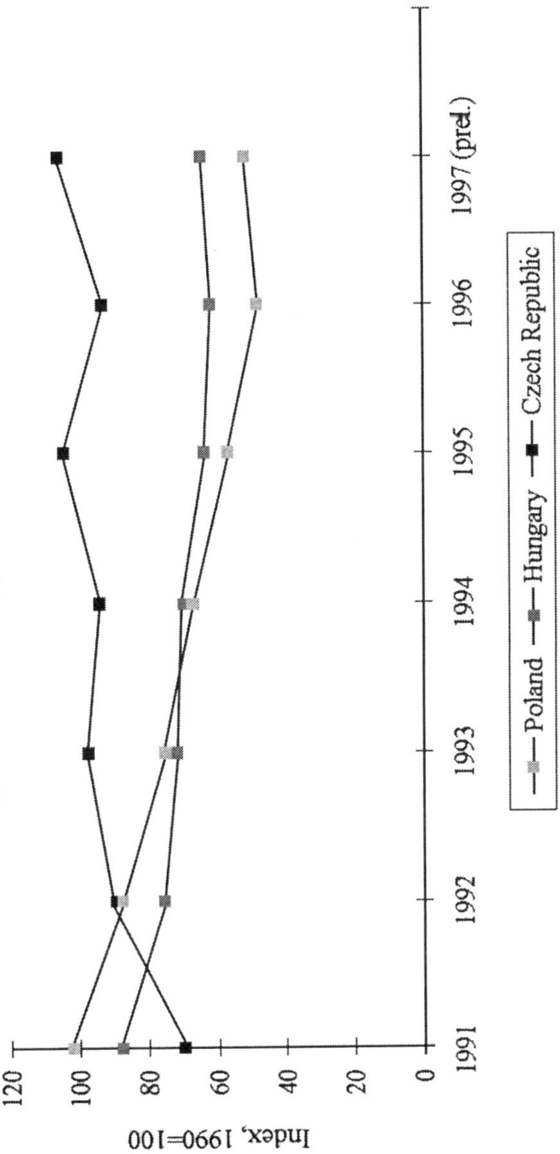

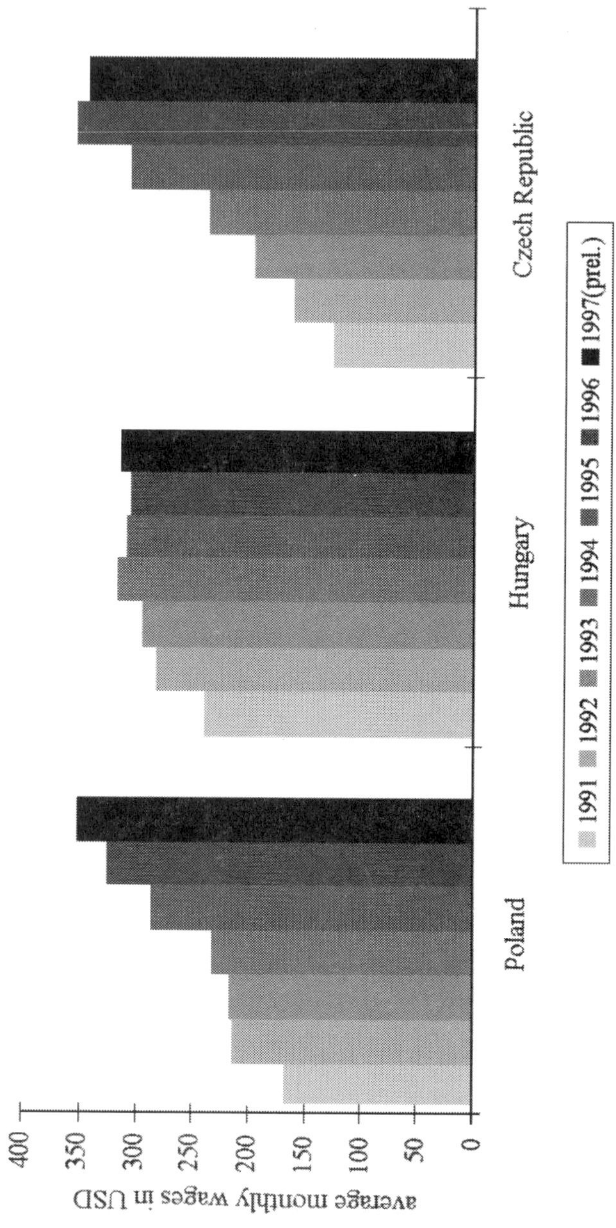


Figure 7: Average monthly wages in USD, at nominal exchange rate, 1991-7 (Source: Podkaminer, 1998)

Figure 8: Unit labor costs, PPP-ajusted, Austria=100 (Source: Podkaminer, 1998)

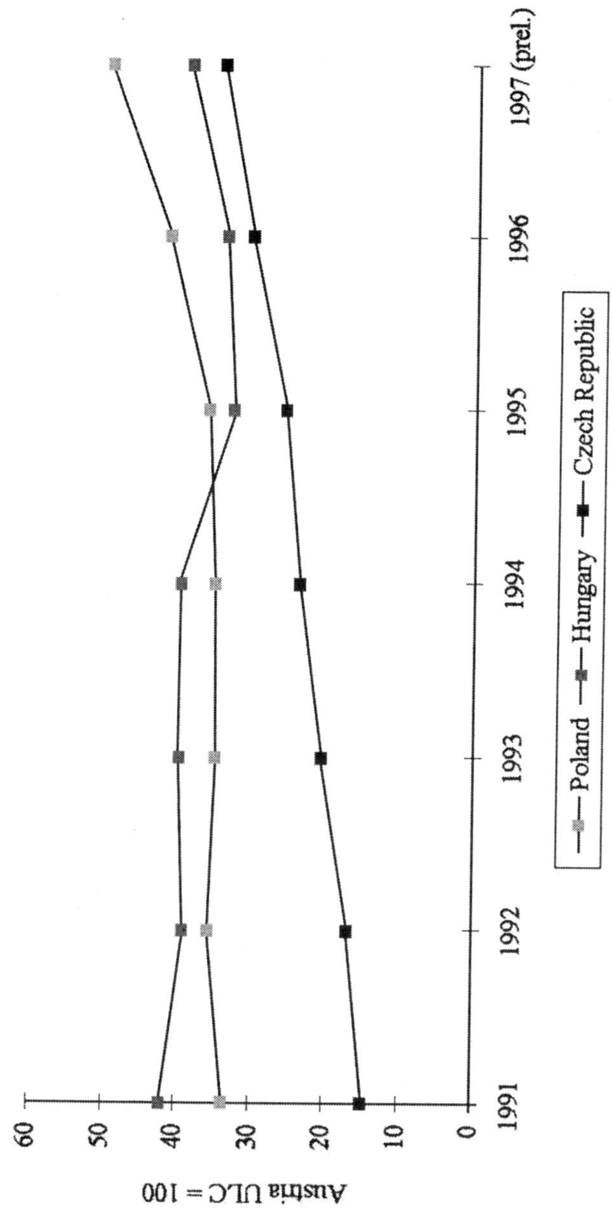

West is remaining stable. As a study by the ECE/UN (*ECE/UN; 1997b*, pp. 57 ff.) shows, this trade remains very concentrated: five commodity groups (in the three-digit SITC classification) accounted in 1992 for 47 per cent of total exports to Western Europe, and 45 per cent in 1996 (Table 2). The list of these commodities remained largely unchanged in each case (except in Hungary, which succeeded in increasing the share of non-sensitive goods in its exports, with equipment and machinery items replacing chemicals and agricultural goods). The most remarkable change in the composition of trade is the increase in exports of machinery and equipment by the Central European countries, from 24 to 33 per cent between 1992 and 1996.

This overall stability may seem very disappointing for the Central European countries. In the socialist past, they always used to claim that their future lay in high-technology exports, and that the unjustified Western embargo on technology exports to the communist countries was preventing them from reaching this aim. Nowadays, while demanding to be integrated in the European Union, they hope to reach the Western European average level of technological development in a few years, provided there is market access for the products of their nascent advanced industries. These hopes will be dashed. Technological development is not just a matter of investments and skills, or even markets. It is also related to being part of industrial international cooperation, through the network of multinational corporations. For the time being the involvement of the Central European countries in the global economy is mainly passive, as there are very few Central European multinationals (see below, last section). Exploring the opportunities of the service sector may be more promising, especially in its most advanced branches (such as business and computer services). But this is still in the future.

## *CEFTA*

Does the similarity among Central European countries allow us to consider them as a specific group? Formally the Central European countries make up what the West is still calling 'the Visegrád group', a phrase, however, which is not very popular among the countries themselves. The Visegrád agreement was indeed signed in February 1991 between Poland, Hungary and the CSFR. The Final Declaration recommended 'free movement of capital and labour', which was to be promoted by 'the development of market-based *economic cooperation*', cooperation in infrastructure

Table 2 : Major commodities in exports of CECs to Western Europe, 1992, 1994 and 1996.

| | | Share in total exports | | |
|---|---|---|---|---|
| | *Commodity group* | 1992 | 1994 | 1996 |
| *Poland* | Clothing (except fur clothing) | 13.4 | 15.6 | 14.4 |
| | Furniture | 5.1 | 6.6 | 8.1 |
| | Road motor vehicles | 3.2 | 5.1 | 7.1 |
| | Coal, coke, and briquettes | 8.5 | 8.1 | 5.7 |
| | Copper | 5.5 | 5.2 | 5.3 |
| | *Total above* | 35.7 | 40.6 | 40.6 |
| *Hungary* | Clothing (except fur clothing) | 13.6 | 12.5 | 9.9 |
| | Power generating machinery other than eletrical | 0.6 | 3.9 | 8.9 |
| | Road motor vehicles | 1.4 | 1.8 | 4.7 |
| | Equipment for distributing elecricity | 2.6 | 3.2 | 4.3 |
| | Other electrical machinery | 1.8 | 3.3 | 4.3 |
| | *Total above* | 20.0 | 24.7 | 32.1 |
| *Czech Rep.* | Road motor vehicles | 6.0 | 5.1 | 8.4 |
| | Machinery and appliances | 3.9 | 4.5 | 6.8 |
| | Electric power machinery | 2.8 | 3.6 | 5.4 |
| | Clothing (except fur clothing) | 7.3 | 6.6 | 5.3 |
| | Furniture | 3.2 | 3.3 | 4.0 |
| | *Total above* | 23.2 | 23.1 | 29.9 |
| *Slovakia* | Road motor vehicles | 2.5 | 4.1 | 14.2 |
| | Clothing (except fur clothing) | 12.9 | 11.6 | 10.0 |
| | Equipment for distributing elecricity | 1.5 | 1.9 | 4.5 |
| | Universals, plates and sheets of iron and steel | 7.1 | 7.2 | 4.1 |
| | Machinery and appliances | 3.3 | 3.0 | 4.0 |
| | *Total above* | 27.3 | 27.8 | 36.8 |
| *Slovenia* | Road motor vehicles | 1.4 | 12.1 | 14.2 |
| | Clothing (except fur clothing) | 16.5 | 12.9 | 10.5 |
| | Furniture | 4.8 | 5.6 | 6.9 |
| | Machinery and appliances | 4.1 | 5.3 | 5.8 |
| | Domestic electric equipment | 4.8 | 5.5 | 5.8 |
| | *Total above* | 41.6 | 41.4 | 43.2 |

Source: ECE/UN 1997 (b), p. 58.

development, and in the ecological sphere. But no explicit mechanism or regulations were established to ensure that the goal be met (*Visegrád; 1991*). Following the signing of the first Europe Agreements in December 1991, which in effect established a separate free trade area between each Central European country and the EC, the 'Visegrád group' also established a free trade area of its own (CEFTA), by an agreement signed in December 1992. (Since January 1993 this group has had four members, following the split between the Czech and Slovak Republics.) Though the CEFTA was hailed in the West as creating a market of 64 million, the main outcome of the new agreement was to level the playing-field a little. Mutual concessions have been devised so as to ensure that mutual trade would not be discriminated against by comparison with trade with the EC. In September 1995 it was decided among the existing members that CEFTA could be enlarged to include new members from Eastern Europe which were members of the World Trade Organization (WTO) and which had signed an Association Agreement with the EU. Slovenia was admitted in 1996, Romania in 1997, Bulgaria in 1998, and the Baltic states have expressed an interest, even though they are not yet members of the WTO. Tariffs for industrial goods had all been eliminated by January 1, 1997, with a few exceptions (such as imported cars in Poland). Agricultural trade has been freed to a lesser extent. As in the Europe Agreements, each member may impose some special measures such as import surcharges in case of balance of payment difficulties.

The Eastern economists who are most in favour of the development of intra-regional trade (or rather the least opposed to it) have advocated liberalizing mutual trade (beyond what is provided for in the agreement), dismantling the existing barriers to regional investment flows, and eliminating the unnecessary costs of mutual trade and in particular the use of Western intermediaries (*Inotai and Sass; 1994*). Poland suggested the liberalization of labour force migrations, and also the establishment of a CEFTA bank on the EBRD model to finance regional investment projects. Slovakia has pleaded for permanent headquarters. These suggestions were never accepted (*Richter; 1997*). CEFTA was thus confined to a minor role. While the share of trade within CEFTA has slightly increased after 1993, it remains very small as compared to the share of its members' trade with the West (*Hrnčíř; 1997*, p.97). In 1997, the share of intra-regional trade in total trade of the CEFTA members had dropped back to its 1994 level, at 14 and 10.5 per cent for exports and imports respectively (*ECE/UN; 1997b*, p. 52). Few people thus recommend a strengthening of CEFTA as a means of reviving mutual trade. One may however ask whether such a strengthening might not help the process of accession to the EU (*ECE/UN; 1996*, chapter 4).

What is the future of CEFTA once integration of the Central European countries is achieved? Few studies have been devoted to the issue. Matejka (*Matejka; 1998*) shows how the selection of the five 'fast-track' countries will cut CEFTA in two parts, when Slovakia (assuming that Slovakia is to remain in the second-round circle), Romania and Bulgaria are left out. Slovakia will in addition be affected by the ending of its customs union with the Czech Republic. Once admitted to the EU, the CEFTA members will have to renounce the agreement and conduct their relations with their former partners on the basis of the Europe Agreement concluded between the EU and each non-EU member. This new status will *inter alia* jeopardise the exports from Slovakia, Romania and Bulgaria to the first round of the EU applicants for agricultural goods and other sensitive products. The same outcome is expected in the case of the Baltic Free Trade Agreement (signed in September 1993) for the relations between Estonia (which belongs to the first round of applicant countries) and its two Baltic neighbours, Latvia and Lithuania (which don't). True, in discussing the impact of enlargement on the EU policies the European Commission has stated in *Agenda 2000* that when the applicants had special arrangements with third countries at the time of accession, the required adjustments should not harm these third countries (*European Commission; 1997a*). Also, the EU should take into account the needs of the latter when adjusting its remaining quantitative restrictions once new members have joined. All these provisions are however expressed in very vague terms. Thus the process of regional cooperation that has been encouraged by the EU in central and eastern Europe in the beginning of the 1990s seems severely impaired by the selective enlargement process.

In fact what has increased the similarities among CEFTA members is a kind of semi-spontaneous, semi-forced coordination originating outside the CEFTA. First, these countries have conducted successful stabilization policies, and reduced inflation as well as the budget deficit, as has been seen, according to the recommendations of the international financial organizations that provided assistance under terms of economy conditionality - so that in order to get funding one had to apply stringent macroeconomic policies. By following these policies, the fall in output that was experienced in the Central European countries to a lesser degree than in the South-Eastern European countries, the Baltics and the former Soviet

Union, was also reversed earlier than in those countries. Though it is claimed that Poland and Czechoslovakia (and later the Czech Republic) have applied shock therapy recipes and that Hungary (until 1995), Slovakia (since 1993) and Slovenia have been more 'gradualistic', the trends in critical indicators such as the inflation rate, the fiscal balance ratio and the growth rate are similar. Though the front-running countries (Poland and the Czech Republic) claim that the stabilization packages have been devised on the basis of domestic expertise, the common denominator here is the advice supported by funding from the international financial institutions, and first and foremost by the Bretton Woods organizations, the IMF and the World Bank.

In a second phase, assistance from the international financial organizations has subsided and is now replaced by the pre-accession assistance granted by the EU to all associated countries. The pre-accession process itself induces all the countries to adopt similar regulations in the framework of the *acquis communautaire* (i.e. the incorporation into national legal systems of all legal texts adopted since the Treaty of Rome in 1957 and still in force), and similar policies in fighting corruption and crime, protecting the environment, building a sustainable social safety net and improving corporate governance. What voluntary co-operation never achieved is being realized though external pressure or coercion.

The EU has also sought to promote regional co-operation in non-economic fields on its own initiative. The Essen European Council launched the Pact for Stability in 1994 (initially a French idea) to deal with border problems and difficulties linked with the status of minorities. A few agreements followed, namely between Hungary and Slovakia, and between Hungary and Romania. In March 1995, the Pact for Stability was handed over to the OSCE (Organization for Security and Co-operation in Europe). In this field the aim of the EU was less to prepare the applicant countries to work together than to settle existing disputes among future members prior to accession.

All these features shape a community of Central European countries as substantially distinct from the neighbour countries. The South-East European countries are still struggling with uncompleted stabilization, and are much more lagging behind in structural transformation (privatization, banking reform, etc.). The Baltic countries are poorer than the Central European countries, and have more slowly recovered from an initial steeper fall in output. The fact that Estonia has been selected for the first round of accession negotiations to the EU is not a sign of its similarity with the

Central European countries, but rather a signal that the Baltic countries should be considered a part of Europe.

The core of the Central European countries, Poland, the Czech Republic and Hungary, have also attracted most of the foreign direct investment (FDI) directed to the East, and most of the portfolio investment. They are thus much closer to being integrated in the global economy.

## *Integration into the global economy*

FDI flowed into the Central European countries immediately following the beginning of transition, as a component of privatization. Portfolio investment expanded later (since 1993-4) as this required the existence of a capital market, however restricted this has proved in reality.

### Foreign Direct Investment

While the centrally planned economies were getting less than 1 per cent of the world FDI before 1989, the share of the European countries in transition (including Russia) amounted in 1995 already to 5 per cent of the world total, and the share of the Central European countries amounted to 3.5 per cent. Table 3 shows the net FDI inflows for the period 1990-7 together with the cumulated inflows and the inflows per capita. The data allow for the following assessments :

a) There has been a very rapid growth in FDI. Overall, the annual inflow (in current dollars) was multiplied by 4.8 between 1991 and 1996.

b) The average ratio of net FDI inflow/GDP was in 1996 and 1997 2.2 per cent in Central and Eastern Europe. This compares with averages (for 1986-92) of 2-2.7 per cent for Spain and Portugal, 3.5 per cent for Belgium and Luxembourg, and 0.8 per cent for the United States. (*Martin and Velásquez; 1997*).

c) In 1997, Hungary, the Czech Republic and Poland had cumulatively attracted 84 per cent of the total FDI in Eastern Europe. In cumulated FDI per capita, Hungary is the leader, having attracted twice as much FDI as the second in line, the Czech Republic*. This may explain why the most

---

* Recent statistics however provide for much higher figures for Poland, with cumulative FDI inflows for the period 1989-97 reaching 19,250 millions US dollars, more than twice the figure yielded by standard central bank data. The gap is supposd to be due to investments-in-kind and reinvested earnings. (*EBRD, Transition Report Update*; April 1998, p. 12.) There is some scepticism surrounding these new data.

Table 3: Foreign direct investment in the CECs, 1991-7 (million US$)

| | 1991 | 1992 | 1993 | 1994 | 1995 | 1996 | 1997* | 1991-7** | 1991-1997 FDI flows per cap. ($) | 1997 FDI flows/GDP in per cent |
|---|---|---|---|---|---|---|---|---|---|---|
| **Eastern Europe** | 2459 | 3005 | 4171 | 3697 | 8991 | 6906 | 8268 | 37497 | 354 | 2.4 |
| Bulgaria | 66 | 42 | 40 | 106 | 90 | 106 | 438 | 888 | 105 | 4.3 |
| Czech Rep. | 612 | 1004 | 664 | 862 | 2562 | 1428 | 1300 | 8432 | 838 | 2.4 |
| Hungary | 1460 | 1471 | 2336 | 1148 | 4453 | 1983 | 2085 | 14936 | 1548 | 3.7 |
| Poland | 117 | 204 | 800 | 942 | 1134 | 2741 | 3034 | 8972 | 221 | 2.2 |
| Romania | 37 | 73 | 84 | 341 | 419 | 263 | 956 | 2173 | 97 | 2.7 |
| Slovakia | 82 | 100 | 134 | 170 | 157 | 200 | 140 | 983 | 192 | 0.4 |
| Slovenia | 85 | 111 | 113 | 128 | 176 | 185 | 315 | 1113 | 572 | 1.6 |
| ***Total CEC (in p.c. of Eastern Europe)*** | 95.8 | 96.2 | 97.0 | 87.9 | 94.3 | 94.7 | 83.1 | 91.8 | | |

* Preliminary
** Cumulated 1991-97.
Source: ECE/UN, 1998.

detailed studies of the FDI have been concerned with the Hungarian case (*Csáki; 1997*) (*Hunya; 1997*) (*Inotai; 1995*). Geography (distance from Western Europe) and size (for Russia) explain this concentration, along with other determinants. However the countries in transition are lagging behind the main host countries for FDI in emerging markets. A USDA estimate for the accumulated FDI stock up to 1996 shows that all the countries in transition taken together (50.6 billion dollars) have received half as much as Brazil ($108.3 bn) and less than a third as much as China. (*USDA; 1997*, p. 3).

d) FDI sectoral distribution in the Central and Eastern European countries is associated with the globalization of production. The FDI flows were from the outset directed towards manufacturing industries, moving gradually from less to more value-added and skill-intensive sectors. OTP has been an important component of FDI. The privileged sectors have been the car-making industry, food processing, pharmaceuticals, and hotels. The service sector is still promising, especially banking and insurance activities, and public utilities (power distribution, air and railways transportation, and telephones).

e) Germany is by far the main investor in the Czech Republic and Hungary (about 30 per cent of the total); while the United States is the first in Poland, with one-fourth of the total.

What are the determinants for the investors into the Central European countries, and particularly the three core countries, Hungary, the Czech Republic and Poland? There have been many case studies (for an overview of the main surveys since 1991, see (*Lankes and Venables; 1996*, pp. 332-3). The usual motivations are listed: the market potential, low costs (especially cheap labour costs), and a geographical determinant, the proximity from the EU. Lankes and Venables also conducted a survey of their own, on the basis of an EBRD project, with interviews by researchers from the IFO institute in Munich. Along with the market and cost determinants, the authors introduce an additional characteristic of the projects surveyed, i.e. the control mode (subcontracting, joint venture, or wholly owned subsidiary). Other variables are taken into account, such as country risk perceptions, tax regime (which is perceived as of little importance), and trade policy of the country. The conclusions of the authors are as follows: one should expect an acceleration of FDI once a critical mass of investment is reached (the 'herding' effect); the share of cost-motivated and export-oriented FDI is bound to increase, while the FDI mainly determined by the size of the domestic markets and the natural resource endowments is bound to recede; and finally, the share of fully-owned subsidiaries is going to increase while the share of joint ventures, a more 'primitive' form of FDI, is bound to decrease (*Lankes and Venables; 1997*, pp. 563-4). The three conclusions taken together suggest that the most successful transition countries in attracting foreign investment are also the most integrated into the globalization process. First, these countries are selected as an export base even when the domestic market is narrow. Second, the cost considerations tend to become essential, and hence the host country cannot afford to let its real dollar wages to increase in comparison with other countries, though this consideration tends to become less important once a critical mass of FDI is attained. Third, the most successful countries in attracting FDI are included into multi-national corporations' global networks up to the point of becoming sub-regional headquarters for multi-national corporations, as Inotai suggests for Hungary (*Inotai; 1995*, p. 119). Such an evolution implies that FDI should decreasingly be linked with the privatization process which has initiated foreign investment in the region.

The countries in transition were initially rather reluctant to accept foreign investment. This may be seen as a legacy of the former system, when FDI was likened with the harmful influence of capitalism. They soon however competed for FDI. The first determinant was the need for capital, in a situation when domestic investment fell still more steeply than output, and when foreign assistance could not match the huge investment needs of the region. But FDI is not only used for investment. Governments receiving cash for a share in the equity of a privatized enterprise may use it for pressing needs such as the servicing of foreign debt or the financing of a trade deficit. As Inotai (*Inotai; 1995*, p. 10) states, there is nothing wrong in that, especially if FDI is financing a 'modernization deficit' arising from high machinery imports. The flexibility in the use of FDI inflows is however bound to be limited in the future, as these inflows are increasingly linked with greenfield investments or increases in stakes of already privatized companies. In Hungary and the Czech Republic, the potential of privatization was nearly exhausted by 1997. Poland, which delayed the privatization process until 1995-6, still has large state enterprises to sell, including some in the telecommunications sector (*Financial Times,* 8 January 1998).

Restructuring needs are generally considered as an essential motivation for FDI in the countries in transition. The foreign partner, even with a minority share, brings a managerial culture, especially in fields very much under-developed in the centrally planned economies (such as marketing or financial management) and fosters the development of new technologies. The benefits deriving from FDI in this respect must not be exaggerated. They are associated with a high degree of exposure of the country to foreign business influences. Hungary is the country where foreign penetration is strongest (with over 60 per cent of export sales and about of 40 per cent in investment: *Hunya; 1997*). However, even in this case, there are limits to the restructuring potential of the FDI. This potential is hindered if the financial sector is not restructured at the same pace as the industrial sector. Research and development is not necessarily enhanced when the foreign partner relies on its own resources (for instance, in the car industry, the most technically advanced technologies, especially automation, remain controlled by the foreign multinational, and this was a major disappointment in the Volkswagen-Škoda venture in the Czech Republic). Foreign-controlled enterprises often use their own suppliers rather than involving local suppliers in their activities. The foreign-controlled sector becomes a part of the global strategy of the foreign owners, with little say from the local governments. In such sectors as food processing or clothing, local producers have been crowded out. Foreign enterprises may create new jobs, but often they reduce employment (a development that is felt as much less critical than in European industrialized countries as downsizing linked with increased productivity is a policy priority in the countries in transition).

The motivations of the foreign investors may contradict the long-term aims of the national governments. When the foreign investor primarily looks at his gains in terms of lower costs, an increase in these costs may prompt him to settle in another location, and here the competition between the developing countries and the countries in transition is high; the latter are exceedingly confident in their specific advantages (geographical closeness to Western Europe, skills of the labour force) which are easily eroded in a context of industrial globalization: distances and human technical skills matter less. When the investor looks at market expansion, often he tries to buy a monopoly position, at a time when the national governments are trying to de-monopolize (*ECE/UN; 1993*, chapter 5: 'Restructuring of state-owned enterprises in Eastern Europe').

There is thus a difficult balance to be maintained between the wish of the Central and Eastern European countries to be fully incorporated into the global economy, and the desire to keep a control on their national industrial and social policies (*Martin; 1998*, p. 23). But this is not a matter of choice for the Central European countries. The preference of the multi-national corporations for Hungary, which seemed likely to be challenged by the Czech Republic before the Czech crisis of 1997, suggests that only Hungary might be included into the global strategy of the multi-national corporations; but still more like a privileged part of the periphery than as a component of the core.

## Portfolio Investment and Other Capital Inflows

Non-FDI capital inflows have accounted for roughly 50 per cent of the private capital inflows into the Central and Eastern European countries (table 4 and *Fischbach and Scattaglia; 1997*). They consist of portfolio investment, and bank or non-bank lending, to which one may add short-term funds and unrecorded movements (errors and omissions) in a broader view. These flows have been driven by several determinants:

- A 'push' has been exerted by the structure of international interest rates. The low level of interest rates in developed countries since 1990 has 'pushed' capital to emerging markets, as analytical studies have shown (*Fernandez-Arias; 1996* and *Fernandez-Arias and Montiel; 1996*). Developing countries, and later (since 1993) countries in transition benefited from such a push. By mid-1997 all countries of Central Europe had received international credit ratings, which added to their visibility, as well as their generally improving creditworthiness. The overall approval (despite occasional reservations for some countries) of the international financial institutions, and the normalization of the most indebted countries' relations with their official and private creditors (as in the case of Poland), have added to this creditworthiness.
- Domestic factors have exerted a 'pulling' effect. Among these factors one finds the domestic macroeconomic stability (measured by the rate of inflation). The movement of the exchange rate also matters: while frequent devaluations suggest instability, a managed float or a crawling peg may be preferred (from the point of view of the investor) to a fixed exchange rate which suggests a risk of excessive appreciation of the real exchange rate and of deterioration of the current account. The impact of the fiscal policy is ambiguous (*ECE/UN; 1997a*, a special study on Capital Inflows into Eastern Europe). A strict fiscal policy is a sign of stability, but a lax fiscal policy, especially when fiscal deficits are financed by borrowing abroad or bond emissions, goes with high interest rates that attract capital inflows. Structural policies also matter, namely the scope, speed and forms of privatization, which impact on the valuation of assets (in case of portfolio

Table 4. Net capital inflows into the CECs, in $bn, 1995-7

| | 1995 | 1996 | 1997* | 1995 | 1996 | 1997** | 1996 | | |
|---|---|---|---|---|---|---|---|---|---|
| | capital account flows, amounts | | | in per cent of GDP | | | in % of gross capital inflows | | |
| | | | | | | | FDI | Portfolio investments | Loans |
| **Eastern Europe, total** | 23,7 | 15,6 | 21,8 | 7,3 | 4,5 | 6,4 | 57 | 14 | 29 |
| **of which:** | | | | | | | | | |
| Czech Rep. | 8,8 | 3,5 | 1,4 | 17,5 | 6,2 | 3,0 | 32 | 17 | 49 |
| Hungary | 7,0 | 0,2 | 0,8 | 15,7 | 0,5 | 2,0 | 63 | 29 | 8 |
| Poland | 2,7 | 5,3 | 8,9 | 2,3 | 3,9 | 6,6 | 57 | 4 | 42 |
| Slovakia | 0,9 | 2,3 | 1,6 | 5,4 | 12,3 | 6,9 | | | |
| Slovenia | 0,3 | 0,5 | 1,6 | 1,4 | 2,9 | 9,1 | | | |
| **CECs, in %** | *83,1* | *75,6* | *65,6* | | | | | | |

Net capital inflows are gross inflows minus outflows (linked for instance with repayment of debt), according to balance of payment statistics.

* Preliminary figures for 1997.

** Extrapolation of January-September data

Source : same as table 3.

investment). The opening and expansion of stock exchanges is an important feature of structural policies that attracts foreign capital.

The emerging markets of Central Europe are still volatile, and very sensitive to world-wide movements. Warsaw was the first booming stock exchange in the region, and also the first to experience a sharp drop in 1994. The Czech Republic was affected by a confidence crisis in the first half of 1997 that was quickly likened to a Mexico-like crisis. In fact it was much more a crisis of transition, as the collapse of the Czech currency and capital markets was not the burst of a speculative bubble, but was rooted in the lack of completion of structural reforms, with an unreformed state-owned banking sector, and an opaque governance of the privatized enterprises. This explains why the Czech crisis did not extend to the neighbouring countries (but for a short-lived attack on the Polish zloty) and could be solved by a quick policy response (although that response itself generated a deep and long-awaited political crisis). When the Asian crisis erupted later in 1997, Central European countries appeared relatively little affected, if only because of the small size of their capital markets. Stock market indices, that fell strongly in the last quarter of 1997, soon recovered, especially in Hungary and Poland. Postponed equity emissions have resumed in 1998. The financial crisis in Russia again rocked the Central European exchanges in mid-1998, especially in Poland and Hungary - the countries that were most exposed, because their banks retained large assets in Russian governments bonds (Russian acronym GKO).

Will the Central European countries go on to attract portfolio investment in the future? They are in 1998 the most credible emerging markets following the Asian crisis and the fears raised by Latin American markets. But these markets are too small to offer a real alternative to other large-scale investments. Too large inflows of speculative capital would in any case be dangerous for the Central European countries, and the relative under-development of their financial and banking system would increase the risks for a financial crisis.

## Conclusion

The question mark in the title of this paper still remains. Of the five countries included in this survey, Poland, Hungary and the Czech Republic have the best potential on a global scale. Slovenia's assets lie in several factors: it is a very small country; it is the most prosperous of the Central

European countries; its agricultural potential is low and thus it is not a menace for the EU agriculture; foreign investment would significantly increase in industry and services if the law was more friendly to foreign business. Slovakia has assets similar to the Czech Republic's, now that it has solved the political problems that blocked (up to September 1998) the normalization of its relations with the EU. It has the advantage of providing a link with Ukraine and the CIS countries.

So far, the whole area has not yet developed its potential. The backyard hypothesis still holds true. Export structures and FDI sectoral concentration point to the same conclusion. Clothing and road motor vehicles, that are the main commodity groups in Central European countries' exports, are controlled by foreign investors. What is going to happen once transition is completed and the Central European countries are integrated into the EU? The special ECE/UN study on OPT (*ECE/UN; 1995*) contends that even after EU accession a shift away from OPT towards direct sales of clothing would be at the same time difficult and risky. As for the car industry, any autonomy for the Central European countries is out of question.

A broader view would have to take into account the overall consequences of EU accession, from the points of view of macroeconomic policies and their impact on growth, connections with the Euro and the way they would constrain the exchange rate policies, the behaviour of EU and non-EU based multinationals, and other factors. Some studies have taken the case of Spain as a significant reference (*Fayolle; 1996, Martin and Velásquez; 1997*). The Spanish example would yield optimistic conclusions: growth has been stimulated (though constrained by macroeconomic policies); productivity has improved; international specialization has improved; the attractiveness of the country for foreign investors has increased. Similar conclusions may be drawn from the Portuguese experience. But are such comparisons really fit for the Central European countries? The initial systemic and economic conditions are different. Now the EU will have to absorb at least five (and perhaps six, if the situation of Slovakia is reconsidered) countries at one time.* The shock of the accession is impossible to assess in advance, especially as the new members would have to take steps towards joining the

* We assume that the accession would take place, if not at the same time for all first-round applicants, at least in very close delays, though the EU Commission has repeatedly stated that the beginning of the negotiations at the same date did not imply a simultaneous conclusion. The political pressure from the applicant countries and the political consequences of a discrimination among them would certainly point to such a conclusion.

European Monetary Union at some point, which would constrain their economic and monetary policies. The incumbent poorer members of the EU could be looked upon as the 'periphery' of the richer European Community even in the years following their accession. The looming accession of poorer countries that have not yet completed their structural transition to the market will create a new 'periphery' within the EU, at least until another enlargement, if there is to be one, reintegrates the Central European countries into the core of Europe.

# Core or Periphery? Economic Factors

*András Inotai*

## 1. Different interpretations of 'Central Europe' in economic terms

Historically, the 'Central European economic space' has always been established around the key modernization anchor of the region at the time. Before World War One, this anchor role was played by the Habsburg Monarchy, and the area covered a vast territory from Northern Italy to Southern Poland, and from Bavaria to the present-day Western Ukraine. Between the two World Wars, and particularly in the 1930s and early 40s, Central Europe became part of the German expansion to the East (*Drang nach Osten*).

Recent interpretations, however, exclude from the economic definition of Central Europe the luckier countries of this geographic area that became part of the Western European security and economic system after 1945 (Western Germany and Austria). Thus, the reference of the term 'Central Europe' moved to the east (by leaving behind Germany and Austria as genuine Central European economic actors), and, at the same time, 'Eastern Europe' moved to the geographically central part of Europe. 'The Eastern bloc' became the most widely used term of description for the area in this new situation, and the bloc was understood to be militarily, ideologically and economically dominated by the Soviet Union. The first attempts to differentiate within this 'bloc', based on an understanding of historical roots, originate from the second half of the 1960s, when the term 'East Central Europe' (referring to a group comprising the small ex-CMEA member countries plus Yugoslavia) emerged in the comparative economic literature (*Berend and Ránki; 1967*).

Nevertheless, the re-emergence of this part of Europe as a new and at least partially 'independent' actor of the continent could only be dated back to the late eighties and early nineties. Already the 'Central European Initiative' (CEI) started by Austria, Hungary, Italy and Yugoslavia in 1988 and extended a bit later to Czechoslovakia and Poland has signalled the rebirth of a new economic space, although the CEI exerted more of a psychological than a genuine economic impact. This was partly due to its limited economic weight, and to the still underdeveloped economic interdependence of the member countries in the late eighties. Also, the CEI could not develop further because the dramatic changes affecting all countries of Central and Eastern Europe suddenly gave a new and hardly to be expected direction to political, economic, social and ideological developments in this part of Europe. The unprecedented opportunity and challenge of systemic transformation produced a twofold and contradictory impact on the question of how to define the 'Central European economic space'. On the one hand, the historically rooted, but, by the force of history, for decades interrupted relations within the traditional 'Central European economic space' experienced a dramatic rebirth, and this moved the geographic borders of Central Europe towards the West (as the latter was understood after 1945). As a result, Germany, Italy, Austria and Northern Italy were again included in this 'pattern of space'. Conversely, though, the systemic transformation common to all the Central and Eastern European countries previously dominated by the Soviet Union at the same time created a dividing line between Austria, Germany, Italy, and their Eastern neighbours, and shifted the reference of the term 'Central Europe' towards the East.

In this context, the new Central Europe was defined as part of the group of countries with systemic change. But how large is this group in reality? There are several criteria which can be used for definition. The broadest one is the group of ten countries that have signed Association Agreements with the European Union (AA-10). This includes three ex-Soviet republics (the three Baltic States), the traditional Central European countries and a part of the Balkan region. (Therefore, the term 'Central and Eastern European countries' (CEECs) would seem to be more appropriate here.) A second approach only considers the CEFTA countries, covering Poland, the Czech and Slovak Republics, Hungary, Slovenia and, most recently, Romania (CEFTA-6).* Finally, a third, and economically probably the most justified definition is based on virtual progress towards sustainable political democracy and market economy, and, more importantly, towards genuine economic (inter)dependence in relation to Germany, Austria and Italy, as indicated by the flow of trade, investment, human resources and tourism. If these are to be our criteria, there is no doubt about Poland, the Czech

* The future and likely enlargement of CEFTA towards Bulgaria and the Baltics will eliminate the distinction between AA-10 and CEFTA, unless, in the meantime, some present CEFTA members become members of the European Union.

Republic, Hungary and Slovenia belonging to the new Central European economic space. Slovakia's membership is overshadowed mainly by political problems, while Romania's enforced catching-up process still has to be put to the test. It would be a mistake to forget about another Central European country, namely Croatia, which traditionally belonged to this economic space, and also its recent economic data are demonstrating this linkage. For political reasons, however, Croatia has not so far been able to become a member either of the AA-10 (because it has no Association Agreement with Brussels) or of CEFTA (where one of the membership criteria is the Association Agreement with the EU). Sooner or later, however, this country is expected to 'return to Central Europe' not only in economic terms, but from an institutional point of view as well.

In this paper, primary attention will be given to the CEFTA-6 group, as the 'Eastern half' of the re-emerging 'Central European economic space'.

## 2. Framework Conditions of an Emerging New Pattern for the 'Central European Economic Space'

Leaving aside the artificial creation of the German *Lebensraum* in the 1930s, Central Europe is, after more than a century, back on the European map of economic growth and structural modernization. However, the conditions of its re-emergence, as well as the framework in which the region is re-emerging, are very different from those that have prevailed over the last century.

Firstly, the 'Eastern part of Central Europe' faces a threefold challenge within one (or, perhaps just half of one) generation. It has to find adequate answers to the systemic transformation in general, and in particular to the modernization pattern, as the second stage of successful transformation. Second, and parallel to this effort, institutional integration into the European Union has to be accomplished. Third, global challenges have to be addressed. Evidently, all three tasks are closely interdependent. The future role of this part of 'old' Central Europe in shaping a 'new' Central Europe largely depends on the character, the timing and the sequencing of answers to the above challenges. For example, the economic policy steps of systemic transformation, as well as answers to global challenges, will influence the future pattern of integration into the EU. This process in turn will also affect the pattern of structural transformation and the scope of global integration.

Second, in the 'Western part of Central Europe' the pattern is very different from that of the last century. On the one hand, the region has become part of a larger Transatlantic framework in security terms, and to a deeply institutionalized (Western) European system in economic (and in the future probably also monetary) terms. As a result, it has lost its independent role as an authentic modernization anchor for the less developed part of Central Europe. More precisely, it can exert such an impact only as an integral part of the Transatlantic and the Western European communities. On the other hand, the challenge of modernization has reached not only the Eastern but also the Western part of Central Europe. There will be a mixture of answers, on national, integration and global (multinational) levels, that are likely to affect the future nature and role of Central Europe quite seriously. Finally, we have to stress that, in contrast with the last century, Europe as such has ceased to be the core growth region of the world economy. Signs of 'peripherization' can be identified not only in the Eastern but also in the Western part of Central Europe and, more importantly, in Europe as a whole: in comparison with North America or the Far East, that is, and despite the substantial financial problems recently observed in some Far Eastern countries.

In consequence, revitalization and catching up to the leading economies and economic trends, has become a common European task, even if the levels, in financial and human resources, from which this catching up process has to start are different across regions and countries. Here, the most important question is whether, and to what extent, Central Europe can play a role in the overall modernization process of Europe. And even more importantly, can the Eastern part of Central Europe become an active player in this process?

At first glance, there is no fundamental change in the historically developed pattern of economic progress for the Eastern part of Central Europe. As in the past, there is no genuine modernization anchor within the region. Thus, it has to be found outside the national economies of the area. In general, this anchor role is expected to be played by the European Union. The endeavour of all countries to become full member of the Union as soon as possible is clear evidence for this. On the surface, the modernization anchor for the region traditionally located in Germany (and the Habsburg Monarchy) has shifted to Brussels. However, under this institutional cover, the same historical roots can still easily be detected. More than half of the Polish, Czech or Hungarian trade with the EU is in fact carried out with Germany, and if Austria and Italy are also taken into consideration, we see that about three-quarters of their trade relations with the EU are still concentrated on the countries representing the traditional Central European modernization anchor.

Also, the relative economic weight of the Eastern part of Central Europe, in comparison with the European Union, is very modest: which seems to support the general view that the successful modernization of this region will be the result of a one-way process, from the Western part of the continent (as the modernization anchor) towards the Eastern part of the continent (the recipients or objects of modernization). In fact, the total GDP of the CEFTA-6 is, even at purchasing power parity, not higher than 5 to 6 per cent of that of the EU-15, and the region's average per capita income accounts for about one-third of that of the EU average. Despite these hard facts, there are a number of important developments which support the view that the Eastern part of Central Europe may, in the not too distant future, become an increasingly important subregion of European modernization.

(a) First, the future of the world economy is decisively shaped by the activities of multinational companies and capital. Some transforming Central European economies, most notably Hungary, have already become preferred locations of multi-national corporations. While the geographic framework of modernization is still represented by Western (and even more by Western Central) Europe, mainly in the form of the free trade in manufactured goods stipulated by the Association Agreement, and conditioned by the prospect of full membership in the EU, the actors of modernization are far more than just European companies. For the first time in its history, the economic modernization of the Eastern part of Central Europe is likely to be co-shaped by non-European factors and by company strategies conceived not only in Central European, or even European, but in global terms. It is worth noting that, according to a number of sources of background information, it was more the pressure by large European and non-European companies than the internal development of the EU which has accelerated the EU's process of thinking in order to start negotiations on accession with the candidate Central and Eastern European countries in the first place.

There are three important lessons on sequencing one can learn from the less than one decade of multi-national corporation activities in Hungary, and to a lesser extent in the Czech Republic and Poland. All three may have substantial implications for the future place of Central Europe in the continent but, to some extent, even in the global division of labour.

First: the entrepreneurial sequencing. After 1989 there was no chance for a genuine 'national' economic development in the transforming Central

European countries. While most modern Western European economies were based on a historical sequencing of creating small national firms that, after a while, could become medium-sized, than large-scale companies and, finally start their international activities, this option was not available for the transforming countries of Central Europe. Although efforts have been made to create a genuine national entrepreneurial class, two fundamental conditions for such an approach are absolutely missing. One is time, because the outgoing 20th century does not leave room for this initiative (nobody has 60 to 80 years to develop a genuine national entrepreneurial structure). The other is the globalizing economy which, from the very beginning, punishes those countries that try to close their doors to it. Without at least a temporary autarchy, however, it is impossible to create the old pattern of national entrepreneurs. The costs of closing down were very high even in the last decades, and under present circumstances it would probably be economic suicide for small, modernising countries in Europe. If this is the basic constellation, the sequencing is clear, although in its final result is still unknown. (We only know that no other approach would have been viable.) The main engine of macroeconomic development has to be the activities of multi-national corporations. If the economic environment is attractive, it will be mainly the multi-national corporations which will create an increasingly broad network of subcontractors, both national and foreign-owned, but all of them located in the given modernising country. Therefore, we see that the modernization impact is crucially coming from the multi-national corporations, but will be multiplied by an expanding network of modern(ized) cells.

Second: the sectoral sequencing. multi-national corporations themselves have been going through a substantive learning process. Since they had very little knowledge of the transforming Central European countries before 1989, they started to base their activities here on the experience gained in less developed countries in other parts of the world. Beside gaining market shares, mainly as a result of liberalization, privatization and the collapse of previous markets, they focused on less qualified or simply unskilled, labour-intensive production (textiles, leather, etc.). Within the space of a few years, however, they have discovered that relative labour costs are even less expensive (and therefore more competitive) in higher-skilled labour-intensive branches (machinery, transport equipment, and parts of the electronics and computer industry). Finally, and most recently, they have started investments in research and development activities as well, for cost advantages in this field are even more attractive (not to mention the innovative capacities in various sectors of economic activity in the transforming Central European region). A fortunate combination of globally moving capital and technology, on the one hand, and the available innovative research and development capacities, on the other hand, may offer a special instrument to Central Europe not only for successful modernization but also for becoming a subregional modernization pole.

Third: the geographic sequencing. Throughout the modern history of Europe, modernization waves have spread from West to East. This process is still clearly manifested in the catching up process of Central and Eastern Europe today. Territorial differences in income levels, economic activities and production structures can be moderated only in the medium and longer term. In order to make the process of modernization sustainable, there is an active role both for the State and for the European Union, in co-operation with the Central European candidate countries. Central Europe's modernization success crucially depends on the speed and scope of the spill-over effects towards Eastern (and South-Eastern) Europe.

(b) Second: major balance-of-power shifts in the European continent are expected to create better chances for a more dynamic role for Central Europe in the shaping of Europe's future. German unification (including the intra-German political shift represented by establishing Berlin as the new capital of Germany), the enlargement of the EU by three EFTA countries, and the Association Agreements signed with most and membership negotiations opened with selected Central and Eastern European transforming countries are the most important elements of a twofold dynamism: from the Southwest (or the Mediterranean area) towards the Northeast (the Baltic Sea); and from the Atlantic coast towards the geographic core of the continent. Around the intersection of these two lines (and, of course, along the two lines as well), the new Europe is in the making. 500 years after Europe turned to the Atlantic, the Eastern part of Central Europe may be the great beneficiary of these shifts. The positive impact will be the higher, the more these countries are able to combine favourable geographic trends with the global opportunities offered by multinational corporations, and with advantages deriving from their status as 'late-comers'.

(c) Third: Central European candidate countries, on their way to full membership in the EU, reveal a pattern different from that of the accession of the Mediterranean economies. In the latter, institutional integration (i.e. full membership) preceded macroeconomic integration into the European structures. In other words, it was the institutional umbrella that created the possibilities for grass-roots integration, by deepening intra-firm relations (partly with the fundamental support of EU financial transfers). In contrast, the Central European candidates have already to a large extent created the micro-economic conditions. Looking at the share of the EU in their total trade, and even more importantly, at the rapidly increasing intra-industry activities, one can state that, in micro-economic terms, these countries are already prepared for membership. However, what is still missing (and it is something more and more required by those who are interested in the sustainability of the recently created micro-economic networks) is the institutionalization of relations, i.e. full membership at the earliest time possible.

At present, more than 70 per cent of the Polish, Hungarian and Slovenian exports are directed to the EU. Geographic reorientation in the last decade was accompanied by substantial market share gains for the candidate countries in total EU extra-regional imports. CEFTA-6 exports in extra-regional imports of the EU grew from 2.6 per cent in 1989 to 7.6 per cent in 1997. In turn, CEFTA's share in extra regional exports of the EU experienced an even more dramatic increase, from 2.4 to almost 10 per cent. Even more importantly, the structure of exports reveals an unprecedentedly rapid change from less processed to more processed goods, away from sensitive products towards final consumption goods and, first of all, towards products constituting the backbone of subcontracting networks. According to 1997 figures, the share of machinery in total exports of CEFTA to the EU amounted to 34 per cent (over 50 per cent in the case of Hungary). Between 1994 and 1997, machinery proved to be the main engine of export growth to the EU, with 57 per cent (in the case of Hungary with 76 per cent) of the total increment of exports. (Data from *Eurostat; External and Intra-European Trade; Monthly Statistics* (various issues) and own calculations.) Looking at Germany, in 1997, CEFTA-6 countries had a total share of 6.6 per cent in total German imports - up from 4.6 per cent in 1993. However, their participation in the German market of final industrial goods increased from 5 to over 8.6 per cent in this four-year period. CEFTA-6 accounts for one-third of German imports of wood products, almost 20 per cent of metal manufactures, more than 16 per cent of clothing, almost 15 per cent of glassware and 10 per cent of footwear and leather products. More important are structural changes taking place in higher skill-intensive and partly also in technology-intensive industries, such as machinery and electrical and transport equipment. Here, the share of CEFTA grew from 2.6 to 5.6, from 3.7 to 8.2 and from 2 to 6.8 per cent, respectively, between 1993 and 1997.

Behind this generally rapid structural upgrading there is a differentiation process unfolding even among CEFTA countries. Due to different patterns of privatization, diverging features of economic policy and the different role played by foreign direct investments, Central European candidate countries have already started to specialise in different product groups. Poland, and increasingly Slovenia too, are specialising in labour-intensive products, while Hungary is leading in specialization in machinery, transport equipment and electronics, followed by the Czech Republic. The growing structural interpenetration is demonstrated by the fact that total German imports grew by 31 per cent between 1993 and 1997, while imports from CEFTA-6 increased by 124 per cent. German imports of machinery and electrotechnical articles from CEFTA-6 increased threefold, and those of transport equipment almost fivefold, while total imports only grew by 30 to 40 per cent. The indisputable engines of export growth of CEFTA-6 to Germany were these three product groups, representing 53 per cent of the total increment of exports between 1993 and 1997. While this share reached less than 20 per cent of Romania's and only 28 per cent of the Polish export increment to Germany, it represented 49 per cent for the Czech Republic, 64 per cent for Slovakia, 73 per cent for Slovenia and almost 80 per cent for Hungary (own calculations based on *Statistisches Bundesamt. Fachserie 7. Aussenhandel. Reihe 3. Aussenhandel nach Ländern und Warengruppen*).*

(d) Fourth: the next enlargement of the EU will be the first one which will not reach the geographic boundaries of Europe. While all earlier enlargements incorporated geographic peripheries into the integration process, the first round of Eastern enlargement will bring geographically core continental countries into the EU. Their transit position, coupled with additional (potential) advantages may generate some relevant impacts on the increasing role of Central Europe in a new Europe of the early 21st century. A basic precondition for playing such a role is, however, that the European integration process will not be interrupted and that no new dividing lines will be created at the new external borders of the Union.

(e) Fifth: the future pattern of Central European co-operation and its influence on European (and partly global) trends will also be shaped by the

---

* Just to mention some Hungarian export figures to Germany, it is not well known that Hungary (and Poland and the Czech Republic even more so) is exporting more manufactured goods to Germany than five EU member countries - Greece, Finland, Ireland, Denmark and Portugal. In 1993, Spain exported 2.65 times more machinery and 75 per cent more electrical articles to Germany than Hungary. Four years later, in 1997, Spanish exports to Germany of these two product categories reached just 80 per cent of the corresponding Hungarian exports.

utilization of selected revealed or latent comparative advantages for the transforming part of this part of Europe. Four elements can be mentioned in this context.

First, the growth potential of the region will become more important for many European countries. Certainly, domestic markets are limited, but structural upgrading and rapid growth of purchasing power* will be important factors. Further liberalization of trade in order to cope with the stipulations of the Association Agreements, parallel free trade within the CEFTA region, elimination of barriers to agricultural trade and, more importantly, membership in NATO and the EU, are additional components of a sustainable high growth both of production and of productivity in the next decade. In contrast, growth in Western Europe is likely to remain modest (the Maastricht criteria underlying the introduction of the Euro may even worsen growth prospects temporarily), while traditional high-growth regions (mainly the Far East) are likely to suffer from financial and institutional crises in the next few years. As a result, even the relatively modest but rapidly growing Central European market can become a major area of attraction, with growth rates 2 to 3 times higher than the EU average, and with near or above double-digit (industrial) productivity growth rates.

Second, rapid structural change of exports has already shown that the comparative advantages of most Central European candidate countries are in their well-educated and flexible labour force. The pattern of international trade between more and less developed countries cannot be applied to the trade pattern between the EU (Germany, Austria) and the candidate Central European economies. Supported by international capital movements and the activities of multi-national corporations, the latter are expected to become important partners and competitors in higher-value-added and technologically more intensive production sectors. The 'mixture' between partnership and competition very much depends on EU strategies towards this part of Europe. It has to be added that a higher level of general education may be an important factor in the generally more efficient absorption of external resources, including would-be EU transfers. (The central geographic location of these countries points in the same direction. Therefore, it is mistaken to measure the (potential) absorption capacity of these countries in comparison with the less developed members of the EU.)

---

* It is often forgotten that the main engine of higher purchasing power in rapidly modernising economies is the appreciation of the national currency, and not necessarily real wage increases.

Third, the international competitiveness of the 21st century will not only be based on economic criteria such as prices, quality, just-in-time-delivery and other factors. To an increasing extent, general social, mental and institutional flexibility will be shaping competitiveness. In this context, the painful years of systemic transformation have shown the vast (although certainly not unlimited) potential of Central and Eastern Europe, also in comparison with Western Europe. It remains to be seen how large this potential really is, and how national governments will be able to exploit it adequately. More importantly, we have yet to see to what extent Western Europe will allow the use of this potential to improve not only Central Europe's position within Europe, but also Europe's standing on the global scene.

Fourth, late comers do usually have some advantages. They derive these from economic factors (relatively lower costs of introducing up-to-date technologies), from the political situation (generally higher level of social flexibility) and, last but not least, from psychological components (the commonly shared need and desire to catch up). Global liberalization and its challenges to national economies on different levels of development should be considered as an important contribution to identify and exploit these advantages.

### 3 . Some remarks on CEFTA's future in Europe

The above-mentioned features and potential advantages are, to different degrees, characteristic of all CEFTA countries. However, for obvious reasons, they cannot be used in the framework of intra-CEFTA co-operation exclusively. Predominantly, they can be exploited and incorporated into a wider pattern of the (Central) European division of labour. In consequence, CEFTA is unlikely to become a 'core region' in Europe, but it has a good chance of becoming a less peripheral area of Western Europe, and a more intensive part(ner) of the European core, facing towards Eastern Europe.

Still, co-operation among CEFTA countries has a substantial potential. Already in the last years, intra-CEFTA trade has started to grow rapidly, and today its share in the total trade of the member countries reaches about 8 per cent (excepting the special trade between the Czech and the Slovak Republics), or twice the historically lowest share immediately after the collapse of CMEA co-operation. There are three major factors affecting further intensive growth of trade (and economic) relations.

First, the commodity structure of intra-CEFTA trade is much less developed than the trade pattern between CEFTA countries and the EU. Sooner or later a fundamental structural upgrading will happen, shifting the commodity pattern from the predominance of agricultural goods, chemicals, raw materials and semi-finished goods towards higher value-added products represented by machinery, final consumption goods and more technology-intensive intermediate products.

Second, membership in the EU will be extremely useful also in increasing intra-CEFTA trade flows. With 8 per cent, at present, intra-CEFTA trade has already reached a level that exceeds the level of economic co-operation between Spain and Portugal before membership in the EU, which has dramatically intensified Spanish-Portuguese economic contacts within one decade. Such a dramatic impact can hardly be expected in CEFTA, but, as a result of accession to the EU, intra-CEFTA trade can achieve a two digit share of 12 to 14 per cent in total trade of the member countries.

Third, multi-national corporations already have a growing influence on intra-CEFTA trade relations. The forthcoming membership in NATO of three CEFTA countries, as well as accession to the EU, will certainly increase the interest of large transnational companies in the regional market. As a result, three different attitudes of the multi-national corporations can be identified. On the one hand, multi-national corporations can establish subsidiaries in one or more of the CEFTA countries, focusing on the domestic (or part of the regional) market. On the other hand, they may consider CEFTA as an integrated market and opt for just one production location to serve the whole regional market. Finally, they could restructure their planned or already established production potential located in various countries of the region in order to develop a regional network of subcontracting, similar to that created between the individual CEFTA countries and (selected) EU member countries in the last years. In the next period, the attitudes described in the second and third point are likely to decisively shape not only intra-CEFTA co-operation but also the gradual integration of CEFTA into the all-European framework of activities of multi-national corporations. As a consequence, not only intra-CEFTA trade relations are likely to be upgraded, but also the contribution of CEFTA countries to an improved global position of Europe could be envisaged.

In this process, subregional growth poles (modernization centres) are expected to emerge in the next few years. They will not become authentic, independent growth centres, since they will remain embedded in and their progress will be essentially defined by the more important decision-making centres either in the EU, in other (Western) European countries or at the headquarters of multi-national corporations. Nevertheless, their dependency pattern will be changing, and it will become gradually more balanced. Dependence on the above-mentioned centres will be complemented by growing independence (or decision-making power) in the regional context. Also the recovering 'national capital', in the first stage mainly linked to multi-national corporations, but, as a result of progress, gradually provided with its own financial resources, marketing outlets, and technological and managerial skills, can contribute to a more balanced relation between dependence (periphery) and genuine decision-making (core). CEFTA countries joining the EU in the first round of enlargement have a chance to play a double role. On the one hand, they can 'internalise' dependency from Western Europe (instead of the 'externalized' dependency pattern of today). On the other hand, they have good opportunities to become core countries in relation to the other European countries still left outside the EU.*

## 4. Problems and prospects

In the last decade of the century, the transforming countries of Central Europe have returned to the long-term development pattern interrupted twice in this century by history (not only in 1945 but already in 1918). Whether they can continue on this way and, at the same time, successfully adjust themselves to the new global and European realities, depends on various tendencies, the outcome of which is, in most cases, not yet clear.

(a) First, the second stage of economic and social transformation, generally called *sustainable* modernization, has only started in a few countries. In most cases, the success of modernization cannot yet be considered guaranteed. This, however, is a major precondition to be able to answer the question whether (this part of) Central Europe will become part of the 'core' or remain on the periphery of European (and global) developments.

(b) Second, it is not sustainable modernization in itself that is needed, but a *managed* modernization, based on a long term strategy of (potential) comparative advantages. Successful modernization can hardly be attained

* This process, though almost unnoticed, has already started. The rapidly growing capital exports from Hungary in 1997 can, to a large extent, be explained by transfers of multi-national corporations located in Hungary to some neighbouring countries. In other words, profits of multi-national corporations earned in Hungary are (co-)financing the expansion of these companies in selected Eastern and Southeastern European economies.

against the main actors of this process, who are external (or not yet 'internalized'). Still, the pattern of modernization is likely to be rather different if carried out by external actors only (although this is probably still better than the absence of modernization), or also by internal or 'internalized' actors. The first calls on the State as a development (and not a redistributional) agent. The second, in the best version, can consist of the EU (once a Central European country becomes a full member) and of those multi-national corporations that will already have upgraded their production structures, and considered the given Central European location as an inseparable part of their world-wide (or at least European) network of activities. The crucial decisions influencing the status of the transforming part of Central Europe on Europe's future map have still to be taken in co-operation with the above-mentioned actors. (The evolving pattern will depend on the relative negotiating skill and power of these actors. )

(c) Third, it is difficult to imagine that Europe will have several growth and decision-making centres in the foreseeable future. More precisely, it is only likely within the European Union and not outside the integration framework. Thus, aspirations based on finding non-European partners to counterbalance the overwhelming power of the EU could turn out, in my opinion, to be rather costly wishful thinking. Non-European investors located in Central European candidate countries have not arrived in order to create a 'second Europe', but because they have firm hopes of becoming part of the existing Europe, i.e. the EU. This does not mean, of course, that Central Europe has to focus unilaterally on Europe. But the sequencing has to be clear: first, integration into the European structures and second, by using these structures create better chances for global activities (either supported by a larger Europe or by trying to eliminate the European rigidities in alliance with interested EU members).

(d) Fourth, decisions in the EU and the present member countries have essential consequences for the future development pattern of Central Europe. Only some of the critical areas will be mentioned here.

(da) The denial of a free labour market for a longish period, even after full membership for the first candidate countries, is likely to have a rather ambiguous impact. While it is hampering the integration of Central Europe's labour markets, most probably it will substantially increase capital flows to Central Europe. In earlier parts of this paper, several factors working in this direction have already been outlined. However, one of the most powerful influences may come from largely restrictive labour market policies in Western Europe. As capital flows cannot be blocked by national or even EU-level policies, more capital may flow to the Central European markets. This could prove to be an extremely helpful instrument to improve the pattern of integration in the Central Europe of the future.

(db) Extreme care has to be taken with those adjustments to the EU rules which promise higher security for Western Europe but less security in a wider Europe. As the candidate Central European countries are at the geographic cross-roads, the consequences of adjustment - and its nature, scope and speed - can substantially shape their future position as core or, maybe, as what we could call 'internal periphery' countries. The implementation of policies designed to establish certain social standards before (i.e. as a precondition for) accession has to be done with consideration for the implications of such policies for the competitiveness of these countries. As long as competitiveness is not threatened, and the higher standards force countries and firms to upgrade their production and, thus to incorporate themselves with more advantage into the process of Central European economic co-operation, the adjustment process has to be supported. If, however, competitiveness is likely to decline because of too quick and broad adjustment, the consequences are likely to be rather negative. The present EU countries may (temporarily) get rid of part of the competitive pressure (without, of course, being able to eliminate the dominating pressure coming from the global markets); but by doing this, they will worsen their global market position and, at the same time, build up a potential of instabilities in the neighbouring countries, as a result of low growth, higher unemployment, real migration capacities, etc.

The results of joining the Schengen agreement may be even more ambiguous. Evidently, this policy is supposed to shift the external borders of the EU towards the East and enhance the stability of the EU member countries. However, the price of this apparent stability could be too high, if, on the new external borders of the Union, a higher level of instability were to develop than the instability supposedly avoided through applying the Schengen rules.

Any requirement that, immediately or within a relatively short period, is expected to generate more costs than benefits, would negatively influence Central European co-operation and reinforce the peripheral position of Central Europe (before enlargement of the Union it would have a negative effect on the Western part of Central Europe; and after enlargement, on the new member countries).

(dc) The Central European candidate countries already have a growing impact on the cost structure of firms with headquarters of subsidiaries in EU member countries. Those firms (and countries) which are using the (cost, geographical, educational, innovative and other) advantages offered by the candidate Central European countries have already obtained comparative advantages vis-à-vis those EU countries and firms which have remained reluctant to enter the new markets. Sooner or later, differences in competitiveness will become manifest among different EU member countries, as most of them are likely to become part of the monetary union. This, however, means that differences in competitive strength cannot be remedied by autonomous exchange rate policies (mainly devaluations). Therefore, frictions in the EMU, due to different levels of co-operation with (and within) Central Europe, cannot be excluded. As, along with multinational firms, German (and to a lesser extent Austrian and North Italian) companies seem to have a predominant position in intra-industry co-operation with the candidate Central European countries, conflicts between deeper co-operation in Central Europe and monetary integration cannot be ruled out.

(dd) Most importantly, the future of Central Europe will be fundamentally influenced by the timing and conditions of accession of (some of) the first-round candidate countries to the EU. Quick accession, largely supported by already dense co-operation among Central European countries on both sides of the EU, could provide a relevant impetus to develop a Central European growth centre within Europe. Such a development would be favourable also for other European countries, both within and outside the EU. For the first group, it could enhance the global competitiveness of Europe, while the second group could get more relevant support in its process of economic modernization. The more the first wave of Eastern enlargement is delayed, the higher will be the costs, both in real terms (to finance growing instability at the Eastern border of the Union) and in terms of foregone benefits (in terms of access to inputs required for higher competitiveness in the global market). However, the most important longer-term implication may be political and concerns the future place of Germany in Europe. Germany's inclusion in Europe, a century-long endeavour of French politics and the result of a 50-year old self-imposed, self-restrictive and enlightening German policy, can only be a successful undertaking for the first decades of the next century if Germany's Eastern neighbours are quickly taken into the EU. The EMU, in itself, will not be able to play this role, because it lacks the security component. The future of Europe, in general, and the predictable and manageable future of Central Europe in particular are not only based on economic, but, to a large extent, also on security criteria.

(e) Fifth, and finally, it is imperative to enhance the stability of the whole of Europe. Therefore, new and long-lasting institutionalized fragmentation is to be avoided. In this context, the treatment of those candidate countries that are unlikely to become members of the EU in the short term (plus potential new associated countries) has to be given careful attention. In this context, Central Europe, including the present and future members of the EU belonging to this geographic area, has a historic task and opportunity. Whether Central Europe will become a core region of the Europe of the next century or will, at least in part, remain a peripheral area, with all the imaginable and still unimaginable consequences for the continent, largely depends on the degree to which it will be able to solve this essential problem.

# Some Comments

*Loukas Tsoukalis*

The two papers by Professors Inotai and Lavigne complement each other nicely. One general point raised by both papers refers to the identity of Central Europe as an economic and political region; and hence as something more than a simple geographical entity. Assuming that a regional identity does exist, would it be limited to the Czech Republic, Hungary and Poland (and perhaps also Slovakia), or would it be more appropriate to adopt a more inclusive definition which would also incorporate other countries such as Romania?

It is true that the countries of the region, however defined, share a similar political and economic past based on more than four decades of communist rule. But they are not, of course, the only ones. They also share a common goal, namely accession to the EU and the progressive integration of their economies in the European system. They already have a high degree of economic dependence on the EU in terms of trade and investment. However, other countries of the former Soviet empire also share the same political goal and they have a very similar degree of openness to trade with the more advanced economies of the European continent. Narrowly defined, the countries of Central Europe have been so far among the most successful transition economies and they also have the best chance of being allowed into the EU sooner rather than later. This is arguably the most important factor differentiating them from the other countries of the wider region.

Is that a strong enough factor to help bring the countries of Central Europe together and thus forge a common regional identity? The level of economic interdependence between the countries of the region is low and likely to remain so. Regional institutions are certainly not considered as a substitute for EU membership. Furthermore, none of the candidate countries on the so-called fast track leading to EU accession is keen on being treated as a member of a group by European institutions. Among the fast runners in Central Europe, Poland presents a very different set of problems in terms of its future accession to the EU, compared with Hungary and the Czech Republic. In many respects, Poland is what Spain used to be in the context of the Mediterranean enlargement. It would be only natural that both the Hungarians and the Czechs, not to mention the Slovenes or the

Estonians, try to separate their application from that of Poland by arguing that their own early accession would present relatively few problems of indigestion for the fat Europeans of the EU. This will not help to foster a spirit of togetherness among candidate countries, even though it seems highly unlikely that any one of them will be able to repeat the Greek act by joining earlier on its own.

Will CEFTA prove to be more than a convenient, low-key transitional arrangement until its members join the EU? In more general terms, will Central Europe have much of an economic and political meaning after the next round of enlargement? I very much doubt it. Earlier enlargements may have created some kind of a Southern European group, especially when it comes to transfers of funds. But it has never been a particularly solid group; and the Central European one may prove to be even less so.

The second general point refers to the nature and speed of the economic transformation in Central Europe. On the basis of all the main indicators, the Czech Republic, Hungary and Poland have been among the most successful transition economies, with all the ups and downs, as witnessed, for example, in the Czech Republic in recent years. Both papers stress the role of multinationals in the economic transformation of the transition economies and the very limited role that governments are likely to be able to play in the future. Will this prove to be a sustainable relationship? And what about the other factors in the equation? Can they be safely assumed away?

Both papers discuss the economic prospects for the countries of the region and especially the nature of their future specialization, and hence their position in the rapidly changing European and international division of labour. To put it in slogan terms, will Central Europe become the economic backyard of the more advanced countries of Western Europe, as suggested by Professor Lavigne, or is it more likely to emerge as an independent growth centre between Western Europe and the other candidate countries left behind on the slow track? Professor Inotai adopts the more optimistic scenario. He sees more possibilities for at least some of the Central European countries getting away from their present position in the international division of labour, which is determined almost entirely by two factors, namely cheap labour and geographical proximity to EU markets; and he expects them to shift eventually to the production of more high-skill and technology-intensive goods.

The realization of one or the other scenario will in turn determine whether Central Europe remains a periphery in political and economic terms or whether it becomes gradually part of the core. This would have major consequences for growth. Continued dependence on cheap labour would not ensure the high rates of economic growth envisaged in Professor Inotai's paper. He refers to rates of growth in the countries of Central Europe being two or even three times higher than those of the EU-15 for the foreseeable future as a means of catching up. This is surely a hypothesis that remains to be tested.

The political economy of economic transformation/reform needs to incorporate political and social factors which will largely determine its success or failure. The identification of losers should be an important part of this exercise; and there have been many losers in this process of transformation/reform in the former communist countries. In some of those countries, they have indeed succeeded in effectively resisting or simply delaying economic change. Those are precisely the countries considered as the least successful transition economies. How will the societies of Poland, Hungary or the Czech Republic react in the future to the ever accelerating pace of economic change? Economists - or indeed politicians - who take social acceptance of economic change for granted do so at their own peril.

The success of the process of economic transformation also depends heavily on the development of institutions and their ability to regulate the economy. The Czech crisis of 1997 has raised basic questions about the regulatory capacity of even the more advanced countries of the region; and hence also about their ability quickly and successfully to make the transition from a command economy to a very different state of affairs in which public institutions interact constantly with the market. It is not simply a question of indulging in the magic of the marketplace. Transition countries have a long distance to travel in this direction.

External factors will, of course, continue to play a very important role. Central European economies are open economies, vulnerable to the ups and downs of the world economy and the vagaries of the international financial system. The experience of the last two years is rather comforting in this respect. The turbulence in international financial markets has had only a limited effect on Central Europe; and so has the financial collapse of Russia. This means that markets increasingly perceive the countries of the region as an adjunct of Western Europe and not as part of the East or the Third World. So far so good, one might add.

My last point refers to modernization. As Professor Inotai correctly points out, modernization is not only about economics. It also has a strong political and social dimension. He argues that most of this process of modernization in the past was imported; and he seems to imply that it will continue to be so in the future, with multinational companies acting as the main modernizer for the countries of the region. Once again, it is the primacy of the economic factor; alternatively, globalization beats governments and societies. This hypothesis too remains to be tested.

I shall add a few comments on modernization and the potential role of the EU. There are perhaps some interesting lessons to learn from the past. Although the process of European integration originated in 'Carolingian Europe', which still remains the hub of political power and economic prowess, EU membership has in many respects meant, and still does, much more for the peripheral and less developed countries, be they Ireland or Greece today, or the Czech Republic tomorrow. It has offered those countries a stable multilateral framework and the opportunity to take an active part in the formulation of European policies; instead of being reduced to the role of simple consumers of decisions taken elsewhere.

The EC, and later the EU, has acted as a force of stabilization and modernization for the young democracies of Southern Europe after the collapse of dictatorial regimes. Active participation in European institutions and the application of common rules have played a major role in this respect. Large transfers of funds have also facilitated the adjustment of previously heavily protected economies. The transformation of the Iberian economies has been truly spectacular; and Greece is now, with some delay, trying to catch up.

Although there may still be a Southern problem, manifested mainly in terms of lower income levels, the gap with the rest of the EU has been gradually reduced. Broadly speaking, the integration of the Southern European countries should be declared a success.

The challenge presented by the countries of Central and Eastern Europe is undoubtedly much greater. There are many more countries involved; the difference in terms of levels of economic development is much greater; democratic institutions and civil society in at least some of the countries are still weak; and last but not least, it is all a question of establishing a new geopolitical order in a region of Europe which contains many sources of potential instability and which happens to lie next or close to the Russian border. Already the prospect of EU membership, distant though it may be for some of the candidates, has played a major role not only in relation to economic policies but also in the treatment of minorities and the respect of human rights.

Preoccupied with internal problems, the EU has continued for too long to treat candidate countries as outsiders who may one day, and preferably it will be a fairly distant day, join in. It has also tended to show relatively little generosity, and even less imagination, in parting with its money. The proposals made by the European Commission in Agenda 2000 constitute a turning point, even though the proposals for the development of structural policies for the period between 2000 and 2006 risk widening further the economic gap between different groups of European countries, and most notably the 'ins', the 'pre-ins' and the 'late-to-be-ins'.

The process of democratization and economic and social modernization of the countries of Central and Eastern Europe will unavoidably be linked to their progressive integration into the European system, of which the EU constitutes by far the most important part. And for this to happen without killing the goose that lays the golden eggs, major internal reforms of the EU will be required, coupled with a more flexible and generous approach towards prospective members.

# 4.
# Central Europe and European Integration

Erik Holm

# Deep Integration or Shallow Integration?

*Helen Wallace*

### Introduction

Nearly ten years since the great changes of 1989 across Europe, the jury is still out on what pattern of integration might emerge in this very different Europe. The jury is out and the negotiators are out too, engaged in discovering what might be the basis for accommodation between the European Union (EU) and the many applicant countries for EU membership from central and eastern Europe. Prognoses proliferate on which timescales might be possible, which countries might accede to the EU, and what new arrangements might be needed to facilitate eastern enlargement. Most of the practitioner discussion is focused on the technicalities of the accession process and especially on the pace of change and adjustment in the applicant countries. The presumption is that most of that adjustment will be unilateral, by the applicants towards the 'standards' and practices of the existing EU and its members.

But this is too simple a version of the story for two reasons, one obvious, the other less obvious. The obvious reason is that the EU is itself involved in a process of change, with economic and monetary union (EMU) the sharpest illustration, and is under pressure to alter some of its policies. The less obvious reason is that we are living in a period in which the 'integration project' in Europe is in a broader sense under test. In essence it can be argued that the particular model of integration which has developed in and around the EU has been the product of a particular phase in European history. That phase fostered a particular synergy of integration dynamics and institutionalization along several complementary dimensions. It became a phase of what I shall describe as *deep* integration. The two questions that follow are: first, whether that model of deep integration is sustainable for a membership something like that of the current EU; and, second, whether the model of deep integration is extendible across the broader continent.

In one sense the answer to the first question seems obvious. The development of EMU seems the clearest testimony possible to the capacity of the West European integration process to become deeper. Moreover the planned incorporation within EMU of so large a number of EU members (with markedly different economic characteristics) suggests that an inclusive pattern of intensified integration might be possible. As long as EMU works (... and as long as public consent for its consequences can be sustained) it is tempting to hang all the rest of the discussion on the fortunes of EMU. And, of course, the counter argument seems to make this self-evident. A collapse of EMU would be a huge set-back with enormous ricochets across the continent and could well jeopardise the enlargement process.

This paper, however, makes a different argument. It takes as its focal point a different analysis, namely that we can understand the west European deep integration model only if we identify the several different dimensions of integration that have characterized western Europe since the 1940s and if we can comprehend the relationship between the emerging European arena of regime-building and the politics of the countries that fall within it. Economic integration generally, as currently intensified by EMU, forms only part of a much wider setting. That wider setting was framed by the division of Europe which facilitated the development of integration across several other dimensions as well. It was the synergy between these different dimensions that produced *deep* integration. Hence EMU on its own is not sufficient evidence of a sustainable further deepening of integration. Moreover the ending of the sharp division of Europe, however welcome, destabilises the synergy in the inherited deep integration process. Hence the answer to the second question, whether the model is extendible to central and eastern Europe, requires us to ask whether we can expect to discover an equivalent pattern of multidimensional integration across the continent.

## The different dimensions of integration

What then are these different dimensions? I shall call them the *functional*, the *territorial*, and the *affiliational*.* They can be characterized as follows:

i. *functional*: the connections of a concrete and substantive kind in the economic and societal domains in which interdependencies have developed and transnational regimes have been constructed, in particular as regards economics, physical resources and infrastructure, and shared socio-economic spaces (e.g. some cross-border regions);

* The argument that is summarised here is drawn from (*Wallace; 1998*).

ii. *territorial*: the management of borders and boundaries between countries and around groups of countries, including the range from the management of borders between contiguous neighbours (France/Germany, UK/Ireland etc.) to the construction of military alliances, i.e. *both* managing 'neighbourliness' or diasporas *and* the big questions of geopolitics; and

iii. *affiliational*: affinities of values, ideologies, and cultural connections across country borders, that form a basis for shared affiliations 'beyond the (nation) state'.

In western Europe these three different dimensions have all been present in the past fifty years as components of the integration process. What has been striking is that connections have developed so extensively and so intensively in all three dimensions. With the exception of those countries that have been 'outliers' in refusing extensive involvement (Norway and Switzerland are obvious, though different, examples), the west European experience has been one in which - over the decades - most west European countries have experienced a strengthening of connections along each dimension.

Nonetheless, we should note that the different dimensions of integration were framed by the division of Europe. Functional connections were set by the distinction between market and non-market economies. Territorial connections were bounded by the iron curtain; thus, for example, making it incontrovertible that for these purposes Turkey was part of 'western' Europe. Affiliational connections were heavily overlaid by the ideological division of Europe.

## Multiple frameworks

The transnational connections that have been built on each of these dimensions have been articulated through a variety of different frameworks and institutional arrangements. It is important for the analysis to realise just how many different kinds of frameworks have been involved. The two most obvious and overarching frameworks have of course been the EU and NATO, operating in a kind of symbiosis, though always with different memberships. Thus the strong territorial connection between Turkey and western Europe has been reflected in Turkey's full involvement in NATO, while its less intense economic connection and contested affiliational connections have kept Turkey outside the EU. Thus the availability of these two 'macro' transnational organizations has enabled different forms of linkage for different countries. It has also created a kind of core group of countries that were full players in both of these organizations.

But my argument rests on not only the complementarity of NATO and the EU. There are in addition quite a number and range of other forms of organized connection in western Europe. Some address functional co-operation issues (the management of rivers and seas, or specific technical and industrial collaborations, such as Airbus, the European Space Agency, etc.). Some manage the territorial concerns of 'neighbourliness' (Benelux, UK-Ireland etc.). Some rest on an affiliational base (the Nordic family). Some of these arrangements are institutionalized and multidimensional, while others operate rather informally or sporadically. One, the Council of Europe, provided a loose political regime for most of the countries of western Europe. Another, the OECD, grew to include 'similar' (western industrial) countries from elsewhere in the word.

Three key points characterise this mosaic of overlapping arrangements. First, they have provided the means to develop differentiated ways of organizing and regulating relationships and connections between west European countries. We can thus observe something of a distinction between those countries that have been involved in all of them and those with looser or more 'lop-sided' connections to the European integration process. Second, the persistence of these other fora seems to indicate some of the limits to the macro organizations in that they have not succeeded in 'taking over' or subsuming the smaller frameworks. In other words, the other fora have provided channels for differently articulated connections, some of which have begun to provided an opportunity structure for the organization of post-1989 Europe - the Nordic/Baltic region seems the clearest example of this. Third, but this is harder to demonstrate, the development of the macro organizations seems to have been dependent on the availability of fora with more restricted memberships to channel and articulate some of the connections between those countries. Here the best example might be the Franco-German partnership, with its separate institutional arrangements to underpin bilateral co-operation, as well as to provide a basis for 'collusion' within the macro organizations.

The broad point which follows is that, although the EU and NATO have been by far the most important of the various west European organizations, they are not catch-all fora in the sense of canalising all of the important connections between the countries that they have engaged. And, of course, NATO is not only a European organization, but a transatlantic alliance, a fact which reflects the lack of autonomy of the European frameworks for handling security. Indeed this provides a large part of the explanation for the failure of the EU to develop a strong regime in the security field.

## Deep integration

None of what has been asserted so far should be taken as suggesting that west European integration has consisted simply of a diffuse and sporadic pattern of connections across western Europe. On the contrary, the proliferation of connections, combined with the overlay of different kinds of connection, has produced an extraordinary pattern of transnational entanglements across western Europe, albeit less intense at some of the peripheries. Moreover the combination of engagement across different integration dimensions with interlocking organizational frameworks has structured integration in western Europe in a distinctive way. Indeed it is precisely this institutionalization of connections that has made a huge difference to the regularization of interdependencies. It is precisely here that the EU has come to represent so central a part of the wider mosaic. It was the particular success of the EU in building institutional and legal commitments that made it emerge as the prime (though not the sole) forum for structuring connections, commitments and interdependencies. Moreover the character of the EU institutions encouraged a political dynamic that propelled integration into new functional areas and opened up an opportunity structure for an increasingly wide range of political, economic and social actors to engage in the process. In comparison all of the other institutional frameworks for collaboration in western Europe are much more limited.

Nonetheless we should note some of the limits to and consequences of this process of deep integration. The EU has gone much further in articulating the functional dimension to integration than it has as regards either the territorial or the affiliational dimensions. Its incursions into the latter domains have been more tentative and, as yet, less productive or certain. The EU has been more successful in building client and agency relationships with actors from the participating countries than it has in building societal and broadly-based attachments, which are still primarily articulated in political spaces at the country (or more local) level. Also, and crucially, the EU has developed a number of 'club' characteristics. Its institutional arrangements and policy regimes are built on a concept of solidarity and privilege for incumbents, combined with discrimination against and exclusion of outsiders. EMU is an important example of this, in that the establishment of a single currency club requires a particular and explicit set of solidarity and privilege arrangements for incumbents. Indeed this feature is already reflected in some discrimination *within* the EU between EMU participants and the non-participants. A key issue here is whether EMU will provoke other forms of policy cooperation (macroeconomic or fiscal) that would reinforce the distinction between those countries inside the currency union and those outside it.

## The domestication of Europe

Briefly, our analysis of the patterns of integration in western Europe depends on how we view the relationship between transnational integration and the capabilities and preferences that emerge within the participating countries. There is a continuing debate on how far the European level of interaction is dependent on (and vulnerable to) what happens at the country level, and thus over how far the integration process has an autonomy of its own that is in the process of altering the character of the countries involved. Without attempting to resolve this difficult argument, two points can nonetheless be made. First, national political and economic agents make choices about which European framework to activate for which of their purposes - e.g. space co-operation through ESA rather than through the EU. They change their minds about which framework is appropriate - border management as regards individuals through Schengen and several other frameworks at first, and only much later through the EU. Second, many, even most, of the same national agents are involved in making collective decisions in European frameworks about whether and how to adapt or extend their collective European regimes. Thus more or less the same people in the participating countries are involved in the discussion of NATO and EU enlargement or in discussion about how to articulate the relationship with Turkey. In this sense the individual frameworks are not autonomous, but locked into an iterative discussion between the national and European levels, although the parallel fora allow national policy-makers some choices about where to delegate powers.

## The implications for Central and Eastern Europe

To return to our earlier questions... Is this west European model of deep integration sustainable? Is it extendible to central and eastern Europe? On the first question, the short answer is that it is sustainable to the extent that the still rather vigorous functional dimension is accompanied by a recasting of the territorial dimension and a reformulation of the affiliational dimension - and to the extent that the institutionalization of deep integration can be adapted to incorporate a larger membership. On this last point two further observations are needed. First, there is an awkward tension between the club behaviour features of the EU and the challenge of enlargement to less familiar partners. Second, the practitioners' debate about institutional adaptation has so far been remarkably sterile and locked into a narrow discussion of particular mechanisms and not at all focused on the systemic issues.

On the crucial question of the extendibility of deep integration to central and eastern Europe, several observations are in order. The extension of a deep integration model eastwards seems to require the development of connections across all three dimensions - functional, territorial and affiliational. The EU partnership links and accession criteria are crucially important for the functional dimension. To the extent that the EU touches the territorial dimension it also impacts there. Somewhat perversely, the new engagement of the EU in seeking to manage borders as regards the movement of persons and as regards the provision of internal security risks creating problems more than providing solutions. Moreover the efforts of the EU to develop loyalty and citizenship ties as a reinforcement of affiliational ties produce a new focus of potential discrimination between insiders and outsiders. These difficulties suggest that there is an underdeveloped discussion on how far the territorial and affiliational dimensions to integration might need to be rethought, so that they could become supports for integration in a broader sense rather than obstacles.

Perhaps inevitably the current practitioner discussion is overshadowed by the technicalities of how Central and East European countries might meet the criteria for EU accession. It is a very one-sided discussion - candidates for accession have to adapt to EU club rules. Two elements are lacking. One is a consideration of how other kinds of connection might be developed, not as distractions from the EU debate or substitutes for it, but as elements necessary to facilitate the EU enlargement process. The second is the need to find a way of shifting from the unilateralist character of the debate to one which would start to explore potential reciprocities. Here much remains to be addressed.

# Central Europe Facing a Union in Crisis

*Ferdinand Kinsky*

The enthusiasm that characterized what was a common, indeed almost a general Central European view on the European Union in the early 90s appears to have diminished somewhat today. Since Austria became a member state, public opinion polls show that the orientation of the overwhelming majority which approved the country's entrance to the European Union appears to have been reversed. Euroscepticism is also growing in Germany. The formerly communist Central European countries had all hoped to 'go home to Europe' (Havel) very quickly after having got rid of communism. They were also convinced that a quick admission to the European Community would accelerate their economic transition. Today the satisfaction about having being included in the first group of candidates accepted for entrance negotiations has not quite compensated for the disappointment of being compelled to spend so many years in the solitary-confinement waiting rooms called 'Europe Agreements', for being constantly overseen by Brussels as far as the correct spending of the EU's financial assistance is concerned, and for being pressed at the same time to implement a complicated mass of transition and EC legislation. There is also a growing fear of the EU's incapacity to overcome its present internal crisis, and of the attendant danger that one or several vetoes might eventually come from present member states opposed to the Eastern enlargement. The history of European integration has shown that progress has often resulted from crisis; but there is no guarantee for the durability of this rule. The present crisis - of motivation, of the institutions and of the decision making procedures generally - as well as deep divergences over the final nature of European unification, could indeed considerably delay the admission of new Central European member states.

## The Crisis of Motivation

The historical reasons for European integration - peace between former enemies, the Soviet threat and the economic advantages of the Common Market - are now out of date. In part the objectives have been reached: objectives such as peace between Germany and her former Western enemies, and the almost complete implementation of the Common Market. On the other hand the collapse of the Soviet empire has removed much of the pressure from outside. The former Belgian Minister of Foreign Affairs, Paul-Henri Spaak, used to call Stalin 'the greatest European'. Today people in the European Union have no common perception of an external threat. In Southern France there may be a widespread fear of Islamic fundamentalism, but this is a subject which leaves Scandinavia, say, largely indifferent. Some Eastern Germans as well as quite a few citizens in the Associated Central and Eastern European countries are still worried about a potential Russian danger; but nobody shares that feeling in France, Spain or Portugal. In France, Europe is often conceived as an instrument against US hegemony, but this view is rarely shared in other member states, where most people have become accustomed to the comfortable assumption that American military intervention - or merely the threat of it - will finally solve all conflicts in Africa, Asia, the Middle East or even Central and Eastern Europe.

The question 'Why Europe?', which my generation has not really even been asking seriously for decades now, since the answer appeared to be so obvious, is again on the agenda today. In the member states the younger generation, which is lucky not to have experienced the Nazi occupation of Europe and the Second World War, does not have the same approach to Europe as their parents and grandparents. There are, of course, good reasons to continue the integration process - by completing Economic and Monetary Union, and by making Pillars II (Common Foreign and Security Policy) and III (Co-operation between Justice and Home Affairs) work. The qualified majority decision-making should be extended with an exceptional provision for opting out instead of issuing a veto. More democracy in the EU's institutional system could be achieved by increasing the power of the European Parliament. The co-decision principle should be extended to Pillar II. Additionally, the Parliament should be given the right to participate fully in the institutional reforms procedure, in co-operation with the national governments. For those who are familiar with the complexities of European integration, the institutional reforms appear to be essential: both to guarantee the European Union's capacity to meet the citizens' expectations and needs, and to enable our continent to face the challenges of globalization and to defend European interests in world politics.

Unfortunately, this need is perceived less and less strongly by the public. While in the past public opinion has usually appeared to be more in favour of Europe than the politicians, the situation now appears to have been reversed. Many Germans consider the Monetary Union to be merely Helmut Kohl's private hobby-horse; the enthusiasm of Jacques Chirac's pro-European rhetoric does not even appear to be shared by his own party; and Tony Blair shows signs of being more European than his voters.

The growing opposition to the loss of national sovereignty (e.g. national monetary identity) often appears as a particularly European expression of general hostility towards any transnational globalization. A parallel observation can be made in North America, where NAFTA and the UN are becoming increasingly unpopular. Like the US citizens and Canadians who criticise NAFTA and accuse the UN of being too costly and at the same time of serving anti-American interests, an increasing number of Europeans is convinced that the EU has become too powerful and expensive and that European integration only serves their neighbours', and not their own, national interest. An example of this was given after the European Council meeting on May 1st, 1998, and the difficult compromise for choosing the President of the European Central Bank. While German Eurosceptics attacked Kohl for having lost a battle against France, French politicians opposed to the Monetary Union accused their President of having accepted German hegemony. Le Pen even called the Euro '*la monnaie d'occupation*' and Chirac a '*collaborateur*'.

Furthermore, the mechanisms of globalization and regional integration, such as those in NAFTA and in the EU, are being held responsible for unemployment. Free circulation of goods, capital, services and persons within the European Single Market has already increased competition in Western Europe, and now globalization is adding another reason for 'rationalization'. But job cutting and unemployment also have other causes, such as automation. Mechanization in agriculture and the introduction of robots in industrial production have more recently been followed by the computerization of services and both public and private administrative networks. Investments are today likely to result in the cutting of jobs rather than in the creation of new ones. In addition, as a result of an increasing crisis of the family and of the educational system, a large number of young people leave school insufficiently prepared for the labour market in the first place.

Besides economic uncertainty, the feeling of insecurity resulting from the increasing rate of crime appears today as one of the major political preoccupations. Of course, the international dimension of crime requires more integration (Europol), but people unfortunately react in the opposite way. They believe that criminals are above all foreigners. Therefore the advantages of free circulation for trade and tourism appear to be less important for many people than the fear of Gypsies, Kurds, Russians, Arabs, Turks, Vietnamese and Indonesians invading one of the other member states and thus gaining free access to whole EU territory.

Xenophobia, though, is not only a reaction to globalization and a wrong interpretation of European integration. It is increased by the media, which favour bad news in order to attract a greater audience. Thus, people get the impression that foreign countries are usually suffering from chaos and inhabited by criminals. These prejudicial clichés exist even within the EU, but they are more widespread where attitudes towards Central European applicants for full membership are concerned. Commercial competition among the media does not only lead to this regrettable policy of favouring 'bad news', but also to the selection of events that might confirm the already existing opinions. Reports on 'Brussels' and 'Strasbourg' on television broadcasts are therefore preferably negative. Hence, citizens get the impression of a non-functioning EU, where their own politicians desperately seek to defend their national interests, both against their rivals from other member states, and against the predominantly foreign Eurocrats. The perception of such news by a significant part of the public is often far from reality, especially when the distance between citizens and the decision-making institutions is well beyond that at the local level. Personal contacts with mayors or municipal councillors may allow voters to understand what local government is about, but the knowledge of international affairs remains very limited. As the annual *Eurobarometer* survey published by the European Commission indicates, most EU citizens are unable to name all the member states, and they are unaware of the powers and sometimes even of the existence of the different Community institutions. Additionally, the complexity of decision making procedures and the highly technical nature of the issues increase the general lack of information and consequently also the general hostility to European integration.

## The Institutional Crisis

As the last newcomers, Austria, Finland and Sweden had to wait until the conclusion and the ratification of the Maastricht Treaty, the Amsterdam Treaty has been conceived as a precondition for the next enlargement. In particular, the Intergovernmental Conference, already planned at Maastricht in order to find answers to all the unsolved questions, was supposed to prepare the necessary institutional reforms to be adopted in Amsterdam in June 1997. The results are clearly insufficient.

Some progress was made, such as a simplification of the legislative procedures (by extending the co-decision right of the European Parliament, which will have a ceiling of 700 members). The President of the Commission will find his position strengthened, and we shall have more flexibility - called 'closer co-operation' - in replacement of the former veto, by allowing member states to opt out instead of blocking decisions in some areas (unfortunately less so in Pillar II). The role of the European Court of Justice was also extended but, as Franklin Dehousse puts it 'with such complex rules that the only thing that seems certain is that some lawyers will make a fortune out of it.'

The most important failure at Amsterdam was the incapacity of the European Council to achieve an agreement on the extension of qualified majority decision to areas where unanimity is still the rule. Everybody knows that the EU does not have a real Common Foreign and Security Policy, as became obvious during the various Yugoslav and Iraqi crises. The timid implementation of Europol is already proving to be inadequate to fight the far stronger supra-national structures of crime. The rapid progress of globalization is constantly limiting the member states' national sovereignty and increasing the need for an effective European economic, social, financial and even fiscal policy. There is of course some progress in Pillar I. The implementation of EMU and in particular the establishment of a common currency will help, but the establishment of monetary union strongly calls in turn for at least a limited form of common fiscal policy. This, though, is precisely subject to a unanimous decision; and several member states continue to consider fiscal policy as a non-transferable part of their sovereignty.

As long as the harmonization of fiscal policy and social security, important decisions on free circulation of persons, and the Common Foreign Security Policy continue to be blocked by national veto, public opinion will become even more sceptical, and the opposition to enlargement will grow within the EU. Several leading politicians in the EU member states have already announced that the institutions and decision-making procedures should be revised before the admission of new members. This is the case for France. When President Chirac last came to Prague he seemed to be very optimistic about the date of the Czech Republic's full membership. He made similar speeches in Budapest, Warsaw and even in Bucharest (without announcing a date there). All this was before

Amsterdam. Today, though, the French President and his Prime Minister, who disagree on many other points, appear to be unanimous in calling for new institutional reforms as a precondition for enlargement.

A new Inter-Governmental Conference (IGC) will most probably start before the end of the present negotiations between the EU and the first group of candidates for admission. One of the unsolved problems is the potential reweighting of the votes in the Council and/or the introduction of a double majority system. The agreement reached at Amsterdam on the limitation of the Commission after the next enlargement to only one member per state will only be implemented if an agreement on reweighting of the votes in the Council can be reached. Otherwise the current system could be maintained. However, the question of a new agreement on the votes in the Council and the number of European MPs per member state, as well as on the size of the Commission, remain questions of minor importance compared to the major problem of the extension of the qualified majority decision procedure. Besides, as the relative failure of Amsterdam showed, two major obstacles continue to make institutional reforms difficult:

- *The weakness of the Reflection Group and/or Intergovernmental Conference method.* Recalling his own experience, Franklin Dehousse says: 'It was not a debate. It was also neither a group, since there was not an agreement at the time about anything, nor a reflection. Most members were satisfied with explaining - and repeating, repeating, repeating - their national position [...] This explains, by the way, much of the very bad drafting of the Treaty, especially in some of the most ambitious parts (the partial communitarization of the third Pillar, the integration of Schengen, the strengthen-co-operation provisions).' A better solution would certainly be to ask the European Parliament to draft a new constitution for the EU. It is however very unlikely that the national governments would accept such a loss of constitutional power. The European Parliament will have some increased influence, then, but power will largely remain in the hands of the member states.
- *The remaining divergences among the member states.* They disagree on the institutional reforms and on enlargement. All new treaties and institutional reforms need unanimity of the member states. Additionally, the financial questions remain unresolved. According to all serious calculations, the immediate implementation of the present Common Agricultural Policy and the compulsory expenditures of the Structural

Funds in the Czech Republic, Hungary, Poland, Estonia and Slovenia would lead to more than doubling the EU budget. Tax-payers in the present member states are reluctant to accept this prospect.

The Commission's legislative proposals for Agenda 2000 are an attempt to indicate solutions, but they are encountering violent reactions within the EU. Farmers and their lobby simply refuse to accept any further decrease in agricultural prices. The Mediterranean countries and Portugal reject the idea that they should get progressively less out of the Structural Fund. The Central European candidates for full membership are now aware of the danger that their proposed admission could eventually not meet the required unanimity in the Council. The uncertainties are not only due to the fear of the cost, or of a paralysing effect on the institutional system. There are also deep divergences amongst and within the member states on the most basic features of the final configuration of European integration.

## Divergences on the future of the EU

Although Tony Blair and most of the New Labour leaders are far more pro-European than were the leaders of the previous Conservative governments, the resistance against the EU, based on fears that it might become too federalist, has not disappeared. Sweden and Denmark remain reluctant to accept further important steps towards any integration going beyond the present Single Market, although they might join the Monetary Union in a few years, following a probable move of the UK in that direction. But Britain, Denmark and Sweden remain opposed to any kind of political union, beyond the present intergovernmental co-operation in the field of the so-called Common Foreign and Security Policy and in important parts of Pillar III.

There is also uncertainty about the next German federal government's European policy. Gerhard Schröder's political rise to the position of successor to Helmut Kohl was partially due to his Eurosceptical speeches, and his long opposition to Monetary Union. He recently changed his rhetoric but uncertainty remains about his future European policy. Before the change of government in Britain and the conclusion of the Amsterdam Treaty, three groups could be observed within the EU:

- The eurosceptics, who welcomed enlargement as an instrument to weaken the EU institutions and to prevent further steps of deepening integration;

- The opponents to enlargement - the farmers, the poorer member states who were afraid to receive less money from Brussels, and those who feared the weakening consequences for the EU institution. For them the mere existence of the first group gave them good arguments against the admission of new members. 'Look who is in favour of enlargement, they could say: the British conservatives and all the opponents to the Maastricht Treaty in the other member states! Therefore, enlargement must be bad for Europe.'
- A third group, composed of the Benelux countries, Germany and Austria supported both enlargement and deepening. They hoped that the Intergovernmental Conference and the Amsterdam Treaty would bring the necessary institutional reforms allowing successful negotiations with the candidates for admission.

Today, those three trends have been partially reversed. The British still favour enlargement, but they are no longer systematically opposed to deepening. In Denmark and Austria a majority of the population now appears to be opposed to enlargement, fearing an invasion of poor and 'potentially criminal' Central and Eastern Europeans. In Germany, xenophobia is reaching an alarming degree, especially in the former GDR, where the population has been more isolated than in other satellite countries of the Soviet empire. There will be a strong resistance in the East German public to extending free circulation of people to Poland, and in particular to implementing the Schengen Agreement at the Polish border.

In a declaration annexed to the Treaty of Amsterdam, three member states - Belgium, Italy, and France - demanded a new debate, including qualified majority voting as a pre-condition for the next enlargement.

## Crisis No Reason For Defeatism

The present rise of euroscepticism, the weakness of the institutional reforms achieved at Amsterdam, and the deep divergence over the question where European integration should go, may lead to pessimistic conclusions about enlargement. Will Central European candidates for admission to the EU have to delay their hopes *ad calendas graecas*?

An objective analysis of the present situation should indeed indicate the difficulties, but this need not lead to exaggerated defeatism. The term *crisis* should be understood in the etymological sense of the ancient Greek, where *krisis* meant 'questioning' or 'judgement'. Crisis does not necessarily mean chaos or the definitive end of a concept, although it could lead to it. There can also be renaissance or renewal.

As was said in the beginning, the history of European integration is full of crisis, and pessimists have often predicted the end of the dream. European integration is a permanent compromise between divergent concepts, ideas, models and ideologies, and between conflicting national interests. Frequent periods of stagnation and inadequate responses to major challenges have often led to solutions which were not perfect but acceptable.

Eurosceptical and sometimes even nationalist politicians changed their mind and became convinced Europeans once elected to govern their countries:

- Helmut Schmidt wrote a rather Eurosceptical book before becoming Chancellor of Germany. His experiences in the European Council changed him into a convinced European federalist.
- Jacques Chirac resigned as Prime Minister of France under President Giscard d'Estaing, partially because of his opposition to Europe. He then took the lead of the traditional Gaullist party advocating a Europe of independent nation states without any transfer of sovereignty to common institutions. Once elected as President of the French Republic, Jacques Chirac became far more European. In a TV interview on May 3rd 1998, after the European Council meeting, Chirac answered the question of a French journalist asking him why he had changed his mind on Europe since he had become President by calling his previous hostility an 'attitude of the heart' while his function as President of France had forced him to 'think'. Chirac obviously became European by reasoning.
- Gerhard Schröder appears to be abandoning his previous Euroscepticism. After having strongly attacked Monetary Union and called for the postponement of the production of Euro, he even welcomed EMU in a recent speech in the German Bundestag, and he voted in favour of admitting the eleven selected countries at the Bundesrat. In an article published by the French daily newspaper *Le Monde* two weeks before his victory in the German legislative elections, Gerhard Schröder called for the EU's transformation to a 'federative' political union, following the constitutional example of the German Federal Republic.

There is, of course, no irresistible force of reality making a positive attitude to European integration compulsory for national politicians once they reach a top position in their country. The sociological law of power continues to be a permanent temptation against transfer of sovereignty to the EU institutions, but the above mentioned examples will certainly give us hope for the future.

The conclusion I would like to suggest to Central European candidates may sound contradictory. On one side they should be vigilant and not give excessive credit to the reassuring rhetoric pronounced by Western European political leaders. The crisis is obvious and real, and successful renaissance will be more difficult among fifteen member states than it has been among six, nine, ten and twelve member states. But Central European candidates should use those friendly declarations as instruments of their own strategy, and they should understand that crisis is simply part of the European integration system.

Additionally, Central European candidates should develop three strategies:

- They should avoid delivering easy arguments to those within the EU who remain opposed to enlargement. Eurosceptical dogmatism *à la* Margaret Thatcher as it appeared with former Prime Minister Václav Klaus' statements is the best way to strengthen fear within the EU about enlargement, which could prevent deepening.
- Central European candidates should show their willingness to accept further institutional reforms and progress in European integration. They will then find allies among those who hope that the prospect of enlargement will finally lead the present member states to accept the necessary institutional reforms.
- Central European governments should make greater efforts to inform their citizens on what entering the EU really means. The lack of information is unfortunately still important within the EU. It reaches an alarming degree in the populations of Central European candidates. The interest about the EU among political, economic and cultural leaders as well as among civil servants in Central Europe is still great, as shown by the number of Central European applications for participation in European studies programmes, conferences and seminars on the EU. The present expectations should be met with better care, otherwise the pessimistic fears of further long delays before admission will lead to a loss of interest.

Finally, Central European politicians, businessmen, academics and journalists should constantly express their indignation about the present two class system of Europe, according to which the lucky ones inside the EU do not appear to care enough about the other Europeans still standing outside in the rain. Central Europeans should tell their Western European colleagues that enlargement is a moral obligation. Applauding the victory over communism is not enough. Czechs, Poles, Hungarians, Slovenians and Estonians are no less European than French, Germans, Italians or British. Neither are Slovaks, Bulgarians, Romanians and the other Baltic nations. Unfortunately politics often runs far away from morality, but even so, morality does not need to be entirely absent from politics. Central Europeans have been through a long and sad experience with a political system devoid of morality. It is precisely this experience which could be useful to the EU. Václav Havel, who has given the proof that resistance in the name of morality can be successful even against a totalitarian system, asked for a new European ideal in his address to the European Parliament five years ago. Successful enlargement, and the parallel transition of the EU to a more democratic system, orientated towards the citizens, could be the realization of such an ideal.

# European Identity and the Enlargement of the European Union

*Ingmar Karlsson*

The European identity is often described in a somewhat high-flown manner as having its foundations in antiquity. Free thought, individualism, humanism and democracy, it is said, all had their cradle in ancient Athens and Rome. However, neither the Greek nor the Roman civilizations of antiquity can really be described as straightforwardly European. Both can more accurately be described as 'Mediterranean' cultures, with important centres in Asia Minor, Africa and the Middle East. When Alexander the Great set out to conquer the civilized world of his time - Egypt, Persia and India - it can hardly have occurred to him that he was acting on behalf of Europe.

Christianity is considered to be another basic component of the European identity. With its roots in Judaism, it was however also originally a Mediterranean rather than a European religion. The Byzantine Empire was a Christian power whose borders marked the limit to Roman claims of sovereignty: and a large part of what would become post-Reformation Europe lay beyond this limit. The schism between Rome and Byzantium resulted in the development of a different culture in Russia and South-Eastern Europe. After the Reformation a large part of continental Europe was preoccupied for several centuries with religious wars and rivalry between Protestants and Catholics.

Historians nowadays play down our antique heritage. Instead, the European ideals are more often traced back to the Renaissance and its concept of the individual as the smallest, inviolable element of society. The Enlightenment and the French Revolution contributed with demands for freedom, equality, fraternity, democracy, self-determination, equal opportunities for all, clearly defined government powers, separation between the powers of church and state, freedom of the press and human rights.

The ideas that are triumphant in Europe today are those of the market economy and democracy. By this definition the USA, Canada, New Zealand and Australia should also be included among the European powers. However, Europe represents not only modernity and tolerance but also religious persecution; not only democracy but also fascist dictatorship

(Hitler was the first to use the concept of a European house), colonialism, racism... and also the collectivist ideals of communism.

In other words, the European identity cannot be defined on grounds of cultural heritage and history, and even less can it be used as the basis for European domestic and foreign policies. The explanation is as simple as it is obvious. Economic and political integration between European national states has not yet progressed to such an extent that it is possible to speak of common interests. On the contrary, the collapse of communism and the disappearance of a uniting common threat, and also the enlargement of the European Union to include new members, will actually slow down the progress towards a common European identity.

Instead of the common identity we hear so much about, there is today a noticeable need for national identity and sovereignty; and this need will probably grow proportionately with the increased levelling of European politics and economics. The greater the sense that diversity is being threatened and that standardization is rising, the greater will be the antipathy to projects that promote integration. The European Community is already a reality as far as production and consumption are concerned, but there is widespread popular opposition to the idea of a culturally standardized community. The more blurred and controversial the future of Europe appears to the common man, the more the nations will mobilise themselves against Europe.

Therefore, a balance must be maintained between enthusiasm for the European project and awareness that for the foreseeable future legitimacy for the EU will be in short supply. However, this view does not have to paralyse efforts towards integration. The phrase 'an ever closer union between the peoples of Europe' could indeed be useful precisely for its generality and vagueness.

Edmund Burke's wise words that a political order cannot be created at a drawing board but has to emerge gradually may also be valid for European integration. This in turn means that politicians and bureaucrats must concentrate on immediate, essential and clear issues, and on measures whose consequences can be judged by the citizens themselves.

Every new competence given to a European institution must therefore be explained in concrete terms in order to achieve acceptance. Consequently, the issues which require a European solution should be carefully examined, since an incorrect decision on, say, the agricultural policy, could have far-reaching consequences, and undermine the credibility of different Union projects.

The EU will only achieve a solid basis of legitimacy when Europeans perceive a European political identity. This does not imply that they would no longer feel themselves to be Swedes, Finns, Frenchmen, Portuguese, Czechs, Poles or Hungarians; but that the sense of a common European destiny had been added to these identities. Even after four decades of European integration, however, this development is still in its infancy.

Nation-states have been evolving over long periods, which have frequently been full of conflicts. The associated national ideas are ideological constructions, and every national identity is ultimately a political standpoint. A prerequisite for a strong national identity is that citizens have a sense of loyalty to their state, based on its ability to redistribute social resources, provide education, infrastructure, a legal system, etc.

The same prerequisites hold true for the creators of Europe. As in the process that led to the creation of the European nation-states, the EU will also be an elite project for the foreseeable future, and the European identity an elite phenomenon. The technocrats and bureaucrats in Brussels are undoubtedly the new European elite: but do they really embody a European culture, or are they, like the UN and its functionaries, merely another international civil service which, with the passage of time, becomes increasingly alienated from the people whose interests it is meant to serve? Is there not a danger that institutional loyalty will become stronger than 'European awareness' and that this feeling might also spread among the elite old member states? The negative stereotypes with which citizens react towards these eurocrats aggravate the problem, as the civil servants are not regarded as the first real Europeans, but only as overpaid bureaucrats interfering in matters that do not concern them.

The creation of national symbols and myths and the rewriting of history were also part of the process by which the European nations were formed. First came the state, followed by the formation of a national community within the territorial framework by means of gradual integration and cultural standardization. The architects of the nations emerging in the 19th century made use of the introduction of national consumption, compulsory education and the supra-regional spread of the growing mass media to establish contact between the centre and the periphery and to create seemingly natural boundaries based on geography, language, ethnicity or religion. Above all, the development of national educational systems and mass media and mass communications contributed to the sense of belonging to a national community.

## Efforts to Create a European Identity

Brussels appears to have had this in mind when taking the decision in 1984 that the EC should improve contacts with its citizens and, so to speak, create a European identity, centrally and from above. At a summit meeting in Fontainbleu, the European Council found it 'absolutely essential that the Community fulfils the expectations of the European people and takes measures to strengthen and promote the identity and image of the Community vis-àvis its citizens and the rest of the world'. The Adonnino Committee was set up for this purpose, with the task of starting a campaign on the theme of 'A people's Europe'. This was based on the above-mentioned quotation from the preamble to the Rome Treaty, 'an ever closer union among the peoples of Europe', and on the Tindemans Report of 1975 which recommended that Europe must be close to its citizens and stressed that a European Union could only become reality if there was popular support for the idea. An outcome of the work of this committee was the decision that the EC should have its own flag. When the flag was raised for the first time at Berlaymont on 29 May 1986, the EC hymn - the 'Ode to Joy' from the fourth movement of Beethoven's 9th symphony - was played for the first time. Thus, by means of a flag and a European national hymn, the Union acquired the attributes of a national state. A European Day was also established. The choice fell on 9 May, the date on which Robert Schumann delivered the speech in 1950 that resulted in the first community, the European Coal and Steel Community. Consequently, the Adonnino Committee appears to have assumed that a European identity could be created on the initiative of politicians and bureaucrats. In 1988 the European Council decided to introduce a European dimension into school subjects such as literature, history, civics, geography, languages and music. Legitimacy for future integration should be created by invoking a common history and cultural heritage. The EU is thus attempting to create a European identity from above. A common European frame of reference is being created by means of a standardized set of symbols and myths. A European driving licence already exists, as does a standard EU passport (although it took ten years to agree on its colour and appearance). The Maastricht Treaty introduced the new concept of a citizen of the Union, though his/her rights and obligations have still to be defined. These activities are incompatible with the often recurring theme that European integration must be a natural process and not imposed from above. Every European people has its more or less genuine historical myths, experiences and view of history. There is no

European equivalent to the *Académie Française*, Bastille, Escorial, La Scala, Brandenburger Tor or the opening of Parliament at Westminster. There is no European unknown soldier. Jean Monnet rests at the Panthéon in Paris. The fame of Robert Schumann's resting place at Scy-Chazelles cannot compete with Colombey-les-Deux-Eglises, where General de Gaulle lies buried. Common history has been experienced by many as events against and not with the neighbours in the great European wars.

The main task of the 'Europe-makers' cannot therefore be to provide Europeans with a common identity originating in antique or mediaeval times, but to develop a political self-confidence and ability to act in line with the role of Europe in the 21st century. This will neither happen by elevating the EU to a free trade zone in accordance with Margaret Thatcher's ideas, nor by turning it into some kind of American-style United States of Europe which is imposed on people against their will.

## Basis for a European Patriotism and Identity

Only a long-term, patient growing together can provide the basis for a democratic Europe accepted by its citizens. For decades the European Community was only a utilitarian community. We are only now *en route* towards a community based on common destiny and experience. If there is any lesson to be learned from European history then it is the lesson that Europe as one entity can only be achieved in agreement with and not against the will of the peoples and what they consider to be their legitimate interests. At present, regionalism and nationalism are undoubtedly stronger than pan-Europeanism. Perhaps Europe needs some 'shocks' e.g. in the form of an aggressive Russia, a new Chernobyl catastrophe or another Gulf crisis or Balkan war that demonstrates our dependency on the USA in conflicts affecting vital European interests. Other problems will also arise that call for joint action and which in due course will aid the establishment of an identity such as the necessity to use our common strength to meet the technological challenge from Japan and the USA and, in the not too distant future, the 'new tigers' and common actions to overcome environmental problems, pressure from immigration and to handle international organised crime. A successful European policy in these and other areas could help in the development of a 'constitutional European patriotism' in the same way that 'loyalty to the Constitution' (*Verfassungspatriotismus*) became a reality in the Federal Republic of Germany; replacing the nationalism that no German was able to feel after the terrors of the Hitler period.

An absolute precondition for developing a common political culture and constitutional patriotism in the EU is that its citizens are informed about and participate in the super-national decision-making process. A European public opinion must emerge before there can be any talk of a European citizenship. As stated above, the European identity has no historical frame of reference. European trade unions do not exist at present, nor other interest groups; nor, and above all, do trans-boundary European parties or a European general public opinion.

The Maastricht Treaty brought this deficiency into focus, negotiated as it was by experts in a European code incomprehensible to its citizens. As a result, the reputation of the EU among the European populations was further diminished. A prerequisite for a solid European identity is therefore the development of European parties, or at least party networks, and a political debate on trans-boundary issues. When employer organizations and trade unions begin to meet at a European level to look after their members' common interests, we will have taken the first steps: because politics will have reached beyond the national level.

The best we could achieve at the end of such a process would be a European 'constitutional state', and EU citizenship that was felt to be genuine and not just an artificial political construction.

The road towards this goal is both difficult and long, however, and more likely to be curbed than speeded up by an enlargement eastwards. It has proved difficult enough to bridge the cultural and linguistic differences between Catholics and Protestants, or between Latins, Germans, Anglo-Saxons and Scandinavians in Europe. The task of integrating the Baltic, Slav and Orthodox Europeans will be infinitely more difficult. The larger and more heterogeneous the membership becomes, the greater the need that will be felt to differentiate between the various member states and to create a Europe moving at different speeds and where the political union, monetary union, common security and defence policy and internal market will not extend over the same geographical areas. A union of up to 30 members at varying stages of economic development can for the foreseeable future only function if it is organized along several tracks and at different levels.

The efforts to create a Europe around the hard core of a monetary union with the Euro as a magnet could also be counterproductive. Magnets work in two ways, either drawing particles towards them or pushing them away. There is a clear risk that monetary union could also have this double effect.

## Cultural Diversity - Obstacle or Prerequisite for a European Identity?

European political oratory often maintains that Europe can only be defined through its unique heritage of diversity and lack of conformity and that, paradoxically, its very diversity has been its unifying principle and strength.

However, European linguistic diversity is probably the greatest obstacle standing in the way of the emergence of a European political identity and thus of the whole European democratic project. Multilingual European democracies certainly exist, the prime example being Switzerland, which however has chosen to remain outside the EU.

A democracy is non-existent if most of its citizens cannot make themselves understood to each other. Rhetoric apart, not even leading European politicians are today able to socialize with each other without an interpreter, and very few can make themselves understood to a majority of European voters in their own language. Not one European newspaper exists, except elitist publications such as 'The European' [now defunct - ed.]and specialized Brussels-based newsletters. There is no European television programme catching a broad audience apart from Eurosport, and most of its viewers watch matches between nations. In short, there is no public European debate, and no European political discourse: because the political process is still tied to the national languages.

The question of language is basically one of democracy. Political discussion would be divided between A and B teams with many excluded because of their lack of linguistic knowledge if only English and French were to be the official EU languages. At the same time, the problem of interpreting is already becoming insurmountable. Over 40 per cent of the EU administrative budget is already spent on language services. Eleven languages make 132 combinations possible in the translator booths. The addition of another 10 Eastern and Central European languages brings this figure to 420. Some form of functional differentiation will therefore be necessary, making some languages more equal than others - although this would have a negative effect on public opinion towards Europe in the small member states.

At present, an average of 66 per cent of EU citizens are monolingual, while 10 per cent speak at least two foreign languages. Ireland is at one extreme with 80 and three per cent respectively, while only one percent of the population in Luxembourg is monolingual and no less than 80 cent speak at least two foreign languages. In order both to function as Europeans and to safeguard our own interests, Swedes and Czechs must become tolerably fluent in at least one other major Europe language apart from English. Swedish and Czech remains the basis of our cultural heritages and domestic political discussions, but in order to play a constructive part in Europe we must develop into citizens of Luxembourg as far as language is concerned.

Consequently, Europe is neither a communication- nor an experience-based community, to use German concepts. Both factors are indispensable in the development of a collective political identity which must be created by sharing experiences, myths and memories, often in contradiction to those held in other collective identities. They are, moreover, often strengthened by the comparison with those that are distinctly different. Not just Robert Schumann, Alcide de Gasperi, Jean Monnet and Konrad Adenauer should be counted among the fathers of European integration, but Josef Stalin as well. The Cold War enabled a sense of unity to be mobilized among Western Europeans, but who can play the role of opponent now in order to provide Europeans with such a common identity? The USA is part of the same circle of culture. Japan is of course a homogeneous and different society but it is too far away, and it does not constitute any political or military threat. And its economic strength is directed primarily at the USA.

There is an inherent danger that Europe will choose to define itself vis-à-vis its surrounding third world neighbours and that the Mediterranean will become the moat around the European fort. The creation of a pan-European identity risks being accompanied by a cultural exclusion mechanism. The search for a European identity could easily take the form of demarcation against 'the others', a policy which leads to a racial cul-de-sac, even though at the same time the mixing of races continues to rise in Europe.

A European identity must therefore be distinctive and all-embracing; must differentiate and assimilate the same time. It is a question of integrating the nations of Europe, with their deeply-rooted national and, often, regional identities and to persuade citizens to feel part of a supranational community and identity. In the ideal scenario for the emergence of a European political union, the European Parliament must first be 'de-nationalized', and this presupposes a European party system. Secondly, it must have the classic budgetary and legislative powers. The Council of Ministers must be turned into a second chamber and the Commission should be led by a 'head of government' appointed by Parliament.

National parliaments would consequently lose their functions and be transformed into region parliaments, like the *Landtage* in Germany, and would thus have the same position vis-à-vis Brussels that those have today. It is however easier said than done to abolish the democratic deficit by giving greater powers to the parliament in Strasbourg, because the dilemma of representation versus efficiency would immediately come to a head. If every parliamentarian represented about 25,000 citizens, as is the case in Sweden, the gathering at Strasbourg with member nations would have to be increased to 15,000. If in the name of effectiveness, the number were reduced to 500, with constituencies of more than a million citizens, and everyone was guaranteed an equal European vote, Luxembourg would not be represented at all and Sweden would have a maximum of 13 representatives in the European Parliament. It might be capable of functioning but could not by any means claim to represent a European electorate. The democratic deficit would continue, and this problem will of course grow with every new enlargement of the Union.

Europe as an entity can only be achieved with the help of and not against the nations. Europe integration will not be completed because of some natural necessity but only if enough political energy is brought to bear. The future of the EU therefore depends on the common interests of member states and not on the political will of the European people, for the simple reason that such a people does not exist.

Regional and national identities will grow in importance in a world that is becoming even more difficult to grasp and which is changing ever more rapidly. Citizens will be living in a state of increasing tension between loyalties towards their home district, state, nation, Europe and the international community; they will be required to think globally but act locally. Revived historical regions and new regions too are emerging everywhere in Europe. By actively supporting the process of regionalization, Brussels and the capitals can show that the EU is taking its institutions closer to its citizens and thereby creating greater scope for cultural and linguistic diversity than the nation states have been capable of doing. By contributing to a new vision - the Europe of diversity and regional government based on subsidiarity - the idea of Europe can be made more comprehensible and attractive.

In this way, the regional identity can strengthen an emerging European identity. Nowadays, when regions are increasingly turning to the EU in order to get resources for regional development and attract investment, it is Brussels and the EU that will be seen as the friends of the regions, rather than their own national capitals. The national state is thus being nibbled at from both ends. At the same time, we are experiencing a renaissance for national states and regions and their gradual merger in a transnational community. Those who support the region and nation must not necessarily reject Europe, but the traditional national state based on common traditions, identity and loyalty will remain indispensable as a source of strength and of political stability. The national states are therefore essential for the legitimization of a new European order; but structural asymmetry, conflicting interests and unexpected courses of development will make the relations between the national state and European integration difficult to manage. Europe will therefore also in the future continue to be squeezed between what the German philosopher Karl Jasper called 'Balkan and Helvetian tendencies', i.e., between Yugoslav and Swiss development models.

Nations are not eternal and created once and forever. They are what Benedict Anderson has called 'imagined communities'. The idea of a European community cannot arise from the German concept of *Blut und Boden*, neither from the idea of a European *Volk*, nor from that of a European 'cultural union'. The European identity cannot be created through central directives from Brussels or from member state's capitals. It cannot be conjured up at seminars and conferences: it will only become a reality when the citizens of individual European states feel that they personally have something gain from integration and thus say yes to the EU in their daily referendum, to use Ernest Renan's classical definition of a nation.

As we have already experienced, a forced unifying process produces counter reactions in all the member countries. A European identity is possible only if and when the citizens share common interests. If this feeling is missing, or is not felt sufficiently strongly, the EU will have a democratic deficit irrespective of what new competences are given to the European Parliament.

The single market will bring about trans-boundary mobility and thereby, albeit slowly, contribute to the emergence of a European identity; but it will be one of many, relativized by different national and regional identities (such as, for example, a Benelux, an Iberian, a Baltic, a Nordic and perhaps even a reborn Czecho-Slovak identity). Immigration will strengthen the multicultural component that is dispensable for a new sense of identity. At the same time, it will nourish social tensions and racist and nationalist currents; and yet it could also lead to political mobilization and the insight that these problems can only be solved at a European level.

A European 'supra-nationality' will only be accepted at a time when there is no hierarchy of national, regional and supra-regional identities, but when every individual regards them as self-evident and as part of his or her daily life. A policy for preserving diversity will thus be a precondition for creating a European identity, which should not become a replacement for a national identity but which could create support and strength for political institutions that are neither national nor just the framework of a European superstate.

The links between state and nation will thus grow looser. From this point of view European integration does not mean that a new superstate will appear. Cultural identities will remain rooted at the national level but will also penetrate down to ever more distinctive regional identities. We will have neither a new European superstate nor sovereign national states. The nations will not disappear but we will have nations with less of a state element attached, and national cultures with softer outer casings. Relations between European and national identities could take the shape of a foreign and security policy in the wide sense as a fundament of a common European political identity, a 'nation' to which one feels a sense of political belonging, without the need to feel part of a European *Volk* or a European 'cultural nation'.

The German concept of a nation would endure at the national level, but in its original form as conceived by Johann Gottfried von Herder in which a nation need not necessarily express itself in the form of a state. By standing on secure and solid cultural grounds, every people with their own distinctive character and cultural achievements can contribute to a European community.

Cultural nations will thus become divorced from a specific territory. People will have a sense of belonging to a special area and its cultural and political history will be theirs, but this area need not necessarily be linked to a national state with defined territorial boundaries. The European political identity could emerge in this way, while at the same time leaving the cultural, national or regional identity intact. In this way European diversity will not only survive but will develop further as well. The democratic deficit can never be abolished unless this kind of development takes place; and nor will the project of a European Union ever be accomplished.

# 5.
# Risk
# Factors

Vladimir Zuev, Alexei Arbatov

# A Moscow Perspective

*Alexei Arbatov*

There are several possible definitions of the term 'Central Europe'. The narrowest includes all the countries between Germany and the Post-Soviet space (i.e. Poland, Czech Republic and Hungary). The broadest version, in addition to these four nations, also includes Slovakia, Romania, Bulgaria, some of the post-Yugoslav states (Slovenia and Croatia), and the three Baltic states (Lithuania, Latvia, Estonia). Moreover, some analysts would unite the term 'Central Europe' (CE) with the term 'Eastern Europe' (EE) to suggest a notion of 'Central-Eastern Europe' (CEE), which includes as well as all the above also Ukraine, Belarus and Moldova, the other post-Yugoslav nations, and Albania.

Apparently, those different frameworks are not just accidental: they are determined by the profile of the research (whether geopolitical, economic or military-strategic), as well as by particular concepts of the history and post-Cold War international arrangements of the European continent.

Primary importance is given to the foundation of the new European order. Will it rely on NATO, WEU, EU, OSCE, or some combination of all these bodies; and what will be the relative contribution and weight of each one? Where will the UN fit into this picture? Will something solid grow out of the *ad hoc* Contact Group? Will the 16+1 NATO-Russian Standing Permanent Council really be a constant factor, working to construct and maintain European security? And last but not least, what will be the role of Russia in all of this? How will it affect Russia's domestic evolution and the search for new external alliances and partners?

## I

There are many myths concerning the 'civilizational differences' between Russia and Western Europe. In particular, it is claimed that such Western concepts as the free market economy, clear-cut private property, and individualist self-interest as an engine of economic prosperity, are all alien to Russians, who are believed to give preference to collective labour, communal or state ownership (especially of land), and a more or less egalitarian distribution of wealth, with charity as a tool to alleviate inequality. In place of political pluralism, democracy, and the division of state powers, Russia is associated with the overwhelming power of a state relying on a huge, powerful army and run by an authoritarian and 'wise' leader, guided not so much by laws as by conscience and enlightenment. Russians are supposed to believe in the special mission of man and the people, and in unquestioning patriotism - be it for building World Communism or asserting Orthodox Christianity - which justifies inexorable Imperial expansion and the sacrifice of legal and human norms for the implementation of this supreme mission. However, this cannot be confirmed by historic evidence.

Despite being located on the extreme eastern part of the European continent, the early medieval Russian state (Kievan Rus') of the 9$^{th}$ to 12$^{th}$ centuries was in no way different from contemporary feudal states in Europe, and was intertwined by broad dynastic ties with European kings and dukes. In fact, it was more advanced economically and politically: in particular such of its parts as the Novgorod feudal republic or the Kiev principality, which were located on the commercial Dneiper river route from Northern to Southern Europe.

Russia adopted Christianity from Byzantium in the 10$^{th}$ century, together with its important tradition of the subordination (or merging) of church to state authorities. Still, at that time the principalities of Rus' were decentralized, and the church was an arbiter, rather than a servant in their constant feuds, just as in Western Europe. Earlier, in Western Europe, Christianity had served basically the same purpose of an instrument of state power for almost two hundred years, before the final collapse of the Roman Empire in the 5$^{th}$ century. It was only after this collapse that the Christian Church raised itself high above the fragmented kingdoms and principalities, largely run by barbarian autocrats, which functioned among the ruins of the Roman Empire.

Another point is that Rus' has adopted Christianity from Byzantium a whole century before the Great Schism, i.e. when the Church was still integrated, and not divided into rival Catholic and Orthodox parts. True, at that time there were plenty of scholastic and political differences between the Eastern and Western branches; but still, there is no comparison with the later break between the Roman Catholic and Protestant Churches, that escalated into the massacres of the Inquisition and the devastating religious wars of the 16$^{th}$ to 18$^{th}$ centuries (which, incidentally, barely involved Russia).

The real principal factor for Russia's deviation from the mainstream of

European development was its vulnerable geopolitical location, on a huge plain, with few natural barriers, such as mountain ranges or sea shores. Constantly fighting for living space with invaders from the west, south and east, Russia acquired a powerful incentive for the unification and centralization of the state - first of all in order to provide for a strong military power, which henceforth became the core and purpose of the administrative and economic organization of Russia, much more than was the case for most other European states.

This centralization, and the unifying ideology of the Orthodox Church, were crucial for Russia's gaining its sovereignty in the late 15$^{th}$ century, now as the Grand Duchy of Moscow, after more than two hundred years of Mongol rule. Those centuries of oppression seriously slowed down Russia's economic and political advance (as in fact was also the case with Spain, Portugal and the Balkan nations, conquered by Moors and Ottoman Turks respectively).

Another consequence of this inherent vulnerability was a permanent territorial expansion, in search of security: a security which was imposed by force on some weaker peoples (Volga and Crimean Tatars, Balts, Finns and Poles, Siberian tribesmen, and Central Asian and North Caucasus Muslims), but welcomed by others for protection from dangerous outside neighbours (Ukraine and Belarus in the 17$^{th}$ century, Georgia and Armenia in the 19$^{th}$ century). Expanding in this way - by conquering, providing protection and exploring - the Russian Empire by the mid-19$^{th}$ century reached as far west as the Polish-German border, as far south as Anatolia, Persia and the Pamir mountain range, and as far east as Manchuria; and even reached out as far as Alaska and northern California.

The extending perimeter, when it did not reach natural land and sea frontiers, encountered growing resistance from outside states, and this created new vulnerabilities. The perimeter of security was again and again pushed back by the revolts of annexed peoples, as well as by other, expansionist, great powers, which sometimes reached as far east as Moscow (in the 16$^{th}$, 17$^{th}$ and 19$^{th}$ centuries, as well as in 1941 - through the invasions of Crimean Tatars, Poles, French and Germans respectively). Regaining the lost space required enormous sacrifice from the people, concentration of resources on military needs, and a more stringent authoritarian political regime, as well as the imposition of an indisputable ideology to justify the cruelty and misdeeds of the Leviathan state machine.

The above considerations should prove that the 'specificity' of Russia is not a result of it being some kind of mysterious mixture of Europe and Asia, and neither of it serving a 'historic role' of being alternatively a 'bridge' or a 'barrier' between the two civilizations. Instead, Russia's unique national qualities - as far as they are more conspicuous than the peculiarities of the French, Germans or British - are mostly the product of its historic evolution as a European nation and state, exposed to particular security challenges. Those have determined its specific domestic economic and political organization, its social psychology and traditions, its culture and its ideology.

Two centuries of Mongol rule, and permanent contact with Turkic ethnic groups thereafter, certainly affected Russian language, habits and cuisine (just as Moorish culture influenced Spain, or Ottoman culture the Balkans), but not its political or economic development, mentality or ideology. In fact, Russian literature, arts, music, architecture, philosophy, science and engineering are an inherent part of European cultural and technological development. Russia imported both its major ideologies - Christianity and Marxism - from Europe, and adapted them to its special environment.

The same goes for the current democratic reforms, whatever their failures and mistakes. In fact, many of those are due to quite a narrow-minded emulation of Western recipes and of the Polish reform experiment, rather than of a more flexible, more gradual and perhaps wiser adaptation to Russian economic and social conditions.

Both the Russian Tsarist Empire and the USSR had a considerable Turkic and Islamic population (up to 25 %), but never accepted their ideological, political or economic traditions, and indeed imposed their own standards. Nowadays, 80 % of the Russian Federation is composed of Russians and other Slavic ethnic groups. Although the predominant part of its territory is in Asia, only 15 % of its population live there, and this is 90 % Russian. In this sense, Russia is much less Asian than Britain was Asian, Polynesian or American with its colonies in India, Australia and the New World.

During the last decade Russia's foreign policy, domestic resources and external environment have changed profoundly, and in many respects irreversibly, at least for the foreseeable future. Ten years ago Moscow still conducted a global power game, and commanded military superiority over its western and eastern neighbours in Eurasia, while relying on authoritarian rule and centralized command of resources in Russia and its colonies in the Soviet Union and in the 'socialist camp'.

Now, and for the foreseeable future, Russia will be mostly engaged in the affairs of its immediate post-Soviet neighbours and only marginally in the adjacent zones of Europe, Asia Minor, South Asia and the Far East. Apart from participation in arms control and non-proliferation regimes, Moscow's global game is over for a long time.

To say nothing of its former American rival, in the west, east and potentially even in the south, Russia will be facing nations and alliances much superior in economic and military power, casting a long shadow over its 'near abroad'. In ten years Russia's conventional military power will at best reach the level of a large European state, and the nuclear forces - whatever their value in the first place - a level closer to third-class nuclear powers than to the USA. Moscow's economic, political and federal situation remains quite fragile, dependent on foreign support and vulnerable to external influence, and this will stay by far the major preoccupation of any Russian government in the years to come. No doubt, this will be a principal and long-term break from four centuries of Russian/Soviet Imperial dynamics in domestic and foreign politics alike.

## II

For over three centuries Central and Eastern Europe was one geopolitical zone of Russia's expansion, in line with the above dynamics. It was also an arena of tough rivalry and wars for spheres of influence between Russia and the other principal European powers (and the Ottoman Empire), and after 1945, between the USSR and the USA. It goes without saying that the American presence was liberal and welcomed, while the Soviet presence was oppressive and hated by the majority of CEE peoples, except for the Communist ruling elites imposed by Moscow.

The late 1980s to early 1990s was the period of final and irreversible Russian retreat from Central Europe, as well as from most of Eastern Europe - at least in the traditional sense of Imperial dominance. Although it was done in a spontaneous and chaotic manner, this was inevitable as a result of the collapse of the Soviet Communist Empire.

However, one point is of crucial importance. Unlike most other empires throughout history, the Soviet Union in 1991 was not defeated in a large war, and neither was it exhausted in small colonial wars. (The quagmire of Afghanistan in 1979-1989, or local clashes in Georgia, Karabakh, Lithuania, and Latvia in 1989-1991 were just the first signs of such wars, potentially in store for the USSR in the future.) What is of utmost importance in understanding Russia's present interaction with other post-Soviet republics, with the CEE states, and with the big powers of the world, is that the Soviet Union was never defeated in the Cold War; and neither did it crash under the burden of the arms race, as some assert.

The Soviet Empire was created and built for war, for the arms race, and for confrontation with the rest of the world. It could have continued like that for a long time after 1991, were it not for its domestic erosion, caused by the forces of its internal contradictions: between a stringent political regime, a dogmatic and non-credible ideology, and an inefficient centralized economy on the one hand - and the growing material, political and spiritual demands of its population, on the other hand. The latter were generated by the very industrialization promoted by the Communist rulers for military purposes, and by the momentum of scientific, technological and information revolutions, as well as through expanding contacts with the outer world during the 1970s and early 1980s.

Mikhail Gorbachev initiated domestic democratization and détente with the West out of his sincere desire to alleviate those internal contradictions, to remove the threat of nuclear war and to use this interval to modernize the Communist Empire. Instead, it collapsed in five years like a house of cards: first, the 'outer shell' of the Communist alliance/occupation system in Eastern Europe; second, the Communist regime in Russia in August 1991; and third, the Soviet Union itself, in December of the same year. It was not the United States, NATO or President Ronald Reagan's Strategic Defense Initiative that finally defeated the Soviet Empire. Rather, it was destroyed by the hands of Gorbachev's Communist reformers and then by the new elite led by Boris Yeltsin - that is, in both stages, by Russia's democratic movement. And that ended the Cold War and the arms race, not the other way around.

In this sense, the Soviet Empire was defeated by détente and attempts at internal reforms, not by outside pressure. Gorbachev had liberated Eastern Europe to sustain political co-operation with the West and to avoid compromising his *perestroika* by external suppression. And then Yeltsin liberated the other Soviet republics in order to do away with Soviet Communist rule and to get Gorbachev out of the Kremlin. The Russian Federation, as a great power, is the principal victorious power in the Cold War - not the West, which only gave it lukewarm and inconsistent moral encouragement in achieving this victory.

The retreat of Russian power from CEE is an event of historic dimensions, whatever the ensuing chaos, excessive costs and damage, conflicts and frustration - for Russia and for many other nations. Potentially it creates a chance for profound democratic reforms in Russia, as well as for the development of new, fair and mutually beneficial relations of Moscow with its close and far European neighbours. Still, there are at least two major interrelated issues, which represent factors of risk for CEE and for the Euroatlantic zone at large. The first is the prospect of escalating conflicts in the huge post-Communist area. The second is the emergence in Europe of new dividing lines, which may become the thresholds of hostility and military confrontation. This might undercut democratic reform in Russia, which could be affected by events around it, and this would have most serious foreign policy repercussions.

### III

As has happened many times before in history after the crash of great empires, the collapse of Communism in the Soviet Union and Central and Eastern Europe, and the disintegration of the Soviet Empire and Yugoslavia, created a huge zone of instability extending from the Balkans to the Pamir mountain range. Nevertheless, there is still no new security system which might embody the new relationships and address the new international agenda. Nothing of the scale of the Congress of Vienna, Versailles, or Yalta has been created to replace the Cold War's bipolar division of spheres of influence and mutual deterrence.

During the first years, in 1992-1994, this problem was being resolved by Moscow's simply following the lead of the USA in world affairs, concentrating on its domestic reforms, and largely ignoring the new volatile environment in post-Soviet space. The USA, and to a smaller degree its allies, have demonstrated a propensity for taking Russia's subservience for granted, treating it more like a defeated country than as an ally. They did not recognize Russia's right to protect its own legitimate foreign and security interests, and ignored or suppressed its humble attempts to assert its own position. This was manifested in attitudes to peace-enforcement in Bosnia, and also in a number of other cases related to arms control and conflict management.

But this could not continue for long. Russia is not a defeated state, and its geographical proximity and historic involvement in many regional affairs made it impossible for Moscow to stand aside from world problems and passively follow the lead of the West.

In the late 1990s, the interaction between Russia and the West in the post-Communist space has been more controversial and messy. This is becoming a serious obstacle in conflict management and peace-keeping in Bosnia, Southern Ossetia, Transdniestria, Abkhazia, Karabakh, and Tajikistan. These conflicts are spreading to adjacent areas, both outside this zone

(Cyprus, Turkish Kurdistan, Iranian Azerbaijan, Iraq, Afghanistan), as well as inside Russia itself (North Caucasus). There is a serious danger of horizontal escalation of conflict, through fresh eruptions in Montenegro, Kosovo, Macedonia and Greece, Transcaucasus, Central Asia, and China's Uigur province (*Xinjiang*), as well as through resumption of violence and wars in Bosnia and the Persian Gulf, or between India and Pakistan.

After the peaceful division of Czechoslovakia, the region of Central Europe (narrowly defined) looks pretty stable, but it could certainly be badly affected by the consequences of potential conflicts in Southern and Eastern Europe and the Black Sea-Caspian basin.

The most important post-Cold War mission of Russia and the West, as well as Central Europe (as a new part of the West) should be close co-operation in managing and resolving those conflicts, and in peace-enforcement and peace-keeping operations. However, with few exceptions, Russia's own involvement in those conflicts so far has been quite inefficient, and also dubious as to its motives, goals and even Russia's ability to keep control over events.

Western powers and international organizations, like the UN and OSCE, have mostly been resisting Russia's involvement. But at the same time they have been reluctant to take on the expensive, dangerous and domestically controversial responsibilities of large-scale peace-enforcement and peace-keeping in the crisis areas of the whole giant post-Communist space.

Due to failures of Russian and Western policies alike, the post-Communist space is becoming more an arena of to-and-fro arguments between Russia and the West than of real co-operation. Hence, clear patterns of new divisions are emerging across vast zones of Eurasia. In particular, Russia has been forming allied or partnership political (and in some cases military) relationships with Serbia, Belarus, Armenia, Iran, Kazakstan, Kyrgyzstan, Tajikistan, India and China. At the same time Russia's estrangement has been widening with the USA, Western and Central Europe, the Baltics, Ukraine, Moldova, Georgia, Azerbaijan, Uzbekistan, Turkmenistan, Turkey, Pakistan and the Taliban conquerors of Afghanistan.

Co-operation between Russia and the West on peace-keeping in Bosnia is considered a success story. Nonetheless, having been quite efficient at the military level, it is not considered in Russia to be a model in a political sense. In particular, the way in which peace was imposed on Serbia through NATO air-raids (against official objections by Moscow), as well as the way in which the Dayton delineation was devised, do not leave a sufficient chance for peace if UN peace-keeping forces are withdrawn. In this sense, the whole operation cannot be considered any more successful than the UN mission in Cyprus, or Russian management of the Transdniestria, Karabakh, Abkhazia, South Ossetia or Tajikistan conflicts. Moreover, the foundation of co-operation between Russia and the West on conflict-management is quickly being eroded by outside events, and above all by NATO expansion. This issue also in itself constitutes a risk factor for Europe.

## IV

The late April 1998 vote of the US Senate in favour of NATO extension to include Poland, the Czech Republic and Hungary made the first stage of expansion an achieved fact. There is a broad consensus in Russia that NATO expansion is not just against Russian security interests, but also violates some of the commonly accepted rules according to which the Cold War was ended. When Moscow agreed to the reunification of Germany and its staying in NATO, to disbanding the Warsaw Pact and then the Soviet Union itself, to deeper reductions of nuclear and conventional forces than the reductions by the West (according to the INF-SRF, CFE, START-I and START-II treaties), and to the hasty withdrawal of half a million troops from comfortable barracks in Central Europe to tent camps in Russian fields - nobody took the trouble to warn the Russians that as a result of all these concessions, the most powerful military alliance in the world would start moving towards the Russian borders.

On the contrary, Moscow was being repeatedly told by the West that it would be accepted as an equal and genuine partner, and that no major decision on international security would be taken without it. The decision on NATO extension came as a clear demonstration that such decisions may and will be taken, and that Russia's opinion really matters only as long as it is entirely in line with the Western position.

It is not that Russians are against NATO as it is, but they would prefer this great military alliance to find other post-Cold War functions, rather than to extend itself to their borders without any plausible or clear explanation for why it is doing so. In the aftermath of the Paris and Madrid summits in May and July 1997 the primary and fundamental question in the Russian mind remains unresolved: if NATO is really expanding as a defensive military alliance, then what is the threat to the new member-states that could warrant such an expansion?

If, on the other hand, NATO is being extended in a new role: as a foundation of a new European security system for peace-keeping - why the haste and why is Moscow's opinion being dismissed? If there is a reason to hurry, why is Russia not seriously contemplated as a member of such a system in the foreseeable future? Why, instead, is it offered only the 'Partnership for Peace' and yet another consultative council? And why are those measures considered insufficient for new members and aspiring states, but good enough for Russia?

At present, NATO expansion to the east is seen in Russia at best as a mistaken policy, pregnant with complications and new controversies, and at worst as a consummation of the 'grand design' of encircling and isolating Russia, achieving an overwhelming strategic superiority over it and finally causing the disintegration of Russia itself, so as to do away with it as a European power once and for all. The start of NATO expansion may well be a turning point in the post-Cold War period, which will seriously strengthen the hand of anti-Western hard-liners in Moscow and start another cycle of Russia's distancing itself from the West. It could deeply undercut co-operation between Russia and the West on conflict-management, arms control and non-proliferation of weapons of mass destruction and missile technologies in the world at large.

Several main arguments in favour of NATO expansion are put forward in the USA, Western and Central Europe, but none of them seem valid.

For instance, it is indicated that Russia may revive its military potential and once again threaten CEE, even though at present such a threat is non-existent. But in reality such a threat is not conceivable for the foreseeable future, that is at least for the next 10-15 years. On the contrary, it is NATO that would most probably enlarge its military power over Russia in relative terms, even if it did not come any closer to Russia's borders in the process of accepting new member-states. During the next 10-15 years NATO would most probably acquire 2:1 to 3:1 conventional superiority over Russia in Europe. It may even be 4:1 or 5:1, depending on the rate of extension, on Russia's force reductions, on military reforms and on the level of defence appropriations. In addition, the USA (together with France and Britain) will maintain a substantial superiority both in strategic and tactical nuclear weapons. Whether the nuclear superiority of the West is 30 %, double or triple depends on the future of arms control treaties and funding for Russian strategic forces. All qualitative measures of the military balance would make it appear still more favourable to the West.

This is certainly a major shift in the military balance in Europe. Less than 10 years ago crack Soviet tank armies were standing in the centre of

Germany, within two days march from the Channel, and the Warsaw Pact was enjoying triple superiority over NATO in conventional forces, double superiority in theatre and tactical nuclear weapons, as well as parity in strategic nuclear forces. The USSR alone was twice as strong in conventional forces in Europe as all NATO armies. Soviet defence spending and weapons procurement were an order of magnitude higher than at present. Even the theoretical possibility that Russia could come close to these levels during the next 10-15 years is close to zero, and a chance of doing it quickly and by surprise is totally excluded.

Another thesis is that, apart from the military balance, NATO expansion would integrate Central Europe into a Western zone of stability, prosperity and common security. However, NATO, as an alliance conceived and structured for collective defence against a common external enemy, does not have an effective capability to resolve conflicts among its members. The dead-locked conflict between Greece and Turkey, which has escalated after the end of the Cold War, provides a vivid illustration of this.

Economic prosperity and social stability is provided not by NATO, but by the EU and the other European institutions. Entering the EU is now a goal of practically all the CEE countries. Poland, the Czech Republic, Hungary, Slovenia, Estonia and Slovakia have the best chances. Latvia, Lithuania, and under certain circumstances also Croatia, Romania and Bulgaria have reasonable though more distant prospects. The motivations of CEE countries here are clear and should be encouraged: through joining the EU they could expect rapid economic growth and social stability, as Spain, Greece and Portugal enjoyed in the 1970s and 1980s. The significant expansion of the common market as a result of CEE enlargement would trigger economic growth in the EU as well.

At the same time, many CEE nations are apparently applying to join NATO in order to enhance their chances of eventually entering the EU. However, NATO membership is not a necessary precondition for EU membership. The EU incorporates a number of non-NATO countries (Austria, Finland, Ireland, Sweden), while Estonia and Slovenia were invited to negotiate their entry into the EU regardless of not having received similar invitations from NATO. Membership in NATO does not represent a sufficient criterion for entering the EU: Turkey's chances for joining the EU remain much smaller than those of non-NATO Cyprus or Malta. But on the other hand, granting NATO membership for certain CE countries could be considered by some Europeans as an excuse for postponing negotiations for EU accession or even as an alternative to EU (especially in the case of

Romania and Bulgaria). Moreover, the requirement for broad rearmament as a consequence of NATO membership could suppress investments into civilian sectors of the economy, and thus impede prospects for economic growth. If so, the CEE countries' ability to join the EU might in fact diminish.

Yet another argument is that, although the CEE nations are no longer threatened by Russia, their 'historical grievances' give them the right to seek protection in NATO. True, during the four decades after 1945, the CEE nations were occupied and oppressed by the Soviet Union, and also suffered many times and for long periods at the hands of Russian Empire before 1917. But history did not start at 1945, and there is no lack of 'historical grievances' in Russia either. It should not be forgotten that Hungary and Romania sent their troops to conquer the USSR with Hitler's armies in 1941, and that they marched all the way to Stalingrad together. It was not Russia, but France and Britain, which sold out Czechoslovakia to Germany in Munich in 1938. Poland is also amazingly selective in choosing to remember its 'historic grievances' towards Russia concerning actions taken after 1945 and before 1917, while apparently having simultaneously chosen to forgive and forget when it comes to Germany, which destroyed Warsaw and built Auschwitz and Maidanek between 1939 and 1945. Of course, Germany is now a democratic country, and not to be compared to Hitler's Third Reich - but exactly the same is true of the Russian Federation with respect to the Soviet Union.

# Eastern Central Europe as a Subject of German Foreign Policy

Joachim Krause

Since Germany's unification in 1990, her foreign policy has become the subject of much speculation. Notably, during the aftermath of the crisis over the recognition of Slovenia and Croatia in 1991/1992, the question of Germany's general foreign policy orientation was raised time and again. Most attention was given to Helmut Kohl's *Europapolitik* (Europe-policy), and to the policy towards Eastern Europe. With respect to Eastern Europe, two fundamental apprehensions were voiced: first, that Germany was restarting a power game with Russia over Eastern Europe; and, secondly, that as a result of this approach, Germany could try to create a zone of special interest in Eastern Central Europe, with a view to the eventual redrawing of international borders.*

This paper attempts to outline the basic approach of German foreign policy towards Eastern Central Europe - sometimes wrongly referred to as 'the lands in between'. The main argument of this article is that, contrary to those apprehensions mentioned above, Germany's foreign policy towards these countries constitutes a marked and radical shift from the policies of Prussia, Imperial Germany, the Weimar Republic and, notably, the Third Reich. It is based on the notion that the co-operatively organized interstate system in Western Europe - which was the result of determined Western policy efforts after World War II - is so much to the benefit of Germany that Germany has become the most enthusiastic champion of internationalism, institution-building and integration in Europe. Given Germany's size and importance, any deviation from that policy, any reversal to a traditional interest-oriented policy, and any attempt to restore a European balance-of-power policy would have such detrimental consequences for Germany in the long run that no reasonable politician would attempt such policies. For East Europeans, this German policy forms an opportunity to join the prosperous and co-operatively organized Western world, and it also gives them an unprecedented chance

* By the term 'Eastern Central Europe', the following areas are meant: the territory of Poland, Czech Republic, Slovakia, Slovenia, Hungary, Bulgaria, Romania and the Baltic states.

to let smaller countries have a relatively higher impact on international affairs. Paradoxically, however, this presupposes that these states and societies will learn to play the rules of open and post-modern societies: i.e. rules under which national sovereignty no longer plays a paramount role. Rather, interconnectivity, interdependence and free trade and exchange will be of the greatest relevance; and the corresponding relevant political decisions will have to be made not within national governments only, but chiefly within international institutions and organizations.

This article starts with some reflections about the co-operative approach towards international affairs as it has developed after World War II and the role the Federal Republic of Germany has played in it. It then turns to the relevance of Eastern Central Europe for Germany's risk assessments after the end of the Cold War. As a third step, it weighs the different policy options that have been discussed during the past decade in regard to Eastern Europe, especially the balance between a policy that seeks to integrate the Eastern Europeans into NATO and the European Union, and a policy that seeks to come to good terms with Russia.

## I. The Development of an International Co-operative Approach

Most analysts of international relations tended to view the development of the international order after World War II mainly in terms of the East-West conflict. Indeed, the East-West conflict was the dominant feature of international politics from the late forties to the end of the eighties. However, with regard to the transatlantic area and the whole OECD world there was also a different order developing, based on co-operation, interdependence, institution-building and even integration. The concept of such an order, initially espoused by the USA on the basis of some of President Wilson's ideas about 'democratic peace', but then adjusted to take account of the lessons learned from the failure of international diplomacy during the 1920s and 1930s, was part of the US effort to restructure Europe after World War II. Its purpose was to avoid the re-occurrence of fascism and communism. This new order was based on a global institutional framework (United Nations, IMF, GATT, Bretton Woods System), that was to be supported by various regional or transregional institutions (OECD). It was aimed at establishing free trade and the free exchange of people and ideas in order to overcome the deficiencies of the old international order, and, last but not least, also to make the Western world strong enough to withstand the Soviet and communist threat.

European integration, which came about as an attempt to reorganise international affairs in Western Europe after two devastating wars, did fit into this picture. It was the European contribution to the creation of a Western zone of peace and co-operation, and it gave an example of how much international relations could change qualitatively. That did not imply that power relations didn't play any role among Europeans or within the Western world. However, their relevance was reduced, in part, because of the deliberate efforts by most governments in the West to downplay the relevance of power; and also as a consequence of the stronger welfare orientation of modern industrialized societies.

For the Federal Republic of Germany, the formation of this special intra-Western international order in combination with the East-West-conflict came as a boon. The liberal intra-Western order allowed for a relatively fast recovery after World War II and it entailed specific opportunities for the traditionally export-oriented German industry. The East-West confrontation implied the partition of Germany, but it increased the political and military value of West Germany and thus allowed for a political integration into the 'international community' that was much faster than many people had thought would be possible after Auschwitz.

Within the Western Alliance and within the European Community a special style of multilateralism was created and carefully fostered. This style again held some opportunities for the Federal Republic of Germany. As there was no more room for traditional German national interest policies in the 1950s and 1960s, West German politicians and the West German diplomatic corps alike became accustomed to, and indeed consciously developed, a kind of consensus-orientated style of multilateral negotiations.

Looking back into recent history, it was not always the case that West Germany was the champion of international co-operation and mutilateralism. This was truly the case within the Western world. However, until the early 1970s political relations towards the 'East' clearly had another orientation. Indeed, when during the early 1960s it became apparent that the East-West conflict was more and more shaped by international endeavours to avoid nuclear war and to preserve the political and territorial status quo, it took some time for German foreign policy fully to comprehend the consequences of that move. Acceptance of the German partition, together with the acceptance of the loss of former German territories in the East, was hard to learn for many politicians; and the necessity of a co-operative approach towards the then Eastern Bloc was moot for a considerable time. But from the time that the Social-Liberal coalition came into power in December 1969, a special variant of the co-operative approach was applied by German diplomacy in this area too: both, that is, in bilateral (*Ostpolitik*) and in multilateral (CSCE) relations.

The co-operative style of West German foreign policy towards the East espoused during the phase of *Ostpolitik* under Willy Brandt and Egon Bahr created, however, certain apprehensions among Germany's West European and American allies in the 1970s and 1980s. The concern was voiced that Bonn might slowly dissolve its bonds with the West: that it was ready to take high risks for only a vague prospect of an eventual reunification; and that a united Germany, or even West Germany alone, might look for an independent international role between the West and Russia. Even the multilateral approach of West Germany's *Ostpolitik* was surmised to be a camouflage for a traditional national-interest-orientated policy. (*Ash; 1992*) As a consequence, subsequent West German Government administrations in Bonn tried to alleviate these concerns by calling for more and qualitatively new steps towards European integration - and especially for steps that would lead towards more commonality in foreign policy. The creation of the European Political Co-operation (EPC) in 1972, which is called the Common Foreign and Security Policy (CFSP) since the Maastricht Treaty, is a clear example of that kind of thinking. The Federal Republic of Germany found in France an ideal partner in pursuing such an approach, and thus the Franco-German tandem became the driving force of European integration from the 1970s on.

This kind of co-operative style, in combination with the tendency to seek for European structures that would bind the growing West German economy and population more closely into Western European integration contributed to the ever-growing confidence that was felt concerning the West German democracy. German positions in many foreign policy areas were usually consulted and pre-shaped not only in contact with the major powers but also with smaller European states. Without such an approach the German unification in 1990 would not have been possible - at least not with the ease that we all witnessed.

Since the end of the East-West conflict, and since the emergence of a new international order, the challenges and tasks for German foreign policy have changed considerably.* The most salient aspect of German foreign policy after the end of the East-West conflict is that it is predominantly orientated towards improving the international structural architecture that has turned out to be so advantageous for Germany. Calls for the deepening of the European Union, the reform of NATO, the strengthening of the WEU, support for OSCE and United Nations, and the continuous improvement of international economic institutions, have been constant features of German foreign policy since 1990.

## II. Risks Associated with Central Eastern Europe

Within this framework, the notion of 'risks' acquires a special meaning. In principle, as far as Germany is concerned, risks are developments that could threaten the stability of the co-operative international order and/or pose a possible danger to the internal stability of Western societies (and not only German society). Soon after the fall of the Berlin Wall, Thinks Tanks and planning staffs in many Western states began to ponder about the possibility of risks arising from Central Eastern Europe. In principle, there were four broad categories of risks that were identified at that time, which are still at the heart of both German and other governments' concerns (*Breska et al.; 1997*, pp. 39-48):

1. The danger that economic and social transformation might fail - with all the concomitant problems resulting from that;
2. the danger of a failure of the transformation towards democracy;
3. the danger of instabilities arising from border disputes and by the lack of a clear foreign policy orientation; and
4. the dangers associated with so-called transnational problems such as organized crime, ecological pollution and labour migration.

---

* Among the literature devoted to this subject the following titles may be of special interest: Karl Kaiser and Hanns Maull (eds.), *Deutschlands Neue Außenpolitik, Band I: Grundlagen*; Munich: Oldenbourg 1993; Karl Kaiser and Hanns Maull (eds.), *Deutschlands Neue Außenpolitik, Band 2: Herausforderungen*, Munich: Oldenbourg 1995; Karl Kaiser and Joachim Krause (eds.), *Deutschlands Neue Außenpolitik, Band 3: Interessen und Strategien*, Munich: Oldenbourg 1996; Wolf-Dieter Eberwein and Karl Kaiser (eds.), Deutschlands Neue Außenpolitik, Band IV: Institutionen und Ressourcen, Munich: Oldenbourg 1998; Wolfgang Heydrich, Joachim Krause, Uwe Nerlich, Jürgen Nötzold and Reinhardt Rummel (eds.), *Sicherheitspolitik Deutschlands: Neue Konstellationen, Risiken und Instrumente*; Baden-Baden: Nomos Verlag 1992.

The possibility of a failure of economic reform was mainly attributed to the lack of experience and know-how of the new economic elites in the post-communist societies. There were two dangers seen: either too much reformist zeal, which would destroy too much of the economic assets of these countries, or too much reluctance to proceed with determined reforms. Both these things happened. However, while it was always possible to redress the damage done by too much reformist energy (as was the case in Poland), the damage caused by putting off reforms as long as possible was felt much more strongly, both economically and socially. Romania and Bulgaria are the most obvious cases of this kind, though we could also mention Ukraine and Russia.

The possibility of a failure of democratic transition was voiced by many sceptics at the beginning of the 1990s, since - with the exception of Czechoslovakia - none of the Central East European states had anything that could even come close to a successful democratic tradition in the past. Besides that, more than 40 years of communist repression had left its marks on the respective societies. Democratic forces were systematically purged and either marginalized or driven into exile, with Poland being the only exception. Instead, new political elites were being formed: mainly out of old communist cadres and new nationalists. Many therefore feared that instead of a rapid transition towards democracy, authoritarian dictatorship might be the likely eventual outcome of the political transition in most of the Central East European countries.

Also, the dangers related to the privatization of the large state sector in practically all Central East European states were another element of concern. Would the new political elites be prudent enough in dealing with this delicate issue, or would they succumb to the various temptations associated with that process, such as personal enrichment and selling out to relatives and cronies? All in all, the danger was seen that instead of a transition towards democracy, a transition towards some kind of Latin Americanization of Central Eastern Europe might set in. As part of this process, new ruling classes would be formed, mainly by people plundering the wealth of their respective countries, and it was feared that such strata would have a predisposition towards authoritarian and nationalistic leadership.

These domestic risks might be compounded by foreign policy uncertainties germane to the area. Most border lines were arbitrarily drawn at some point of history and ethnic and minority conflicts abound in Central Eastern Europe. By the same token, non-democratic domestic forces in individual Eastern European countries might resort to hostile foreign policy rhetoric in order to divert attention from their poor record of governance. Since these states had never before in history had a clear sense of where they belonged in terms of foreign policy affiliation (at least, not of where they *wished* to belong), with some of them having had rather traumatic experiences of being repeatedly occupied, the likelihood of erratic and irredentist foreign policies was considered to be very high.

In connection with these risk factors mentioned above, the danger of additional ecological problems and of increased organized crime activity was seen as significant.

All these risks actually materialized in one way or another, and there are many instances which could be quoted here. The economic transformation was actually loaded with many problems, and especially in Romania and Bulgaria the lack of progress in comparison to Hungary and Poland is evident. The privatization of state enterprises never went off very smoothly, in many states there was a strong element of crony-capitalism, and especially in Slovakia under Mečiar a coalition of new nationalists and old functionaries enriching themselves and their cronies were actually threatening the democratic transformation. Hungary needed a long time until it was fully ready to accept its existing borders, and in 1991, Poland saw a presidential election campaign in which a candidate who made strong nationalistic statements and who demanded nuclear weapons for Poland in order to fend off both the Russians and the Germans managed to attract the votes of about one third of the electorate.

It was not one single risk that frightened analysts and politicians alike, but the combined and mutually reinforcing effect that such developments might have when taken together. Most of these risks, though, have been prevented so far, and the dangers imagined from the combined effects of various risks have not materialized. The responsibility for this positive development lies to a great extent - though not exclusively - with German foreign policy. The possibility of the economic and political destabilization of the region, with resultant secondary consequences then being felt mostly by Germans; the prospect of armed conflicts in her immediate neighbourhood and the necessity to accept huge masses of refugees from these areas; and, not least, the possibility that, after a long period of uncertainty and instability the region might once again fall under Russian influence: all have contributed to the strong role that Germany has assumed with regard to Central Eastern Europe in the years since 1990. As one US observer put it, instead of a *Drang nach Osten* the Germans rather felt a *Zwang nach Osten*, i.e. the necessity to do something in order to help these countries to overcome these risks (*Asmus; 1991*, p. 70, *Larrabee; 1993*, p. 124).

However, a broad approach of assistance and conflict prevention was needed and Germany was not able to shoulder this task alone. Although Germany had the largest share in aid granted to these countries, and although German companies invested strongly in that region, one of the most salient features of German policy since 1990 was the attempt to multilateralize the policy towards Central Eastern Europe as much as possible. This was not only done with the intention of avoiding any impression that Germany might consider that part of the world as her 'zone of influence'; it was also necessary in order to share the huge burden of economic aid. By the same token, given the fact that many competencies in the field of economic assistance and international trade were already in the realm of the European Union, Bonn was more than happy to consider the assistance for Central Eastern Europe as a joint task. Again, it was France which, after some initial hesitations, joined Germany and took over an active role in shaping the European foreign policy *vis-à-vis* Central Eastern Europe.

The most important contribution towards giving the Central East Europeans a foreign policy orientation, however, came from NATO's offer to accept new members (as was reaffirmed during NATO's summit meeting in July 1997). Again, the first major Western government to give the strongest support to the notion of NATO enlargement was the German government, where then Defence Minister Volker Rühe already in early 1993 demanded that Poland and others should soon be allowed to join the Atlantic Alliance.

There were four main areas of bilateral and multilateral policy towards Central Eastern Europe:

- Association agreements with the European Union, which opened the EU markets for the Central East Europeans and which gave them the prospect of eventually joining the Union.
- Bilateral and multilateral aid and assistance in the economic field, in the build-up of infrastructure, technology, administration and legislation and in the field of assistance for democratic transition.
- A strategy of conflict prevention aimed at dealing with border disputes and minority conflict.
- The enlargement of NATO through members from Central Eastern Europe.

At the heart of these undertakings was a broad understanding of the nature of 'security' and of 'security risks', something often referred to as a *comprehensive security approach.* Also a close link between conflict prevention on the one hand and *democracy building and human rights* on the other hand was pursued. In order to achieve these goals, a multilateral, co-operative approach was chosen, which envisions international organizations as important tools of preventive diplomacy and where a division of labour among them should be possible *(interlocking institutions)*.

Special importance was given to the Organization for Security and Co-operation in Europe (OSCE). Through it, a *top-down conceptual approach* by which common principles and procedures are developed among all European states was pursued, which turned out to be important with respect to conflict prevention. Among the measures implemented were:

- efforts towards the creation of a general framework of norms and standards to guide states in their foreign and security policy;
- the establishment of a regime of military confidence building measures;
- assistance in the build-up of democratic institutions (elections, creation of democratic institutions, parties etc.);
- assistance in setting up democratic control over armed forces;
- assistance in settling minority problems in a civilized and peaceful manner;
- mediation and observer missions to prevent conflicts from becoming violent;
- international measures to prevent conflicts from escalating.

As these instruments clearly demonstrate, the Germans and the other Western Europeans have tried to act through the Union, through the CSFP or through other international organizations and institutions. The amount of aid money transferred, the number and quality of various assistance programs, and the political capital invested by Germany and other Western European governments was enormous.

The strongest *lever* the EU states had in making their policy a success was their declared unwillingness to let any state enter the European Union that was not able to launch reasonable economic and democratic reforms, that was not respecting human rights, or which was not willing to settle its internal or external conflicts in a peaceful and civilized manner. The Copenhagen Summit of the EU made this very explicit, as did the *Pact on*

*Stability* in Europe, which was adopted at a special conference in Paris in May 1995.

It would be wrong to credit only the determination of the Germans and the other Western Europeans and their use of the above mentioned lever as an explanation for the success of such policies. It must also be emphasised that the West European efforts often fell on fertile soil. One could even dare to state that both elements supported what was already a strong tendency in the Central East European states: the determination to follow the example of the successful Western European states and to mend fences over all the small- and medium-sized conflicts that had bedevilled Central Eastern Europe for centuries, and which had traditionally provided a vector for the influence of foreign powers.

## III. Weighing Policy Alternatives

This strong interest in Eastern Europe, brought about by strong German interest and international pressure, but also felt and appreciated by many other Western European governments, was by and large a success story. However, there are also shortcomings and pitfalls associated with this policy, which need to be weighed against the obvious advantages. One of these derives from the logic of enlargement, which always implies that enlargement will have to come to an end. The other relates to Russia

If the main instrument of stabilising the adjacent region of Central Eastern Europe was to hold up - and eventually implement - the prospect of integration and membership in NATO and the EU/WEU, then there must be a limit to any enlargement process. Depending on where this limit is to be drawn, this might exclude countries that desire membership and which might face serious internal and external stability problems if the prospect for membership were to be taken away. The Ukraine, Romania and Bulgaria are such states, where EU-membership is currently inconceivable - as might be their membership in NATO also. The accession of the Baltic states to NATO seems to be a long way away for the time being, too. Slovakia is still an open issue as regards membership in NATO and EU. There are good reasons for both NATO and EU not to open its gates for membership to all those who simply express the desire for it. In the main, the internal cohesion and efficiency of these organizations has to be maintained, and their institutional logic has to be adapted first, before new members could be accommodated.

The example of Turkey demonstrates that the protracted holding out of the prospect for membership in the EU without making good on this promise can have disastrous consequences. Since Turkey's membership in the EU was put off virtually indefinitely during the Luxembourg Council meeting in 1997, Turkey has felt rejected and insulted by the Europeans - something that could have long lasting domestic consequences in a country where the process of secularization is still disputed by large segments of society. The same could be said about those Central East European states which, for different reasons, might not make it into the ranks of either NATO or EU. Has anybody really anticipated, for instance, what it would mean for the internal stability and international standing of Romania if she was to be left out of both organizations? These are questions which have to be put in the future and where the reference to earlier decisions on criteria and conditions is only partially helpful.

The other problem relates to Russia. The current Russian leadership has made it crystal clear on various occasions that it is has absolutely negative feelings about the enlargement of NATO. The strategic rationale behind this Russian attitude might be questionable, since Russia really has more important things to worry than NATO's enlargement. Most likely, the negative attitude towards the enlargement of NATO has to be seen against the backdrop of the extremely difficult economic and political situation within Russia - something the current political leadership as well as the majority in the Duma bear the responsibility for. Maybe the resistance against NATO enlargement is again an expression of great power aspirations, thus bearing witness to the fact that Russia is in the process of jettisoning the lessons Gorbachev drew from the failures of the Soviet Union. It might also be that Russia simply feels excluded and isolated from processes that are important but increasingly incomprehensible both for Russian elites and for the man in the street.

Anyhow, the growing resistance to NATO's enlargement and the tendency of the Russian political elite to signal to the West (especially to the USA) that they have the will and the ability to 'strike back', and even to open up a new Cold War, is already posing a major international problem. It shows that the approach by which the Western zone of peace and co-operation is being extended to other parts of the world has its limits in the structural and functional requirements of those international institutions and organizations that form the backbone of this zone. This is a problem to which Germany has not found any solution to so far; and neither have any of her friends and allies.

5

# 6.
# Issues of Identity

Iver Neumann, Pierre Hassner

# Forgetting the Central Europe of the 1980s

*Iver B. Neumann*

Central Europe is a political term. She who says 'Central Europe' maps a particular piece of territory, with a particular set of human collectives and institutions, and sets it apart from other possible mappings. Saying 'Central Europe' is a way of making place out of space: a way of forging a certain collective self, and charging that political self with political power. Since political discourse feeds upon other kinds of discourse, just saying 'Central Europe' is a political act, regardless of what kind of discourse this happens within. When 'Central Europe' is used as a demarcation on a road map, or as a statistical point of reference, one effect is the political one of confirming a world view where this Central Europe exists and has certain functions; which at the same time confirms that other, rival selves which present themselves under different names have a weaker claim to relevance than has Central Europe. Central Europe is as it were spoken into existence, and maintained as a relevant political term by dint of its continuing use, this text being an example of how the verbal expression and typographical mememe of Central Europe is continuously used, contested, negotiated and ultimately either confirmed in one of its usages or changed in its terms of reference.

In this paper, I will ask three questions. First, what is the history of the term? Secondly, what makes its use possible? Thirdly, how does it function politically, and what empowers it?

## The History of the Term

I want to address the history of the term Central Europe for two reasons. The first reason is to demonstrate that the term has meant different things at different times, depending among other things upon which other terms it functioned in relation to. If it has meant different things at different times, having as its reference points different human collectives, different spaces and different political practices, there is every reason to believe that its referents may change again. In short, there is not one Central Europe, either from a historical or a contemporary perspective, but many Central Europes, and they all compete for political importance. The second reason for addressing the history of the term is that past usages echo within present usages, in the sense that the term Central Europe, like any other term, is not simply a technical one, but carries with it a certain political baggage, which is the weight of its own history.

Although one may trace a debate about where its centre is to the first usages of the term 'Europe' and its relatives, the first concerted claims to occupying it seem to emanate from the project for a protectionist economic zone drawn up by the German political economist Friedrich List (*List; 1904 [1841]*), with inspiration from Fichte (*Fichte; 1979 [1800]*). The claim of these authors was that Germany was placed in the middle or centre of Europe, so should play a central role in its economic and hence also in its political affairs. In spatial terms, List's *Mitteleuropa* includes places like Belgium. The political campaign for a *Mitteleuropa* received a boost on the eve of the First World War, when the Germans were discussing in which direction to expand; with a programme for *Mittelafrika* now also contesting the one of *Mitteleuropa*. The central plea for the importance of *Mitteleuropa* came from Friedrich Naumann (*Naumann; 1915*). It is highly apposite to our discussions that historically there has not always been a hard and fast line between the German term *Mitteleuropa* and the English term Central Europe. For example, recent writings on Central Europe such as Mutton (*Mutton; 1961*, vii) are economic in tone, and still include Belgium.

I mention this since, at the turn of the century, the term Central Europe seems also to have been used about the Habsburg empire or constellations of territory, and about human collectives resembling the Habsburg empire. Looking back at the struggle of these two projects, we tend to call them *Mitteleuropa* and Central Europe, respectively, but that is anachronistic. At the time, this demarcation was not clear. This is a rather obvious point, since this struggle played itself out overwhelmingly in other languages than English, and so the English term could not of course have been used very often. Since, however, the English term 'Central Europe' is often projected back in time and applied to these debates, this may still be a point worth making.

After the Second World War, the term *Central Europe* was used by Hungarian and Polish intellectuals such as Czesław Miłosz, this time as a cultural term. The central point about this usage is that it took place within the overall discourse of the Cold War, with its political two-camp division of Europe and the world into the camp of socialism and the camp of capitalism. In this setting, the Central European discourse acted as a countermove to these stories of the politically constituted selves of socialism and capitalism. Pointing to historical periods previous to the Cold War, the term Central Europe was a reminder that other ways of mapping the world did exist. As already noted, this usage of Central Europe coexisted with a usage like that of Mutton's, i.e. of Central Europe as a German-centred economic project.

Around 1980, the setting now being one coloured by the emergence of the Solidarity movement in Poland, there was a marked reinvigoration of the cultural use of the term Central Europe. The best known example of this usage is the essay by Milan Kundera, originally written for a Swedish journal and called 'A Kidnapped West'. It was published with this title in Britain, but also by *The New York Review of Books* as 'The Tragedy of Central Europe' (*Kundera; 1984*). Kundera wrote in the following vein: 'Russia is not just as one more European power but as a singular civilization, an *other* civilization [...] totalitarian Russian civilization is the radical negation of the modern West...'. Kundera had then already written extensively on the topic, as had a number of other Czech, Hungarian and Polish artists and intellectuals (see *Neumann; 1998a* Chapter Five for an extensive overview). As already mentioned, it is a point of no mean interest that these texts were often made available to a European-wide readership in English, as well as in other languages; this discourse on Central Europe was now definitely a trans-national and indeed European- and Atlantic-wide one.

In the 1980s, however, we can also trace the resuscitation of the other major usage of the term in this century, namely that of Central Europe as a German-centred economic and political project. It was only during the 1980s that two different usages were stabilized to denote these two different projects: Central Europe for the cultural discourse emanating from the Czech Republic, Poland, Hungary etc., and *Mitteleuropa* for the economic-political discourse emanating from Germany.

With the end of the Cold War and the dissolution of the Soviet Union, the Central European discourse spread from being mainly the preserve of those artists and intellectuals who were self-proclaimed Central Europeans, to also involving West European intellectuals and Central European politicians (who, by the way, at this stage of the game were themselves sometimes also artists and intellectuals). It also changed from being an overtly cultural (and only covertly political) concept, to one which was explicitly and overtly political, in the sense that specific political ends for 'Central Europe' began to be named. Two examples will suffice. First, a quote from Timothy Garton

Ash, offering itself as an appeal to the EC's Maastricht summit (*Ash et al.; 1991*, 19):

> *Historically and culturally, Poland, Hungary, and Czechoslovakia belong to Europe. A Europe which contains Crete but not Bohemia, Lisbon but not Warsaw, is historical nonsense. [...] It makes plain, practical sense to start 'the expansion of the EU' with those that are nearest, and work out to those which are farthest. Poland, Hungary, and Czechoslovakia are nearest not only geographically, historically, and culturally, but also in the progress they have already made on the road to democracy, the rule of law, and a market economy.*

In January 1990, Václav Havel had voiced to the idea that Central Europe was a cultural concept in search of realization when he told the Polish Sejm that

> *there is before us the real historic chance to fill with something meaningful the great political vacuum that appeared in Central Europe after the break-up of the Habsburg Empire. We have the chance to transfer Central Europe from a phenomenon that has so far been historical and spiritual into a political phenomenon. We have the chance to take a string of European countries that until recently were colonized by the Soviets and that today are attempting the kind of friendship with the nations of the Soviet Union which would be founded on equal rights, and transform them into a definite special body, which would approach Western Europe not as a poor dissident or a helpless, searching amnestied prisoner, but as someone who has something to offer...*
>
> (*Havel; 1990*, pp. 56-57)

This discourse was a very productive one, in the sense that the term 'Central Europe' was very soon adopted by Western politicians too. In record time, the idea established itself that Central Europe self-evidently had a place at the head of the queue for EU and NATO memberships. This turn in the debate was so swift and decisive that it was very soon suppressed that the three countries involved - the Czech Republic, Poland and Hungary - had with equal naturalness been universally known as parts of 'Eastern Europe' only a few years before. As this successful semantic gambit played itself out, one could see a wild scramble all over the former Eastern Europe and also in certain parts of the former Soviet Union as intellectuals and officials alike tried to find reasons for having their country too subsumed under the suddenly very user-friendly term 'Central Europe'.

Whereas one reason for this scramble was a perceived need to partake of the success of the Central European enterprise of the 1980s, there was also another additional reason. As pointed out by Maria Todorova, after 1990, 'Central Europe' was no longer presenting itself simply as being different from Russia, but also as being different from that other half of the old 'Eastern Europe', namely the Balkans. The Balkans has become a new 'other' to Central Europe, 'sometimes alongside with, sometimes indistinguishable from' Russia *(Todorova; 1997*, p. 160). She produces as particularly convincing discursive evidence for this a quote from the debate about the pacing of NATO enlargement, where it was argued that NATO

> *cannot suddenly open its doors to anyone at all [...] the contiguous and stable Central European belt borders both on the traditionally agitated Balkans and the great Eurasian area, where democracy and market economics are only slowly and painfully breaking away toward their fulfilment. In short, it is a key area for European security.*
>
> (Václav Havel in New York Times 17 October 1993, p. E17, quoted in (*Todorova; 1997*), p. 156).

One Balkan response to this othering was to fight the exclusion from Central Europe by trying to be included in it, that is, by fielding itself as an alternative Central Europe.

Another significant development of the 1990s was that the debate about *Mitteleuropa* became a central part of ongoing German negotiations about the place and identity of Germany itself in its European setting (*Staun; 1998*). The move of the capital from the *Bundesdorf* Bonn back to Berlin is often presented as the epitome of this process, and so a quote from one of Helmut Kohl's Berlin speeches may be used as an appropriate example:

> *In Berlin kreuzen sich die Wege vom Norden in den Süden, vom Westen in den Osten Europas. Wir Deutsche haben mehr Nachbarn als jedes andere europäische Land. Die geographische Mittellage Deutschlands hat zur Folge, dass es uns nicht gleichgültig sein kann, was um uns herum geschieht.*
>
> (Kohl, 13 March 1991, quoted in (*Staun; 1998), p.* 37)

At present, then, representations of 'Central Europe' take on three major forms. First, there is the politically successful one which denotes three countries - the Czech Republic, Poland and Hungary - as Central Europeans *and hence* as countries correctly accepted into NATO and also at the front of the queue for EU membership. We have here a self-representation which has been recognised by Western Europe. Secondly, there is a politically ambitious representation of Central Europe which is entertained by the belt of countries from Estonia in the north to Bulgaria in the south, and which insists that Central Europe does not only include these three countries, but also something more: and most particularly of course the country where this new and improved representation is being forged, be that Slovenia, Romania or somewhere else. Ukraine, perhaps. However, it is interesting to note that here we have a self-representation which is usually not recognised by Czechs, Poles and Hungarians, and only accepted in a partial and variegated manner by Western Europeans. One could say that negotiations over this representation are intense. Thirdly, there is another politically successful representation: that of the version of Central Europe known as *Mitteleuropa*, centred on Germany and usually not seen as comprising other spaces. This is a self-representation which is generally, if usually grudgingly, recognised in all other European countries, and so it is a politically successful one on the whole.

## What Makes the Representation of Central Europe Possible?

Representations do not simply exist. They pop up for a reason, they are maintained for a reason, and they are challenged for a reason. Since 'central' is an epithet of 'Europe', in order to be effective one should think that any representation of Central Europe should be subsumable under the broader category of Europe. Discourse on Central Europe must be compatible with parts of discourse on Europe at large to be credible and effective. This should mean that discourse on Europe presents a universe on which discourse on Central Europe not only can, but must draw. To be more specific, the European discourse forms the raw material out of which Central European subject positions must be formed, and draws a set of boundaries outside of which Central European subject positions cannot be formulated.

For two shorthand examples, let us refer to the Polish debate on civil-military relations and the Estonian debate on minority policy. In Poland, the prestige of the military has traditionally been high. This is probably to do with factors such as the importance of the traditional warfighting *szlachta* (nobility) as a nation-bearing element in the nineteenth century, and the role of J. Pilsudski in the inter-war period. When President Wałęsa's political base crumbled, it was, therefore, not surprising to see him look to the military for support (that this happened despite Solidarity's experiences with the imposition of martial law only adds to the strength of this argument). One of Wałęsa's lines of attack was to play down the need for clear-cut civil control in his dealings with the military. When the opposition was still rather efficient in fighting this gambit, it was partially because they could refer to the existence of a European 'standard' where civil-military relations were concerned, and the need for Poland to adhere to that standard in order to be treated as *Beitrittsfähig* by the EU, and also by NATO. Thus, Polish internalizations of what was represented as European 'standards' played a role, perhaps a decisive role, in defeating a ploy which had the strength of growing out of national traditions.

In Estonia, discourse about Russians in the late 1980s and early 1990s had a heavily racialist strand. Estonians at home and abroad would go on in conversation about how Russian women had been raped by Mongols and Tatars for centuries and so were 'contaminated' by 'an Asiatic gene pool', etc. At present, this strand has not necessarily disappeared, but it has at least been forced further underground. How did this happen? One major reason was the existence of a European standard of discourse where such views were deemed to be impermissible. The cultural hegemony of a European standard against racialist discourse (which is no less a standard for not being always adhered to) worked in the direction of changing this particular strand of Estonian politics. As witnessed by the case of Estonian citizenship laws, this is not to say that the European standard for minority policy as it is held up by the EU, the OSCE, etc. is being fully adhered to. The point, however, is that the political discourse of one applicant state was partly changed. A further point may be that by not adhering fully to the European standard in question, Estonia's chances of integration into the EU have probably been hampered. Be that as it may, the two examples should demonstrate that overall European discourse has certain boundaries for what goes and what does not go, and that a country, in order to be recognised as European (and that includes Central European), has to represent itself by means available within those boundaries.

But this also means that it is no coincidence that Central Europe is represented as it is, and recognised as it is. Saying 'Central Europe' is an appeal to Europe at large for being recognised as part of the European self, on the terms within which that European self represents itself. We have here, therefore, a case of isomorphism, whereby discourse on central Europe replays certain parts of discourse on Europe.

Having investigated the noun in the term Central Europe, I now turn to the adjective 'central'. In order to tell a credible story of yourself as 'Central Europe', you have to pass yourself off as central in one or more ways. Central America does this by having a geographical position between North America and South America; the Central African Republic seems to do it by an appeal to geography as well, and Central Asia does it mainly by being politically placed between the five historic major historical empires in Asia.

Is the Central European representation put forward by Czechs, Hungarians and Poles warranted in placing Central Europe in the centre of Europe? Geographically, it depends of course on where one draws the boundary to the East. Interestingly, in order to be centrally placed geographically, Central Europeans should have to follow Peter the Great and his geographer Tatishchev's lead and draw the boundary at the Urals, thus including a 'European' part of Russia (see *Neumann; 1998a*, Chapter Three). In political terms, however, this is exactly what a number of advocates of Central Europe want to avoid. They want Russia to be outside of Europe altogether.

Kundera *et al.* argue that Central Europe is central to Europe in a cultural sense or, more specifically, that it was so around the turn of the century, and that Europe therefore cannot be culturally whole without including Central Europe. This may or may not be so, but the issue of wholeness does not rest on the metaphor of centrality. The same pleas has been made by Norman Davies, when he refers to Poland in a book title as being the 'Heart of Europe' (*Davies; 1984*). The metaphor here is an organic one, which stresses the supposed wholeness of a supposed European organism, but which at the same time would seem to sabotage the metaphor of centrality: wherever the heart is, at least where the human species is concerned, it is not placed in the spatial centre of the body.

Kundera also insists that the powder tower at *Náměsti republiky* in Prague is the dead centre of Europe, because east-west and north-south trading routes ostensibly crossed there at some historical point. István Bibo and Jenö Szücz have made similar claims for Hungary on grounds of historical sociology. These are claims for inscribing specific practices at specific points in time with contemporary relevance. It is hardly the case that Central Europe is central to European cultural and economic life overall today, and so presenting it as being so on historical grounds necessarily includes a lot of bracketing of other historical experiences.

The one discourse where this representation of Central Europe has almost consistently been held to be central is the geopolitical one. Bismarck and Haushofer both pointed to Bohemia as being the centre of Europe. During the Cold War, military strategists placed the central flank here. Ironically, then, this representation of Central Europe can be said to be central in one sense only, namely in a military-strategic sense, and then only as long as the Soviet Union, Russia or any other political entity occupying an overlapping space is said to be Western Europe's enemy, so that there can be a room in which a centre can be lodged, and over which the two parties can contend. Thus, this representation of Central Europe would seem to depend logically on accepting a state of affairs which does not seem to be accepted or wanted by a number of the people who in fact sustain it.

One must then ask how central to Europe the two other representations of Central Europe are. The one presented by countries from Estonia in the north to Bulgaria in the East run into a number of the same problems as does the one presented by Czechs, Hungarians and Poles, and also into the additional problem that discursively, the latter three are trying their best to hog this space for themselves.

The presentation of Germany as central to Europe is, however, very hard to challenge. Along an east-west as well as a north-south axis, Germany does indeed occupy a central space or *Mittellage*. Germany is Europe's largest economy and is thus central to the European economy overall: and it is the central state in a general political sense as well. Culturally, it is less central than at some other periods, but in the cultural sphere the decentering of Europe has proceeded further than in any other sphere anyway, so this may not be so relevant. Crucially, Germany is recognised as central by a welter of other European state and non-state actors, however grudgingly. *Mitteleuropa*, then, is central to Europe in a whole number of ways in which Central Europe is not.

## How do the Representations of Central Europe Function Politically?

Having drawn up a rough sketch of the representations of 'Central Europe', and having specified the discursive space in which Central Europe is negotiated, I now turn to the question of empowerment. What are the overall political patterns traced by these representations?

The currently dominating representation of Central Europe as consisting of the Czech Republic, Poland and Hungary was an appeal issued by Central European artists and intellectuals to the West during the Cold War. It carried a double message: First, it argued that Central Europe was a self different from the rest of what one tended to accept as the unity of the Soviet Bloc. That is, Russia was othered as something not only different, but qualitatively different from Central Europe. In the negotiations over the central European self, some held that it was only different from the Soviet Union, and not also from tsarist or capitalist Russia, and some argued that it was merely different, and not wholly different, from the Soviet Union. Nonetheless, the representation that Central Europe was wholly different from Russia emerged out of these struggles as the dominant representation. Secondly, it was argued that Central Europe was part of the European self, and a part without which the European self could not be whole.

Since this representation has played a role in furthering Czech, Hungarian and Polish NATO and EU applications, in an institutional sense - and that is a crucial sense in a situation where Europe is becoming ever more tightly institutionalized - this representation is a political success story. Why did it succeed? One reason is that it spoke to fears of Russia which are parts of the overall discourse on Europe. Another is that the historical argument that these countries were sold down the river (not the Mississippi, though; perhaps the Danube?) at Yalta, and that the shortcomings of Yalta should be overcome now that the order to which this sale gave rise has fallen, has a certain appeal. Yet another is that the institutions of NATO and the EU could do with some new members to demonstrate their relevance in the post-Cold War circumstances. Obviously, the representation was also convincing in the sense that transition to the general European political and economic models of democracy and capitalism could convincingly be represented as being quicker here than elsewhere; and so the representation succeeded, and in terms of its own choosing (*Neumann; 1998b*).

It seems, however, that this vastly successful Czech, Hungarian and Polish representation of Central Europe, which came to the fore in European politics in the 1980s, is about to be hoisted on its own petard. What suggests this is, first, the very success of the undertaking of becoming an institutionalized part of the European self, and second, the way in which this success lays the discursive space of Central Europe open to infiltration by elements of the two other representations which are currently in circulation.

First, the success. The Czech Republic, Poland and Hungary are now fully fledged members of NATO, with the geopolitical implication of this being that they have thus become members of the 'Atlantic Community'. Although membership in the EU seems unrealistic before 2006 at the earliest, these three countries are widely believed to be on their way in: in terms of political and economic integration, the three countries are drawing closer to the previous members of the EU by the month. All this seems to suggest that the representation of these three countries as a part of Europe without which Europe cannot be whole has actually been recognised by West European countries. This bond, furthermore, has been institutionalized.

There are two ways of describing this in terms of geographical metaphors like 'west' and 'central'. One is to say that NATO and the EU will now consist of Western and Central Europe, and not only Western Europe as before. However, what packed the power into this representation of the Czech Republic, Hungary and Poland as 'Central Europe' was among other things the ideal of their having been temporarily cut off from Western Europe. With integration into West European structures, one of the perceptions on which this whole representation was predicated can therefore be expected to disappear. Instead of saying that Central Europe is joining Western Europe, it would therefore make more sense to say that these three countries are being integrated into Western Europe.

Another reason why this may be a more helpful way of describing matters is the existence of the two other representations of Central Europe - German *Mitteleuropa*, and the belt of states from Estonia to Bulgaria. With the Czech Republic, Hungary and Poland safely ensconced within Western Europe, we can already discern an attempt by the rest of the former Eastern Bloc to invade the Central European semantic space left unoccupied by those who are decamping for the West. Indeed, in terms of the only sense in which these three countries could be said to be central to Europe, namely in the geopolitical or military-strategic one, they will cease to be central and begin to be part of the West from the moment NATO membership takes effect. The central geopolitical space between Russia and NATO - to the extent that it can be said to exist at all as a contested area - will be taken up by the three Baltic states, Ukraine, and other states which have mostly been excluded from the Central European project. This will inevitably strengthen the claim of these countries to make up Central Europe, and it will strengthen it in the very terms formulated by Czechs, Hungarians and Poles during the 1980s and 1990s. At the same time, there is every reason to believe that Germany's *Mittellage* will confirm its role as the central

European state - and perhaps it will turn out to be even more central than one can see at the present juncture.

## Conclusion

For these reasons, Central Europe seems to be moving away from Prague, Warsaw and Budapest, in the direction of Tallinn, Riga, Vilnius and Kiev on the one hand, and in the direction of Berlin on the other. Of course, the representation of the Czech lands, Poland and Hungary as 'Central Europe' may continue to co-exist with a representation of these countries as Western European ones, in the same way that the five Nordic countries manage to be both Northern European and Western European at the same time. Which identity comes to the fore is, after all, contextual. However, with two other representations pitching for the same ground, there may not be any more political mileage to be had out of the representation of Central Europe for the elites of the Czech Republic, Poland and Hungary, and so this particular representation seems destined to lead a rather shadowy political life in future compared to the other two. This move from 'Central' to 'Western' was, however, ostensibly what the Czech, Polish and Hungarian artists and intellectuals who resuscitated the term twenty years ago ultimately wanted. Now that it is happening, it confers on the Czech Republic, Hungary and Poland the onerous task - known for a long time by other peripheral states in Western Europe such as the one I know best - of proving to be central in some specific issue area or other. It is nice not to be too central, particularly not to be too central in a military-strategic sense. It is not nice, however, to be a forgotten country on the periphery of Europe. As members of NATO and the EU, these three countries will still have to take the many small steps that will place them centrally in all those flows which make up European politics. In this, they may take Finland's EU record as an example of how well it is possible to navigate, and Sweden's as an example of how easily chances are missed. In terms of identity politics, then, the Czech Republic, Hungary and Poland cannot afford to rest on their Central European laurels, but must start forging other central European roles.

# Isn't Central Europe Dead?

## *A Response to Iver Neumann's 'Forgetting the Central Europe of the 1980s'*

*Maria Todorova*

It is a pleasure to agree with most of the preceding analysis of the notion of Central Europe. It is an even greater pleasure and challenge to disagree with some of the basic premises of this intelligent interpretation. One of these differences concerns the fundamental approach to the concept of Central Europe. Iver Neumann treats it very much as a *nomen nudum*, that is, as a taxonomical category (as usually reserved for the worlds of botany and zoology) that has not been validated by full description, and can therefore be utilized to label new species. Thus, the central thesis posits that Prague, Warsaw and Budapest have lost their Central European soul, but the soul now seems to be in search of a body, and is expected to be reincarnated in two hypostases: as an aspiring new Central Europe shifted geographically to the east and encompassing the belt from the Baltics to the Balkans; and as an established one, situated directly and 'bequem'ly in the German *Raum* of *Mitteleuropa*.

The first part of this statement is utterly convincing. The recent Central European discourse is, indeed, a phenomenon of the 1980s, but I would be more historically pedantic than Iver Neumann and would insist on precise dating. It is not that 'after the Second World War, the term Central Europe was used by Hungarian and Polish intellectuals such as Czesław Miłosz as a cultural term.' This usage and the ensuing discourse were exclusively confined to the 1980s. To be more precise, the Central Europe idea came into vogue in the early 1980s with the almost simultaneous publication of three works by well known authors representing the voices of the three countries claiming partnership in the idea - Poland, Hungary and the former Czechoslovakia: Jenö Szücs's 'The Three Historic Regions of Europe,' Czesław Miłosz's *The Witness of Poetry*, and Milan Kundera's 'The Tragedy of Central Europe'. In their articulation of the Central European idea, Kundera and Miłosz defined the region in cultural terms, and Szücs stuck to a more historical approach, while all described it in opposition to Russia. Russia was becoming Central Europe's constituting other. At this stage, however, membership in Central Europe was not restricted to the former

Habsburg realm: it implicitly, and sometimes explicitly, subsumed all of non-Soviet Eastern Europe. In fact, the Central European idea of the 1980s was an emancipatory idea, 'a metaphor of protest' in the words of Claudio Magris, which in itself was a sub-species of a genre dealing with 'Europeanness' in general that has been represented in different periods and with different intensity in virtually all European countries. The main issues addressed were the inclusiveness or exclusiveness of Europe as a phenomenon and as a concept, and since much more was at stake in this discussion than merely intellectual prowess, it was conducted passionately.*

In the second round of the development of the Central European idea prior to 1989 - the Eastern European *annus mirabilis* - its followers elaborated on different aspects of it, without moving out of the purported cultural parameters of the idea, and generally replicated the perspectives of the founding fathers. It has been suggested that Central Europe should be interpreted as a case of region-building, 'which is itself a subgroup of what may be called identity politics, that is, the struggle to form the social field in the image of one particular political project.' (*Neumann; 1993*, p. 350) Being undoubtedly a search for identity, *Traum oder Trauma*, the debate over Central Europe was hardly a region-building attempt, precisely because it never came up with a particular concrete political project for the region *qua* region, outside of the general urge for liberation from the Soviets.

Why the 1980s? The rise of Solidarity and the imposition of martial law in Poland *without* a Soviet invasion was a clear signal that Moscow's tactics had changed from the ecumenical worries about the unity of 'the socialist camp' which had motivated the invasion of 1968 to a more differentiated approach. Moscow was ready to consider alternatives to direct interference; it was already openly treating its satellites differently: and this prompted attempts at piecemeal emancipation. Thus, while we have no difference in reading the rhetorics of the 1980s as a primarily emancipatory discourse, I maintain that there is a basic analogy but no continuity between the emancipatory ideas immediately following World War II until the 1970s, on the one hand, and the Central European idea of the 1980s, on the other hand. As I have attempted to show, until the 1980s the preferred term was 'Eastern Europe' but even when 'East Central Europe' was employed, it referred to all the small states of what once was considered the *cordon sanitaire* against

---

* For a detailed textual analysis of the three master narratives of Kundera, Miłosz and Szücs, see (*Todorova; 1997*), pp. 141-148.

Bolshevism, and what after World War II became a quasi-independent *cordon sanitaire* against capitalism (*Halecki; 1950*, *Halecki; 1963*).

To go farther back, the 'Central Europe' of the 1980s was not a new term, but it did refer to an entirely new concept, fundamentally different from its nominal counterparts of the interwar period. *Mitteleuropa,* as most explicitly developed by Joseph Partsch and Friedrich Naumann, had always had Germany at its core. Even before the war, Partsch had conceived of a Mitteleuropa with Germany and Austria-Hungary as the nucleus, around which would revolve Belgium, the Netherlands, Switzerland, Montenegro, Serbia, Romania and Bulgaria. Greece and Turkey were excluded from his vision (*Partsch; 1904*). Naumann, the most famous proponent of *Mitteleuropa*, foresaw an enormous political body from the North Sea to the Alps, and then down to the Adriatic and the Danube valley. In the first version of his plan he excluded Romania, Bulgaria, Serbia and Greece, but also Switzerland and the Netherlands; in his second version, only one year later, Bulgaria was deemed ripe to be included.*

While *Mitteleuropa* had been a German idea, the interwar Central Europe was an East European (and implicitly also an anti-German) idea. The Central Europe of this era existed in different varieties and competing visions. *Střední Evropa* was essentially an expression of Czech political thought. For Tomáš Masaryk it was a 'peculiar zone of small nations extending from the North Cape to Cape Matapan' and including Lapps, Swedes, Norwegians, Danes, Finns, Estonians, Letts, Lithuanians, Poles, Lusatians, Czechs, Slovaks, Magyars, Serbo-Croats and Slovenes, Romanians, Bulgarians, Albanians, Turks and Greeks; but no Germans or Austrians.** In this period Poland was more concerned with Polish matters than with Central European political geography and the Hungarians clung to their 'fanatic revisionism; at best they envisioned a Danubian Europe revolving around their own nation.'***

Eastern Europe *in acta* ceased to exist after 1990, but its demise

---

* (*Naumann; 1915*, *Naumann; 1916*) On *Mitteleuropa*, the most solid study remains (*Meyer; 1955*).

** Quoted after T.G. Ash, 'Does Central Europe Exist', *In Search of Central Europe*, p. 196. On Masaryk's relentless critique of Austro-Hungarian policy in the Balkans, and on his views on the South-Slav question in particular, see (*Skilling; 1992*), pp. 213-233.

*** (*Meyer; 1986*), pp. 123-124. On the other hand, the Hungarian politician Elemér von Hantos was trying to promote closer ties between Hungary, Austria and Czechoslovakia, although he also considered Poland, Romania and Yugoslavia as Central European.

inaugurated a third round in the development of the Central European idea of the 1980s - one in which it became a political reality. Now, one could begin exploring the Central European idea not only in thought but also in action. The post-1989 world gave the Central European idea the chance to actualize itself as a region-building opportunity; but, despite the Visegrád fanfare and the series of summit meetings, concrete co-operation failed to materialize. As Kristian Gerner observed, 'the liberation from Pax Sovietica 1989-1990 revealed that there did not exist any "Central Europe".'* The ideal of intellectual solidarity in the region all but disappeared. It is also remarkable how the transformation of the Central European concept from an emancipatory idea to a politically expedient tool was accompanied by a parallel transformation of the concept of Europe from a cultural definition identified with liberalism and democracy into 'the international solidarity of capital against poverty.'

Why do I insist so much on these seemingly insignificant distinctions between the different utilizations of the term Central Europe? After all, hasn't Iver Neumann pointed out that Central Europe 'has meant different things at different times, having as its reference points different human collectives, different spaces and different political practices,' and that therefore 'there is every reason to believe that its referents may change again'? But it is precisely the universalizing nature of this statement that I object to. It is not simply 'different things' at 'different times'; it is, to be precise, three concrete things at two discrete times, the 1920s and the 1980s. Central Europe did not exist as a term before this century, and I would argue that the long term quest for the heart or the *Mittel* of Europe is different from *Mitteleuropa*. Therefore, I do not see an urgent reason to believe that it will stay suspended in the air and wait for new referents to employ it.

After all, as Iver Neumann himself convincingly shows, Central Europe as a notion is the function of an European configuration in which the space between Western Europe and Russia was seen as a stabilizing region within a system of balance-of-power. This is elaborated in more detail and properly historicized in the contribution of Miroslav Hroch. He demonstrates that at the Congress of Vienna, in Metternich's conception of the 'concert of powers,' the political balance between the Western powers (France and Britain) and the Eastern power (Russia) was to be guaranteed by the intermediary space, coinciding in his particular vision with the Habsburg empire. According to Hroch, Central Europe was not only a macroregion

* Quoted in Neumann, *Russia*, p. 364.

but a 'construct assigned with a mission in the general interest of all Europe.' He further shows that this system reached a crisis point with the unification of Germany in the latter half of the nineteenth century when the area between two centres of political and economic expansion became itself an expanding centre.

Today, however, the political conjuncture is fundamentally different. First and foremost, the notion of balance-of-power is totally dissipated. Already in the post-World War II bipolar era, while the notion was still used, it had a completely different connotation: the precarious equilibrium between two opposing systems, two poles which did not tolerate an intermediate neutral arbitrating or balancing zone. In the last decade, while, formally, the primary units in the international power game are still the nation states, the real play is launched at the supranational level, with multinational or global military and financial organizations. The fear of Russia today is mere rhetorical inertia; the real one is fear *for* Russia, i.e. fear arising from the danger from its further disintegration and the putative appearance of a multitude of unstable states and parastates.* For the states of Eastern Europe, on the other hand, who see themselves in terms of NATO and the formerly anti-Soviet military alliance of the USA and its clients, despite the rhetorical argument for security from future Russian expansion, the Alliance is primarily seen as the only side door leading to the coveted courtyard of the European Union.

It is worth recalling that immediately after 1989, Eastern European governments joined Germany in a call for a pan-European collective security system; there were also various Polish and Czech initiatives, all in the framework of the CSCE (now OSCE). As convincingly argued by Daniel Nelson, it was primarily the 'NATO-first' position of the United States which severely limited the CSCE's structure, staff and budget, and forced the East Europeans 'to back away from pan-European solutions, recognizing that the only path compatible with USA views was NATO.' This prompted a frantic activity among the East Europeans to look for 'new bilateral and regional alliances and associational ties with every existing "Western" institution, while simultaneously turning up the heat for NATO membership.' (*Nelson; 1996*, pp. 459, 461-462.)

It is within this specific context of strongly competitive individual attempts at integration with the West that one can see a newly acquired anti-Balkan edge to the Central European rhetoric: something which was

---

* On the notion of the parastate, see (*Liotta; 1998*).

conspicuously absent in the pre-1991 period. The argumentation for Central Europe's special status is based on two pillars: asserting the affinity of the region to the European system of values, and the exploitation of the ominous threat of a possible take-over in Russia by imperialist, chauvinist, anti-democratic and anti-market forces. In this context, invoking Central Europeanness became a device entitling its participants to a share of the privileges of the West.

The Balkans were evoked for the first time (alongside Russia) as the constituting other to Central Europe. The reason for this was the annoying proclivity thus far to treat Eastern Europe as an indivisible entity. Scholars who wanted to trace structural changes in the newly emerging democracies of the former Warsaw pact preferred to pursue their analyses in the framework of the whole of Eastern Europe. Scholars' blunders may be annoying, but more painful was the early European Union's decision to treat the emerging democracies in a package deal: as of 1 February 1995, the association agreements of the Czech Republic, Slovakia, Romania and Bulgaria (which joined the earlier admitted Poland and Hungary) with the European Union went into effect. This *en groupe* treatment annoyed the Czechs: in an interview published in *Der Spiegel* on 13 February 1995, Havel said that admission to NATO was more urgent for the Czech Republic than joining the EU. If the West accepts that certain, particularly Central European, countries belong to the Russian sphere of influence and thus should not be allowed to join NATO, Europe is heading to a 'new Yalta,' Havel warned. One would suppose that the logical alternative to this is that if these 'particular Central European countries' were admitted to NATO, but the rest were relegated to the Russian sphere of influence, a 'new Yalta' would be avoided. If the notion of a *limes* between the civilized west and 'les nouveaux barbares' is accepted as unavoidable, the question is where exactly should the *limes* run. For someone like Kapuscinski, there is no hesitation: 'the *limes* normally drawn in Eastern Europe is the frontier between the Latin and Cyrillic alphabet.' (*The New York Review of Books*, 17 November 1994)

It is a rule that any social perception (of an out-group by an in-group) tends to construct differences along dichotomic lines. But it is only the degree of institutionalization of these perceptions, or their relative importance and strength for the collective whole which perpetuates them and makes them potentially explosive. The exclusivist rhetoric of NATO expansion and the practical politics following from it is a concrete step in the direction of institutionalizing perceptions. The July 1997 Madrid decision to expand NATO to Poland, Hungary and the Czech republic made these countries viable candidates for second-class European status while firmly excluding the rest of Eastern Europe and relegating it to third and lower classes. This was enhanced when, in December 1997, the EU disclosed its Luxembourg decision to open accession talks with the Czech Republic, Estonia, Hungary, Poland, Slovenia, and Cyprus, and, in an open snub to Turkey, which it did not include even on the waiting list, formulated a booby prize category for long-distance aspirants, comprising Bulgaria, Lithuania, Latvia, Romania and Slovakia. It is symptomatic also that once agreement to NATO accession of the Czechs, Poles and Hungarians was secured, the anti-Balkan edge of their Central European rhetoric subsided, to remain shrill only in the overtures of 'Central European' Croatia, which has not yet secured its place even on the waiting lists.*

On the Western side, while there are two philosophies behind the pro and con arguments, based on different assessments of the balance of power and different final goals, it is symptomatic that they come from across ideological and political party lines.** It is essentially a debate between *Realpolitikers* (concerned with the prospects of alienating Russia, about the costs of expansion, as well as the danger of institutionalizing exclusiveness) versus a brand of moralizers (arguing that NATO expansion is a small price to pay for the strong desire of countries for which the West was harbouring feelings of guilt because of 1938, 1956 and 1968, guilt feelings which were also deftly cultivated by the Central Europeans themselves). Sceptics would argue that the moralizers are actually *Realpolitikers* since, at least in the American case, 'NATO is understood to be the *sine qua non* of American presence in Europe' and the most important lever for keeping Germany in check. (See *Nelson; 1996*, pp. 463, 465, 469, and *Perez; 1997*). In addition,

---

* It is entirely absent, for example, from Havel's emotional plea for 'The Charms of NATO' on receiving the Fulbright Prize in October 1997. Instead, Havel confines himself to sardonic incomprehension at 'a certain large Euro-Asian state, which for some reason is afraid of the alliance.' (*The New York Review of Books*, January 15, 1998, p. 24). On EU membership, see (*Whitney; 1997*).

** The best fora to follow the discussion have been *The New York Times, Foreign Policy,* and *European Security*. For a review of opinions, see (*Steel; 1998*). See also the reactions by Igor Maslov, 'Russia and NATO: A Critical Period,' Ivan Eland, 'Enlargement or Largesse? NATO Expansion Will Be More Expensive than Clinton Admits,' and Ted Galen and Barbara Conry, 'Time Bomb for an Expanded NATO: Hungary and Its Neighbors,' (in *Mediterranean Quarterly*, vol. 9, No. 1, Winter 1998, pp. 1-53); Richard F. Staar, 'Why NATO should expand,' (*Mediterranean Quarterly*, vol. 9, No. 3, Summer 1998, pp. 25-33); Senator D. P. Moynihan, 'NATO Expansion and the Nuclear War,' (*ACE (Analysis of Current Events)*, vol. 10, No. 7-8, July-August 1998, pp. 5-6).

a considerable part was played by the internal Polish vote, and, finally, expanding by only three countries is a fair price to fend off criticisms of exclusion and to still look good.

Let me go back to this part of Iver Neumann's statement that we agree upon: Poland, Hungary and the Czech republic utilized the culturally expressed idea of Central Europe for political purposes: accession to NATO and the front seats in the line for the EU. As Iver Neumann aptly expresses it, it is 'a self-representation which has been recognised by Western Europe.' But the whole point about the Central European representation was to argue that it was an organic part of Western Europe (or just Europe) taken temporarily hostage by the East, by 'a different civilization.' It is useful in this respect to recall that complex notions (like nation, race, gender, continent, etc.) are socially constructed systems of marked and unmarked categories. The complex notion of Europe comprises both marked categories and unmarked categories. 'Eastern Europe' is a marked category. Its history is being taught at Western European and American universities as a subfield of European history. 'Central European' or rather 'East Central European,' and 'Southeast European' history and literatures occasionally emerge as marked subcategories within this subfield. The rest of Europe is not represented by the categories 'Northeast European' or 'Southwest European,' not even by 'Western European,' but simply by 'European.' These are, then, unmarked categories. But marking out is not an innocent act. What happens is that the marked categories become marked as different while the unmarked categories retain their power as the standard against which the rest have to position themselves. And it is the unmarked categories which actually dominate and are discretely at the centre of the general notion. It has been demonstrated that the need to define as well as to define oneself is born from a sense of marginality. While Hungary, Poland, and the Czech Republic made ultimate use of the marked category of 'Central Europe,' *i.e.* in their case it became a 'politically successful representation' in the words of Neumann, the whole pathos of the Central European idea at this time was aimed at dissolving itself as soon as possible into the unmarked category of (Western) Europe.

So, the next question is whether (as Neumann wants us to believe) the strategy of this 'politically successful representation' is going to be mimicked by the outer belt from the Baltics to the Balkans, in an attempt to duplicate the success of the first tier. I dare to doubt it, although in at least one case, this certainly seems to be the case. In his latest performance on the same theme, President Tudjman recently reiterated his main stance about the Central Europeanness of his country. He is averse to any kind of participation in South-Eastern European (or Balkan) region-building, and he views Western counsels in this respect as treacherous. At the opening session of the Central Committee of his governing party (the HDZ) on December 7, 1998 in Zagreb, he firmly rejected unwarranted demands by unnamed centres abroad to encroach on 'the sovereignty of the Croatian state' and warned other countries to mind their own business. He stated that he will allow no one to establish a Croatia serving 'outside interests' and regarding itself as part of the Balkans, instead of a Central European country (*RFE/RL Newsline, vol .2, No. 235, Pt. II, 8 December 1998*).

Of the numerous states forming the outer belt (at least 15 of them),* though, this is the only one to entirely conform to the stated expectation. Neither Estonia nor Slovenia got into the first bandwagon because they utilized this kind of rhetoric: they got in because of their manageable size and good economic performance. Cyprus certainly didn't, because it couldn't, but the point is that it didn't need to anyway. The Baltic countries are following a much more practical strategy to forge direct links with northern Europe. Slovakia had been downgraded from the Visegrád group, and the objections against it have concerned its internal policy, but there was no question that it did not belong to the 'Western values' club.**

Extending a protective arm around the old centres of the Habsburg empire, the West, motivated in part by sentiment, followed neatly the new trench lines outlined by Huntington. According to Tony Judt, this will create 'a sort of depressed Eurosuburb beyond which "Byzantine Europe" would be made to fend for itself, too close to Russia and Russian interests for it to be prudent for the West to make an aggressive show of absorption and engagement.' (*Judt; 1997*) Of the former non-Soviet members of the Warsaw pact, this left two Balkan states unaccounted for: Romania and

* Albania, Belarus, Bulgaria, Bosnia-Hercegovina, Croatia, Estonia, Latvia, Lithuania, Macedonia, Moldova, Romania, Slovakia, Slovenia, Ukraine, Yugoslavia.

** To the frustration of its critics, the Slovak economy was doing surprisingly well, and its past tradition of rabid Catholicism put it firmly in the camp of Western values. Its minority problem with the Hungarians has been handled relatively well, so Mečiar's heavy-handed rule seemed to be the only hurdle to acceptance by the West. Lately, moreover, even before the last elections which removed Mečiar from power, there was a strong chorus of voices against the exclusion of Slovakia, led by Austria, and supported by Hungary and Poland. At the summit meeting in Levoca, Slovakia, Austria's President Thomas Klestil announced that 'We cannot imagine Europe without Slovakia,' and in Hungary's President Árpad Göncz's words 'Slovakia has its place in Europe.' (*RFE/RL Newsline, vol. 2, No.18, Pt. II, 28 January 1998*).

Bulgaria.* Even the exclusion of the Balkans was not consistently observed, however, because it employed a cultural argument which is always arbitrary.

Romania, if not in practice, at least on paper got temporarily off the hook of its Balkanness. France argued strongly for Romanian admission on linguistic grounds. Even if one might argue that this was a tactical move on the part of a France aiming after that to wash its hands of responsibility toward the Visegrád troika, the significant issue is the employment of a completely irrational, not to say silly, argument for Romanian participation: its so called Latin heritage. In the aftermath of Madrid, Clinton found it expedient to assuage Romanian, but not Bulgarian disappointment. Meeting Clinton in Bucharest, Ciorbea assured him that 'Historically and culturally, we believe we belong in the West' and the *International Herald Tribune* had the nerve to add that Romania had a 'Latin heritage which contrasts with that of the neighbouring Slavic countries.' (*International Herald Tribune*, No. 35, 571, July 12-13, 1997, p. 4.) This malapropism in the best case shows ignorance about Romania's Orthodoxy or about the Slavic character of neighbouring Poland, and in the worst case is a demonstration of unabashed old-fashioned ethnic racism.

The most interesting part of the exchange was, however, the rhetoric employed by the Romanian leaders. Throughout, it referred to a direct link to the West, an organic partaking in the European experience - but not via Central Europe. To be sure, the Central European argument is also exploited in Romania, but in a manner not even close to the exclusivist and shrill notes of the Croatian discourse. Romanian politicians have been careful to participate actively in all Balkan initiatives while, at the same time, cultivating their Central European neighbours.

Bulgaria, on the other hand, has never resorted to the Central European argument, and I see no symptoms that it ever will. As I have argued elsewhere, Bulgaria is the only Balkan country which gives serious consideration to its 'balkanness' (which is, *ipso facto*, exclusionary to a claim of Central Europeanness). There are geographical and historical reasons for this, among them the fact that the Balkan range lies entirely

---

* The former Soviet republics were not considered at this point, because their proximity to Russia makes the anti-Russian edge of NATO expansion too obvious, but at least rhetorically, the ground is being prepared for overtures to the Baltic republics, again based on their partaking in the 'Western value system.' Criteria like minority treatment, especially in the case of Estonia, are not voiced, apparently because countries of the 'Latin heritage' are judged by a different standard than countries of the 'Greek' /'Asian'/'Byzantine'/'Oriental'(?) heritage. For a summary, see (*Goble; 1998*), (*Shtromas; 1997*); for a strong reaction (*Maslov; 1998*).

within Bulgarian territory, and that the mountain and the name have became a symbol for nationhood. Being Balkan is a Bulgarian predicament, from which Bulgarians not only cannot escape but which they have in fact found a way to aestheticize. Yet, even while accepted, the Balkan identity is ambiguous, and still subordinated to the claim of Europeanness.

This was clearly reflected in the attitudes toward NATO membership in the country. Despite the polarized political life after 1989, there was complete consensus from the start on the desire for integration into the European institutional framework. This was not the case with NATO, and not for the reasons which abound in the Western press: that Bulgaria is traditionally pro-Russian, or that it is congenitally undemocratic, illiberal, un-Western etc. etc., since it is on the wrong side of the Huntingtonian cultural border (Orthodox *cum* Slavic). While the promoters of NATO saw it as a back door to the EU (exactly as their counterparts in Central Europe did), the opponents pointed out several aspects, among them the following with direct bearing on Turkey, based on the United States' global strategy in which Turkey figures as a main strategic partner, and Macedonia as the key to Balkan peace: 'in the case of ethnic problems in Bulgaria, a NATO solution would be imposed, in line with the American position favouring Turkey and Macedonia.'(*Vinshnata politika na Bilgariya sled 10.IX.1989*, Sofia: Natsionalen institut za mezhdunarodni izsledvaniya, Fondatsiya „Friedrich Ebert," 1997, p. 127)

There were two different and opposed visions of the direction Bulgaria should take in its search to fill the great power vacuum: one with more pronounced European, and particularly German leanings, which in the Balkans wants to promote especially good relations with Athens; the other with stronger American leanings, and a greater openness toward Turkey. Yet, at the height of the romantic love affair of Bulgaria with the United States, the former American ambassador to Bulgaria, William Montgomery, was asked during an officers' course at the Bulgarian Defense Ministry what guarantees Bulgaria would receive in case of an eventual attack by a NATO country. The response was: 'A peaceful policy will give no reason to a neighbouring country to attack Bulgaria, but if that happens, Bulgaria can expect the sympathy of the whole world. There are no other guarantees.' For the record, the Bulgarians have no oil; instead they have Turks. The candid answer cannot fail to strike one as very different from the rhetoric of emotional concern for the sovereignty of the Central European states were they to be threatened by the as yet non-existent Russian danger.

Today, the Bulgarians have joined the supplicants for NATO accession, and have been granted second wave status.* The remarkable thing about the long-winded accompanying rhetoric is that it never once employed the Central European motif. Instead, the aspiration to join NATO was fashioned as 'our civilizational choice.' President Peter Stoyanov, during his visit to Washington in February 1998 told reporters at the National Press Club that this was not just to go along with the 'fashionable infatuation of Eastern [sic! not Central: M.T.] Europe lately of "let us go and join NATO". For us, it is a strongly motivated choice, a cultural choice, a choice of civilization and a strong wish to return to where we belonged 45 years ago and from where we were cut off by force.' Everything in this rhetoric is in place: the cultural argument, the motif of violence or rape, the 'return' to the fold. Yet, not even a mention of Central Europe. The plunge is direct: 'We share the Atlantic values and we are determined to participate in their development and defence.' (*Lyle; 1998*) 'Civilizational choice' has become a byword with mantra-like qualities, and the president, with matchless perseverance and invincible faith in the power of words, keeps on repeating it at every possible occasion.**

The developments at the latest EU summit meeting at the Hofburg Palace in Vienna (December 1998) seem to bear out this scepticism about the effectiveness of the Central European strategy. No firm dates for entry were set; most likely dates will have to be postponed until the union has transformed its own finances. The year 2000 which had been circulated by some members of the first group as a possible beginning of the accession process will be postponed, most likely to 2005 but very possibly even later. This pushes the second-wave countries to at least a decade further down the road. As commentators have put it, 'Brussels may well have calculated that enlargement later, rather than sooner, is the least painful course to follow.' (*Walker; 1998*, *Whitney*; *1998*) The cultural rhetoric notwithstanding, in the end economic calculations are setting the pace for all practical

* Parliament had adopted a declaration on Bulgaria's desire to join NATO in 1993, but this was blocked by the socialist government which came to power in 1994. On February 1998, a declaration was issued by the President, Parliament and government of Bulgaria asking for full membership.

** (*Kaplan; 1998*). In an interview with Kaplan, Stoyanov resorted to his latest supplication: 'Now we badly need encouragement from the West, for we have made a civilizational choice to be part of NATO.' Bulgaria's application to NATO is already referred to euphemistically and ironically in the Bulgarian press as 'the so-called civilizational choice of our country' (*Deneva; 1998*).

developments.* And while the final historical verdict may still be that the Central European strategy was a 'politically successful representation' with qualified achievements for three particular countries in the decade after the end of the Cold war, it seems to me that the present diagnosis is valid: Central Europe is dead.

* The Bulgarian press (the case I know in detail) is remarkably level-headed about this. With the exception of the unfortunate presidential phrase about the 'civilizational choice', which is handled with a chuckle as a diplomatic ploy, there are serious and realistic analyses about the significant and increasing economic differences between the countries of Central Europe and the rest of Eastern Europe, the Balkans in particular. The chances for Bulgaria's accession are measured exclusively in economic and, to a much lesser extent, geopolitical, terms. (*Kirilov; 1998*, *Dermendzhiev; 1998*)

# Afterword

Slavenka Drakulić

# A Trip Back to Europe

*Slavenka Drakulić*

After spending a year in the USA recently, I came back to Europe. In America, it seemed so natural to say 'Europe' when I was asked where I was going. And also, during my stay there, it had seemed natural enough to declare that that was where I was from, too. Europe: just Europe.

But am I really a European? The question, in my experience, is either easy or very difficult to answer, and it entirely depends on which side of the new EU border you happen to find yourself.

If you happen to be, for example, in the USA, the answer seems easy enough. I spent a year there, teaching in a college for women. Among the American students, there were also Soros students from Croatia, Slovenia, Russia, Georgia, Romania, Bulgaria, Hungary, and ex-East Germany, as well as from Ireland, Denmark, France... This was their first visit to the USA, and they were all very disappointed. Nothing was as they expected it to be, after their exposure to American movies. They landed in a small private college, in a small town in the South. All of them came from big cities, and they missed having a city centre, asphalt, and the urban way of life. They could not get used to a landscape of scattered, isolated one-storey houses, with shopping malls, highways and billboards in between. Sure, they missed boys as well, but not as much as a city itself. Urban life represented Europe for them. It was a surprise for them to find that there are comparatively few cities on the American continent (for it is not just a state, but a continent as well, although we rarely think of it in those terms), and that even those cities, not to mention the smaller towns, have a different kind of identity than the corresponding places in Europe. For example, good public transportation is more of an exception than the rule. Villages, too, look very different. They are far away from each other, planted in waste land, and surrounded by wild, untamed nature. The Eastern European girls missed cafés, where you can get an espresso, hang around for a while, read newspapers and meet friends - and they laughed at the Americans they saw eating and walking at the same time, or carrying paper cups of coffee. Perhaps they were not quite aware that this might all be in store for them in their own countries pretty soon too. But most of all, they missed bread. Plain, old-fashioned, freshly-baked bread: the crusty loaf you buy every morning in the local bakery, and not that tasteless, odourless American sponge full of chemicals that you can keep refrigerated for a month. Curiously enough, they also considered bread as something European, and not exactly because it is impossible to find good bread in America: rather because buying it daily is not part of the normal habit of life, so that one has to go out and look for it specially. And then, what about a cup of strong coffee, some good cheese, some proper wine, or maybe even some nice home-made beef soup...

Their concept of themselves as Europeans also had to do with the look and behaviour of the American girls. The Eastern European girls were more careful about their clothes and make-up, and their appearance generally; and the American girls looked much more casual in their jeans and T-shirts. They behaved more casually too. In class they would bring drinks, chips, cookies and fruit, and they would happily gnaw at an apple or slurp at a Coke during the lecture. The girls from Eastern Europe considered this behaviour improper and even rude, and they would sneer at the American girls, who, in their opinion, had no manners. None whatsoever. Indeed, our favourite pastime was gossiping about the Americans, with their peculiar habits, their bad food and their parochialism. On the other hand, being there made it look as if we Europeans all knew exactly what Europe is about. It has something to do with our urbanity, our better food, a more refined style of life, more *culture*... and of course our troubled history has something to do with it too. Anyway, in opposition to the Americans, this was enough of a common denominator for the whole group to consider itself 'European'. (Needless to say, all these 'Europeans' spoke English among themselves.)

I suspect, however, that this comfortable European identity of theirs - of ours - had already started to fade away on the plane back to Europe. When you board an aeroplane in, say, Washington's Dulles Airport, as I did, you already notice differences among the 'Europeans' - and I am using quotation marks for this word from now on. Your experience and your senses tell you that the particular accent, or just the looks, the clothes, a gesture or something will soon reveal that the man next to you is Polish, while the one behind you is British. You will probably make this East-West division first of all (because you are so used to doing so), and then the more subtle divisions will follow. Or maybe you'll spot a pale skin colour, or notice a particular shape to a face, and you'll already have started to differentiate more closely still. But you won't have only geography on your mind: you will also conceptualize that person in terms of history and politics, including all kind of prejudices about the particular nation as well. Because in Europe people all live so close together, they can detect the smallest differences, and in fact insist on these. At this point, you, a passenger returning to 'Europe', subconsciously start the process of division and exclusion: us/them, friends/enemies, better/worse.

Once your plane lands in Frankfurt there is no longer even such a notion as 'Europe': for no-one uses that name any more. There is Germany, there is France, there is Bulgaria or Romania for that matter, but from now on you see that *once again there are two Europas, and there is no way not to notice it*: no way to avoid instantly becoming conscious of this fact. As soon as you land, you have to go through passport control, and that means going through separate booths for EU and non-EU citizens. There, at Frankfurt Airport, you can see quite clearly this new division of Europe, and at that very moment the identity you have established in America starts to crumble. As a non-EU citizen, facing this new division, you must ask yourself who the hell you think you are exactly anyway? Does 'non-EU' have something to do with being an 'Eastern European' or something? And the answer that you are bound to find out sooner than later is that by implication yes it does, because if you are from the former Eastern Bloc, then everybody knows that your country has never been in a position to *choose* not to belong, like Norway or Switzerland for example. There is nothing you can do about it.

So, finally, upon your return from the States, you face it. The words are written in neon, in yellow letters on a blue background and surrounded by stars, for everyone to see and take notice. Fellow-passengers from the aeroplane - the neighbour you were chatting with so pleasantly - take a step to the left (EU), while you take a step to the right (NON-EU) and wave him good-bye. Your line is long and moves slowly. You watch the EU line disappearing. The people flash their passports and the policemen barely even look at them. While you wait, a very familiar feeling of frustration arises in you. You know it all only too well; that policeman's very careful look at your face and your passport (and you are quite aware that you don't look much like your picture: especially not so early in the morning), the checking of your name against the invisible list of criminals, drug smugglers and spies, a possible question about your ticket, about what brings you here (business? pleasure?) and the intended length of stay... A familiar dryness in your throat... A familiar knot in your stomach...

Again? Yes, again.

It is not just that the sign above your head informs you that there is no longer one 'Europe', as you have imagined to be the case since the fall of the Berlin Wall: it is even worse than that, for perhaps what it tells you is that now only the EU is really 'Europe', while the rest of the continent somehow fails to qualify. At that moment, it is of little consolation to you when you see Norwegians or Swiss (or Japanese or Americans) standing in the same line with you. There is a difference between you and them, and you know it. They too will be waved through - because they don't need a visa.

Visa: yet another word that has to do with identity, that represents an invisible barrier, an invisible border. It makes you think that at least now you *can* travel, even if you do need a visa. But it also makes you think of those long queues you see in the street in front of foreign embassies, and the humiliation of standing there waiting, as if you were begging for something. And yes: indeed you are. You are begging the citizens of the EU to let you visit their magic land. They might let you in, or they might not. After all, you are a non-EU citizen, and now you belong to a different category, almost another class. You belong to the class of those excluded from the EU and who therefore need special permission to enter it. From now on, you are part of some unspecified remnant of the continent: the part of Europe that remains outside the EU. You belong to *them*, you are somebody else. That is, the 'other'.

Suddenly, as you are approaching the NON-EU booth, you feel an urge, almost a physical push to leave that line, turn back and get on the first aeroplane going back to the States. There you could simply be a European again, and feel European, and nobody would question your identity, even if you do come from a country no-one has heard of. Back in Europe, though, you are defined as a 'non-' person. As if you were non-existent. The power of language to exclude hits you hard, maybe because you see it so clearly for the first time.

The newspeak language of the Brussels bureaucracy haunts you. You wish they had invented another, better and more neutral word. That NON-EU suggests many things. Not only does it immediately make you feel like an outcast, like a pariah (by a policeman's look which says that you are nothing but an intruder, someone who just wants to stay and steal a job in these times of unemployment), but it carries a heavy load of historical and political prejudice as well. In every country there are people who are non-us, who do not belong, who are the 'others'. Usually they belong to an ethnic minority, or they are Gypsies or Jews, and we all know what *that* means. These non-us people or 'others' are being marked out for not being *us* (or for being NON-US) and because of that from time to time they are also designated as the people to be resettled, ethnically cleansed or killed.

This non-us means nothing good, then. It is not just an innocent word. There are no words like that anyway. It is even worse to use such a word after the fall of communism, especially since none of the ex-communist countries is included in the EU, or not yet. It is in a way a kind of *déjà-vu*, you think, as you stand in front of that very visible new-old border. However, it feels worse than before because you did not expect to be treated like one of the 'others' any more. For a brief moment, we - all the Eastern European nations - were treated like heroes. But when the post-communist reality settled in, we discovered that we are still the 'others' of 'Europe'. One might argue that there is a difference between, say, Poles or Czechs and Albanians - and by the way, does anyone now remember the pictures from the summer of 1992 when tens of thousands of Albanians got into ships in an attempt to escape from Albania; or what happened to these people once they reached the shores of Italy? It is true that differences exist, but our general and common 'otherness' is nevertheless still there too. It only takes a policeman, a shopkeeper and your accent for them to discover that you are... well, different. It would be OK if one were only different, actually, but the problem is that there is always a value attached to this difference. For Eastern Europeans the word 'Europe', used alone, actually means Western Europe. For Western Europeans it is the same. Indeed, for the majority of people inhabiting this continent, the word 'Europe' means quite simply Western Europe; it is so for historical, economic and political reasons, or perhaps because our mentality does not change as quickly as the political system. Whatever the reasons are, it is evident that this has not changed as a result of 1989. And so, while the effects of the revolutions of 1989 and the collapse of communism have not yet had a chance to establish themselves, a new division has been created. Even if from a geographical point of view the eastern part of the region is in fact still Europe, whoever is there who is only talking about geography? We are using the notion of Eastern Europe to include geography and history but also politics, to include our prejudices and complexes, and our new and old frustrations...

But if we are NON-EU citizens as far as 'Europe' is concerned, then what is 'Europe' to us? This has to do with dreams, illusions and myths more than with any reality of Europe. It also has to do with language, and with the desire expressed in language: the desire to belong. Sometimes it is even funny to see it: you can walk down the street in Prague or Zagreb, Budapest or Warsaw, and you notice all these hotels, shops, cafes, or just holes in the wall named Europe, Paris, Hollywood, Hemingway, Four Roses, White Horse, or whatever it might be... As if the sheer magic of these Western names and the use of a foreign language would instantly transport us right there where we belong: *i.e.* in 'Europe'. I remember that there was even a proposal in the Croatian parliament to ban all foreign names in public life. 'A tourist might be confused about whether he was in Zagreb or London,' said the MP who proposed the law. Hardly likely, unless he was completely drunk; but nevertheless, he had a point. Cities were soon visibly changed by that desire - and then the foreign companies came in, anyway.

This desire to belong, or rather to be recognised as belonging to Europe (meaning the West) is the reflection of what we - and now I mean Eastern Europeans in general - imagined that 'Europe' was, while we were all living under communism. I remember a scene from the living room of an Albanian family, with two teenage daughters waiting eagerly for the Italian TV advertisements, their only window to 'Europe'. They imagined it as a place populated by beautiful young people with white teeth and shining hair, driving fantastic cars and having fun. 'Europe', they thought, would be like this TV image: bright and beautiful, rich and pleasant... and I am not sure that they - or we in general - were aware just how unreal that image was. Like smelling a bit of French perfume and imagining that all of France must smell heavenly. It doesn't; it often stinks: but how could people, who must always hope for something better, afford to believe it? When I was small I collected sweet wrappers; but only from foreign sweets. (Ours didn't have wrappers.) And how precious those small pieces of cellophane were! How beautiful they smelt in among the pages of my school exercise book!

That imagined 'Europe' smelled, tasted and looked better. It *was* better: more advanced, more developed, more civilized. Our imagination - and this imaginary image - were easily fed on isolation and deprivation; and the other side of the coin was mythology. In our favourite myth, 'Europe' was the solution to all our problems. Once we were there, they would all disappear. Just like a good fairy that could rescue us from enslavement by an evil dragon, and bring long-deserved justice and plenty into our lives. 'Europe' figured as a kind of Utopia; and moreover, it still continues to serve that function in the post-communist popular imagination, replacing the communist Utopia of the 'better future' we already knew, and which we were forced to live with. But somehow this 'Europe' is still needed. It is as if people who experienced communism are not ready to take full responsibility for their future. Not yet.

Its role in our dreams and illusions is reflected in the language. 'Europe' has become an adjective. If you want to point out some good quality (in music, a film, a book or a painting; or just in an idea, a concept, a hotel, a dinner...) you will say it is 'European', indicating that it partakes of standards that are higher than the local ones around you.

It is hard, then, to convey the disappointment we faced after 1989, and the way some of the post-communist countries slowly and painfully learned that the 'Europe' we imagined, dreamed about, and saw on the TV screen was an illusion. And that happened in spite of all our enormous efforts to prove otherwise. Look, we said, we Czechs are different; after all, Prague is to the west of Vienna... Or it might have been we Poles, or we Slovenes... It all helped, of course it did, but even so we are still very much determined by communism, our common denominator.

Another example showing that this 'Europe' does not exist, that it is a construction and not a country (although it remains a continent) is, of course, the recent war and ethnic cleansing in Croatia and Bosnia, and now in Kosovo. War is very much about manipulating a concept of non-us, of 'otherness', in this case that of ethnic minorities; and that is precisely how it started. But I want to make another point. It was quite pathetic to watch how the unarmed and unprepared Bosnians expected 'Europe' to help and rescue them from Serbian aggression. 'Europe will not let us down,' they said. They sincerely believed that they were in 'Europe'. They were fatally mistaken. Germany, France and Great Britain did not share this opinion. They had other political interests. There was no such entity as 'Europe', and anyway, this war was happening to 'others', somewhere else. It did not have anything much to do with their idea of what 'Europe' is or should be...

To the disappointment which greeted our discovery of the fact that the 'Europe' we had imagined did not exist was soon added another. We discovered that there was no automatic way for us to be counted as European. We would be expected to fulfil certain conditions. Yes, it is presented at first simply as a matter of joining this or that union or organization, from the European Council to NATO or PHARE: these seemed to be the magic words of the newspeak we had to learn. But in that case our European belonging and our European identity would be reduced to a matter of mere politics and economics. And of course, some countries are closer to fulfilling these conditions, and others are much further away. And this creates divisions and subdivisions, so that we find that there are now 'others' among our own numbers, among ourselves: the poor, the underdeveloped, and those hit by war. Indeed, we take very good care not to be confused with 'them'. Who wants to be in the same category as Serbs or Albanians, after all? And so the pattern repeats itself, as we compete to get *in*, to get a visa, to pass behind that booth for NON-EU citizens, to cross the threshold to paradise and get away... from what? Into what? Certainly not into the 'Europe' we thought we knew so well.

Standing in that line in Frankfurt, I worry about my Eastern European girls, who are coming back from America too. Where are these girls now and how did they feel waiting in the same line in Frankfurt or wherever it was, just so they could enter one of the fifteen EU countries? Do all of them have the right to call themselves 'Europeans' - or only some of them? And if so, then how would this be reflected in the newspeak? Certainly, such a change in language would indicate a change in their identity. 'Europe' has been taken away from most of them, and in future, like me, they will have to go back to the States (or Africa, or Japan) to become 'Europeans' again.

As usual, the devil is hidden in the language. What has happened here with the language, and it occurs to me while I am showing my passport (The same distrustful look. The same long staring at the passport.) is *the expropriation of the name Europe*. It has been expropriated by the more powerful, in order to exclude other, less powerful, Europeans. From now on there will be two kinds of identities: Europeans who are compatible with EU citizenship (French, German, Italian...), and Europeans who are not compatible with EU membership (the others).

And yet, except in purely legal and economic terms, however we might try to define Europe, the EU is not Europe. It is only Western Europe, and could better be named WEU if that name were not already in use by another similarly exclusivist organization. I feel afraid: afraid of my Europe being snatched away from me; afraid that I will lose the small yellow (or are they really gold?) stars that make a magic circle around it. I know that I should not be afraid; that it would make more sense to wish that my country too could become one of the stars, that the circle should get bigger and bigger till we were all included... And while all of 'Europe', Western Europe, that is, is preoccupied with its new identity, nobody thinks about the identity of those who are left out. They will probably have to figure it out by themselves, redefining their identity once again in the light of this latest fresh exclusion.

Perhaps 'Europe' should be defined not in terms of geography or history, of politics or even of culture, but just as a dream; as something to fantasise about: Utopia. The nice thing about such a definition would be that everyone would have equal rights to a dream like that; and this time it would be a dream that could never be stolen away from you.

# Articles and books referred to

Ash, Timothy Garton *In the Name of Europe*, Oxford: Oxford University Press 1992.

Ash, Timothy Garton, Michael Mertes & Dominique Moïsi 'Let the East Europeans in!', *The New York Review of Books*, 24 October, 1991.

Asmus, Ronald *German Unification and its Ramifications*, Santa Monica: Rand Corp. 1991.

Baldwin, Richard E., Joseph F. Francois and Richard Portes, 'The costs and benefits of eastern enlargement: the impact on the EU and central Europe', *Economic Policy*, no. 24, April, 1997, pp. 127-76.

Boia, Lucian *Istorie si mit in constiinta romaneasca,* Bucharest: Humanitas, 1997.

Bourdieu, Pierre *The Field of Cultural Production*, Cambridge: Polity, 1993.

Breska, Erich von, Petra Brunner, Martin Brusis, Josef Janning and Barbara von Ow, *Neue Ostpolitik - Strategien für eine gesamteuropäische Entwicklung*, Gütersloh: Verlag Bertelsmann Stiftung, 1997.

Čapek, Karel *President Masaryk tells his story*, London 1941, New York, 1971.

Čapek, Karel *R.U.R. (Rossum's Universal Robots)*, tr. Paul Selver, London, 1923.

Čapek, Karel *War with the newts*, tr. Ewald Osers, London, 1998.

Corado, Cristina *Textiles and Clothing Trade With Central and Eastern Europe: Impact on Members of the EC*, London: CEPR, Discussion Paper no. 1004, August, 1994.

Csáki, György 'L'investissement direct étranger en Hongrie', *Revue d'Etudes Comparatives Est-Ouest*, vol. 28, 1997. no. 2, pp. 39-69.

Davies, Norman *Heart of Europe. A Short History of Poland* Oxford: Oxford University Press, 1984.

Dermendzhiev, Borislav „Ponyatieto Iztochna Evropa zagubi ikonomicheskoto si znachenie,“ *Kapital*, 5-11 December 1998, pp. 31-34.

Deneva, Karmelita „Petir Stoyanov na otchayan shturm za NATO,“ *168 chasa*, December 1998, pp. 4-10.

Drábek, Zdeněk 'Regional and Sub-Regional Integration in Central and Eastern Europe: An Overview', in Teunissen (ed.) (1997), pp. 11-77.

EBRD *Transition Report*. London: EBRD, 1997.

ECE/UN *Economic Survey of Europe in 1992-1993*. New York and Geneva, Economic Commission for Europe, United Nations, 1993.

ECE/UN *Economic Bulletin for Europe*, vol. 47, New York and Geneva, 1995.

ECE/UN*Economic Bulletin for Europe*, vol. 48 (1996). New York and Geneva, 1996.

ECE/UN *Economic Survey of Europe in 1996-1997*, New York and Geneva, 1997.

ECE/UN *Economic Bulletin for Europe*. vol. 49 (1997), New York and Geneva, 1997.

ECE/UN *Economic Survey of Europe*, no. 1. New York and Geneva, 1998.

Eliade, Mircea *The Myth of the Eternal Return: Cosmos and History*, London: Penguin, 1954.

European Commission *Agenda 2000,* 2 vols. Brussels: European Commission, document Com (97) 2000 final, 1997.

European Commission *Avis* on the applications for accession from the associated countries. Brussels: European Commission, documents Com (97) 2001 to 2010 final, 1997.

Fallada, Hans *Little man, what now?*, tr. Eric Sutton, London 1933.

Fayolle, Jacky 'Rattrapage, convergence, intégration: quelques enseignements à partir du cas espagnol', in Jacques le Cacheux (ed.) *Europe, La nouvelle vague. Perspectives économiques de l'élargissement*, Paris: Presses de la Fondation Nationale des Sciences Politiques, 1996.

Fernandez-Arias, E. 'The New Wave of Private Capital Inflows : Push or Pull?', *Journal of Development Economics*, vol. 48, no. 2, 1996.

Fernandez-Arias, E. and P. Montiel 'The Surge in Capital Inflows to Developing Countries: an Analytical Overview', *The World Bank Economic Review*, vol. 10, no. 1, 1996.

Fichte, Johann *Der geschlossene Handelsstaat* Hamburg: Felix Meiner, 1979 [1800].

Fischbach, Mireille, and Maria Scattaglia 'Financial Flows to Eastern Europe: Determinants, Volatility and Sustainability Issues', in *Moct-Most*, special issue, 1997, pp.67-99.

Gellner, Ernest 'Islam and Marxism: some comparisons', *International Affairs* 67:1, January, 1991, pp. 1-6.

George, Stefan *Das Jahr der Seele*, Stuttgart, 1982.

George, Stefan, *Der Teppich des Lebens und Die Lieder von Traum und Tod*, Stuttgart, 1984.

Goble, Paul 'From the Unthinkable to the Inevitable,' RFE/RL Newsline, vol. 2, No. 12, Pt. II, 20 January, 1998.

Halecki, Oscar *The Limits and Divisions of European History*, London and New York: Sheed & Ward, 1950.

Halecki, Oscar *The Millennium of Europe*, Notre Dame, Indiana: University of Notre Dame Press, 1963.

Hamilton, C.B. and L. Alan Winters 'Opening up Trade in Eastern Europe; *Economic Policy*, no. 14, 1992.

Hammelmann, H. A. and Osers, Ewald (tr.) *The correspondence between Richard Strauss and Hugo von Hofmannsthal* Collins, London 1961, Cambridge 1984.

Hankiss, Elemer *Az emberi kaland: egy civilizacio-elmelet vazlata*, Budapest: Helikon, 1997.

Hašek, Jaroslav *The good soldier Švejk and his fortunes in the World War*, tr. and intro. Cecil Parrott, London, 1993.

Havel, Václav 'President Václav Havel's Speech to the Polish Sejm and Senate. January 21, 1990', *East European Reporter* 4 (2), 1990.

Havlik, Peter 'Exchange Rate, Competitiveness and Labour Costs in Central and Eastern Europe', Vienna: WIIW, *Working Papers* no. 231, October, 1996.

Hindley, Brian *Helping Transition Through Trade? EC and US Policy Towards Exports From Eastern and Central Europe*. London: EBRD, Working Paper n 4, March, 1993.

Hrnčíř, Miroslav 'The Global and Regional Outlook in Eastern Europe', in Teunissen (ed.) (1997), pp. 93-126.

Hughes, Gordon and Paul Hare 'Competitiveness and Industrial Restructuring in Czechoslovakia, Hungary and Poland' , *European Economy*, special issue no. 2, 1991, pp. 83-110.

Hunya, Gábor 'Large privatization, restructuring and foreign direct investment', in OECD (1997), pp. 275-300.

Huxley, Aldous *Brave New World*, London, 1994.

Inotai, András 'Foreign Direct Investment in Hungary : Experience, Critical Crossroads and Strategic Options', in Tamás Ferenczi, ed., *The Path to Economic Development,* Budapest: Institute for World Economy of the Hungarian Academy of Sciences, no. 77, 1995, pp. 107-122.

Inotai, András, and Magdolna Sass *Economic Integration of the Visegrád Countries : Facts and Scenarios*. Budapest: Institute for World Economics, Working Papers, no. 33, May, 1994.

Jowitt, Ken: *New World Disorder: the Leninist Extinction*, Berkeley: University of California Press, 1992.

Judt, Tony *A Grand Illusion? An Essay on Europe*, quoted in *New York Times*, January 24, 1997.

Kaplan, Robert D. 'Hoods Against Democrats,' *The Atlantic Monthly, December 1998, p. 36.*

Keegan, John *A History of Warfare*, London: Pimlico, 1993.

Kertzer, David I. *Ritual, Politics and Power*, New Haven CT: Yale University Press, 1988.

Kirilov, Kiril „Novata zhelyazna zavesa minava iztochno ot Praga" *Kapital*, 5-11 December 1998, pp. 31-34.

Kraus, Karl, *The Last Days Of Mankind*, tr., abr. and ed. Frederick Ungar, New York, 1974.

Kundera, Milan 'The Tragedy of Central Europe', *The New York Review of Books*, 26 April, 1984.

Lankes, Hans-Peter, and Tony Venables 'Foreign Direct Investment in Economic Transition: The Changing Pattern of Investment', *Economics of Transition*, vol. 4, no. 2, 1996, pp. 331-47.

Lankes, Hans-Peter, and A. J. Venables 'Foreign Direct Investment in Eastern Europe and the Former Soviet Union: Results From a Survey of Investors', in OECD (1997), pp. 555-65.

Larrabee, F. Stephen *East European Security after the Cold War*, Santa Monica: Rand, 1993.

Liotta, P. H. 'Balkan Fragmentation and the Rise of the Parastate,' *Mediterranean Quarterly*, vol.9, no.3, Summer 1998, pp. 61-81.

List, Friedrich *The National System of Political Economy* New York: Longman, 1904 [1841].

Lyle, Robert 'Bulgaria: President Presses for NATO Membership,' Radio Free Europe/Radio Liberty, 12 February, 1998.

Mach, Zdzislaw *Symbols, Conflict and Identity*, Albany NY: SUNY Press, 1993.

Madách, Imre, *The tragedy of man*, tr. George Szirtes, Budapest, 1988.

Makkai, Laszlo, Mocsy, András and Szasz, Zoltán (editors): *Erdely tortenete* (3 Vols.), Budapest: Akademiai, 1986.

Mann, Michael *The Sources of Power: The Rise of Class and Nation-States 1760-1914,* Cambridge: Cambridge University Press, 1993.

Martin, Roderick 'Central and Eastern Europe and the International Economy: The Limits to Globalization', *Europe-Asia Studies*, vol. 50, no. 1, 1998, pp.7-26.

Martin, Carmela and Francisco J. Velásquez 'The Determining Factors of Foreign Direct Investment in Spain and the rest of the OECD: Lessons for the CEECs', CEPR, Discussion Paper Series, no. 1637, London: CEPR , June 1997.

Maslov, Igor 'Russia and NATO: A Critical Period,' *Mediterranean Quarterly*, vol. 9, No. 1, Winter 1998, pp. 1-15.

Matejka, Harriet. 1998. 'L'élargissement de l'UE à la République tchèque: Quelles conséquences pour la Slovaquie?' *Le Courrier des Pays de l'Est*, no 430, June, pp. 30-7.

McNeill, W. H. *The Pursuit of Power,* Oxford: Blackwell, 1983.

Messerlin, Patrick 'The EC and Central Europe: the Missed Rendez-Vous of 1992?', *Economics of Transition*, vol. 1, no. 1, 1993, pp. 89-109.

Meyer, Henry Cord *Mitteleuropa in German Thought and Action, 1815-1945*, The Hague: Martinus Nijhoff, 1955.

Meyer, Henry Cord '*Mitteleuropa* in German Political Geography', *Collected Works*, vol.I, Irvine, CA: Charles Schlacks, Jr., 1986.

Meyrink, Gustav *Die Erstürmung von Sarajewo*, in *Des deutschen Spiessers Wunderhorn, Gesammelte Novellen, 1. Bd.,* Munich, 1913.

Miłosz, Czesław: *The Witness of Poetry,* Cambridge MA: Harvard University Press, 1983.

Musil, Robert *The man without qualities*, tr. Sophie Wilkins and Burton Pike, London 1935.

Mutton, Alice *Central Europe: A Regional and Human Geography* London: Longman, 1961.

Naumann, Friedrich *Mitteleuropa* Berlin: Georg Reimer, 1915.

Naumann, Friedrich *Bulgarien und Mitteleuropa*, Berlin: G. Reimer, 1916.

Nelson, Daniel N. 'America and Collective Security,' *Medunarodni problemi*, Beograd, vol. XLVIII, No. 4, 1996.

Neumann, Iver B *Uses of the Other. 'The East' in European Identity Formation* Minneapolis: University of Minnesota Press, 1998.

Neumann, Iver B. 'European Identity, EU Expansion and the Exclusion/Inclusion Nexus' *Alternatives* 13 (2), 1998.

Neumann, Iver B. 'Russia as Central Europe's Constituting Other,' *East European Politics and Societies*, vol.7, No. 2, Spring 1993.

Neven, Damien *Trade Liberalization with Eastern Nations, How Sensitive?*, London: CEPR, Discussion Paper no. 1000, July, 1994.

OECD *Lessons from the Economic Transition, Central and Eastern Europe in the 1990s*. Edited by Salvatore Zecchini. Dordrecht: Kluwer Academic Publishers, 1997.

Offe, Claus 'Agenda, Agency and Aims of Central East European Transitions', in Stefano Bianchini and George Schöpflin (editors), *Europe and the Balkans: How They View Each Other, Vol.1,* 1998.

Orwell, George *Nineteen Eighty-four*, London, 1993.

Partsch, Joseph *Mitteleuropa*, Gotha: J. Perthes, 1904.

Perez, Jane 'Blunt reason for Enlarging NATO: Curbs on Germany,' *The New York Times*, December 7, 1997.

Podkaminer, Leon et al. *Transition Countries: 1997 Deficits Lower than Feared, Stability Again a Priority*. WIIW, Vienna Institute for Comparative Economic Studies, *Forschungsberichte*, no. 243, February, 1998.

Quaisser, Wolfgang 'Der Außenhandel Mittel- und Osteuropas mit der Europäischen Union in den sensiblen Sectoren', Osteuropa-Institut München, *Working Papers*, no. 198, December, 1996.

Richter, Sándor *European Integration: the CEFTA and the Europe Agreements.* WIIW, Vienna Institute for Comparative Economic Studies, *Forschungsberichte*, no. 237, May, 1997.

Rilke, Rainer Maria *From the Book of hours: „Das Stundenbuch"*, tr. Babette Deutsch, Norfolk, Conn., 1941.

Rilke, Rainer Maria *The book of hours*, tr. Stevie Krayer, Salzburg, 1995.

Rilke, Rainer Maria *The life of the Virgin Mary: Das Marienleben*, tr. Stephen Spender, London, 1951.

Rosenstein-Rodan, P. N. 'Problems of industrialization of Eastern and South-Eastern Europe', *Economic Journal*, June-Sept., 1943, pp. 202-211.

Roth, Joseph *The Radetzky March*, tr. Eva Tucker, London, 1974.

Schöpflin, George 'Civil Society, Ethnizitat und Staat: eine dreiseitige Beziehung', in Brix, Emil (editor) *Civil Society in Osterreich* Vienna: Passagen, 1998, pp. 447-63.

Schöpflin, George *Nation, Identity, Power*, London: Hurst, 1998.

Shtromas, Alexander 'To Expand Beyond Enlargement,' *ACE (Analysis of Current Events)*, vol. 9, No. 12, December 1997, pp. 5-9.

Skilling, H. Gordon 'T.G.Masaryk, Arch-Critic of Austo-Hungarian Foreign Policy,' *Cross Currents*, No. 11, 1992.

Staun, Jørgen *Mitteleuropa - Centraleuropa - Mitteleuropa - Tysklands genkomst i midten af Europa* Copenhagen: Unpublished manuscript, 1998.

Steel, Ronald 'Instead of NATO,' *The New York Review of Books*, January 15, 1998, pp. 21-24.

Szucs, Jeno: *Vazlat Europa harom torteneti regiojarol,* Budapest: Magveto, 1983, partially translated as 'Three Historical Regions of Europe' in John Keane (editor), *Civil Society and the State,* London: Verso, 1988, pp. 291-332.

Teunissen, Jan Joost (ed.) , *Regionalism and the Global Economy, The Case of Central and Eastern Europe*. The Hague: FONDAD, 1997.

Tilly, Charles (ed.) *The Formation of the National State in Western Europe*, Princeton NJ: Princeton University Press, 1975.

Todorova, Maria N. *Imagining the Balkans* New York: Oxford University Press, 1997.

USDA *Newly Independent States and Baltics Update, Spotlight on Foreign Direct Investment,* Washington, DC: USDA Economic Research Service, 1997.

Visegrád Summit Declaration, *Report on Eastern Europe*, Radio Free Europe/RL Research Institute, 1 March, 1991, pp. 31-2.

Walker, Christopher 'EU Enlargement: "Hurry Up and Wait",' RFE/RL Newsline, vol. 2, no. 238, Pt. II, 11 December, 1998.

Wallace, Helen *Whose Europe is it anyway?*, the Stein Rokkan Lecture, delivered to the ECPR Warwick Workshops, March, 1998, to be published in the *European Journal of Political Research.*

Wang, Zhen Kun and L Alan Winters *EC Imports from Eastern Europe: Iron and Steel*, London: CEPR Discussion Paper Series, no. 825, October, 1993.

Whitney, Craig R. 'European Union Taps 5 for Talks on Membership,' *The New York Times*, December 14, 1997.

Whitney, Craig 'European Union Delays Decisions on Ex-Communist Countries,' *The New York Times*, 13 December, 1998, p. 11.

World Bank, *From Plan to Market, World Development Report 1996*.

Washington DC: World Bank, and Oxford: Oxford University Press, 1996.

Zweig, Arnold *The Case of Sergeant Grischa*, tr. Eric Sutton, London, 1947.

Zweig, Stefan *Amok: Novellen einer Leidenschaft*, Leipzig, 1923.

Zweig, Stefan *Erstes Erlebnis: vier Geschichten aus Kinderland*, Leipzig, 1928.

Zweig, Stefan *Passion and Pain*, tr. Eden and Cedar Paul, London, 1924.

Zweig, Stefan *Verwirrung der Gefühle*: drei Novellen, Leipzig, 1928.

# Contributors

Alexei Arbatov is a member of the State Duma of the Russian Federation.

Christopher Cviic is Associate Fellow of the European Programme at the Royal Institute of International Affairs (Chatham House) in London.

Slavenka Drakulić is an internationally famous novelist and essayist, well-known as a commentator on the political and cultural life of post-communist Europe.

Eliška Fučíková is Director of the Historic Monuments Department of the Office of the President of the Czech Republic.

Erik Holm is Director of the Eleni Nakou Foundation.

Miroslav Hroch is Professor of History at Charles University, Prague.

András Inotai is General Director of the Institute for World Economics of the Hungarian Academy of Sciences.

Ingmar Karlsson is Ambassador of Sweden to the Czech Republic.

Ferdinand Kinsky is Director General of C.I.F.E., and Professor at the European Institute for Advanced International Studies, Nice and at the University of Southern Europe, Monaco.

Joachim Krause is Deputy Director of the German Society for Foreign Affairs Research Institute, Bonn.

Marie Lavigne is Emeritus Professor of Economics, University of Pau, and Senior Research Fellow, ISMEA, Paris.

Christopher Lord is the author of some rather obscure philosophical and literary works.

Iver Neumann is head of the Russian Centre at the Norwegian Institute of International Affairs.

Ewald Osers is a leading translator of Czech literature into English.

Otto Pick is First Deputy Minister of Foreign Affairs of the Czech Republic.

George Schöpflin is Jean Monnet Professor of Political Science and Director, Centre for the Study of Nationalism, School of Slavonic and East European Studies, London.

Maria Todorova is Professor of History at the University of Miami.

Loukas Tsoukalis is Venizelos Chair at the European Institute of The London School of Economics and Political Science.

Helen Wallace is Director of the European Institute at the University of Sussex.

**Abbreviations**

| | |
|---|---|
| AA | Association Agreement |
| CECs | Central European countries |
| C&EE | Central and Eastern Europe |
| CEE | Central Eastern Europe |
| CEFTA | Central European Free Trade Area |
| CEI | Central European Initiative |
| CFSP | Common Foreign and Security Policy |
| COMECON | Council for Mutual Economic Assistance |
| CPI | consumer price index |
| CSCE | Conference on Security and Cooperation in Europe (1973-1994) |
| ECE/UN | Economic Commission for Europe of the United Nations |
| EBRD | European Bank for Reconstruction and Development |
| ECE | East-Central Europe |
| EEC (EC) | European Economic Community/ European Community (until 1993) |
| EFTA | European Free Trade Association |
| EMU | European Monetary Union |
| EPC | European Political Cooperation |
| ESA | European Space Agency |
| EU | European Union |
| FDI | foreign direct investment |
| GATT | General Agreement on Tariffs and Trade (until 1994) |
| GDP | gross domestic product |
| GNP | gross national product |
| GSP | General System of Preferences |
| IGC | Inter-Governmental Conference |
| IMF | International Monetary Fund |
| NAFTA | North American Free Trade Agreement |
| NATO | North Atlantic Treaty Organization |
| OECD | Organization for Economic Co-operation and Development |
| OPT | outward processing trade |
| OSCE | Organization for Security and Cooperation in Europe (from 1995) |
| PFP (or PfP) | Partnership for Peace |
| PPI | producer price index |
| PPP | purchasing power parity |
| SITC | standard international trade classification |
| ULC | unit labour costs |
| UN | United Nations |
| USD | United States dollars |
| WEU | Western European Union |
| WTO | World Trade Organization (since 1995) |